1000
SAUCES
dips and dressings

1000 SAUCES

dips and dressings

Nadia Arumugam

APPLE

DEDICATION

For Papa, a man who likes his sauces.

AUTHOR BIOGRAPHY

Nadia Arumugam is a writer, recipe developer and cookbook author. She was born in Malaysia, grew up in England and currently lives in New York City where she is a food columnist for Forbes.com. Nadia has Masters degrees in English literature from Oxford University and in Journalism from New York University. She trained at Leith's School of Food and Wine in London after which she worked with the renowned chef Anton Mosimann. She has written for Saveur, Fine Cooking and Epicurious.com among other publications. Nadia is the author of *Chop, Sizzle and Stir*.

A Quintet Book
1000 Sauces, Dips and Dressings
Copyright © 2013 Quintet Publishing Limited.

This edition published in 2013 by
Apple Press
74-77 White Lion Street
London, N1 9PF
www.apple-press.com

ISBN: 978-184-543-524-0
QTT.TSDD

This book was conceived, designed and produced by
Quintet Publishing Limited
6 Blundell Street
London N7 9BH
United Kingdom

Photographer: Simon Pask
Food Stylist: Val McArthur
Designer: Jacqui Caulton
Project Editor: Julie Brooke
Art Director: Michael Charles
Managing Editor: Emma Bastow
Publisher: Mark Searle

10 9 8 7 6 5 4 3 2

Printed in China

CONTENTS

INTRODUCTION

Sauces. Dressings. Dips. What do they have in common? All three possess an important quality; they can turn a mundane, humdrum meal or snack into an exceptional gourmet experience. While developing these recipes, I was especially mindful of one thing – a general lack of time that plagues each and every one of us. With this at the forefront of my thinking, every recipe is devised to be as streamlined as possible. Most can be completed within half an hour, many within a matter of minutes, and almost all within the time frame it would take you to prepare a simple meal.

Sauces

We have the French to thank for the many classic sauces that we frequently see on restaurant menus. It was the founder of French haute cuisine, Marie-Antoine Carême who devised a system to categorise these sauces in the early 19th century. He referred to the principal basic recipes as 'Mother Sauces' and variations on these with added flavourings and ingredients, as 'Daughter Sauces'. The original four Mother Sauces are: Béchamel, Velouté, Espagnole and Tomato sauces. The chef Auguste Escoffier later added Hollandaise as the fifth Mother Sauce in the 20th century. For example, Béarnaise and Choron are Daughter Sauces of Hollandaise sauce; Aurora and Mushroom are variations of the Velouté sauce; and Mornay and Nantua are derived from Béchamel.

These true classics aside, sauce-making has grown to encapsulate many new classics such as mayonnaises, vinaigrettes, fruit coulis and dessert sauces, not to mention the panoply of sauces inspired by global, ethnic ingredients.

THICKENING SAUCES

Some sauces, such as béchamel, begin with a thickening agent called a 'roux'. This is a mixture that is composed of equal parts of melted butter and flour. It is important to cook out a roux for a minute or two before adding a liquid such as milk or stock. For a classic white sauce such as a béchamel, the roux should be no darker than a pale golden, blonde hue. For a velouté sauce, you can cook the roux a little longer, just until it is a sandy, biscuity colour. The end result is a silky, viscous sauce. Other sauces might be thickened with the addition of cream that's then reduced by boiling the mixture until the desired consistency is achieved.

Flour and butter come together in another thickening method in a mixture called a *beurre manié*. Here slightly softened butter is kneaded into flour in a ratio of two to one. Pieces of the paste are whisked into a hot sauce until the mixture is thickened just right.

Then there's the use of cornflour, which is added to a finished sauce. Before adding to hot liquids, cornflour must be 'slaked', which means it needs to be combined with a little cold water and stirred until a smooth paste is formed. Once added to a saucepan, the sauce mixture must be stirred while it simmers to prevent the liquid from becoming lumpy (if it does, straining the cooked mixture through a fine sieve will usually rescue it) and the liquid will thicken after a minute or so. It's important to cook out a cornflour-thickened sauce for a couple of minutes to get rid of the 'raw' taste of the cornflour. Sauces thickened with cornflour tend to lose their clarity and become a little opaque. If you prefer a clear, but thickened sauce, use arrowroot instead.

Cold butter, alone, cut into cubes, and whisked into a hot sauce off the heat will also thicken it. Also, the butter will enrich the sauce and give it a nice sheen. This technique, widely used in professional kitchens, is known in French as '*monter au beurre*'. Don't bring the sauce to a boil or the butter will separate from the sauce and form a greasy film on the top.

CONSISTENCY

I think there is no ideal when it comes to the consistency of sauces. You should go for what you like; whether it's a thinner and fresher sauce or a thicker, more unctuous one. As a general rule, if you're looking for what is generically referred to as a 'pouring consistency', your sauce should do just that; it should pour easily. A technique chefs use is to dip a wooden spoon into the mixture then run a finger down the back. If the sauce eventually runs back into the path you've drawn with your finger after a few seconds, then the consistency is about right. There are some sauces where you want a thicker consistency, such as a rich cheese sauce. In this instance, you want the sauce to thickly coat the back of a spoon, and if you draw your finger down the back, the clear path should hold its own and not flow back. This is known as a 'coating consistency'.

SEASONING A SAUCE

A common mistake cooks make when they create a sauce, especially one that requires significant reduction, is that they add too much salt too soon. The end result is then far too overpowering. The lesson here then, is to wait to season until the finishing stages of the recipe when the sauce has boiled away to the right consistency. Remember you can always add salt, but it is impossible to take it away.

Saying that, there are a couple of things you can do to correct a slightly over-seasoned sauce. You can begin by adding some lemon juice or vinegar. If that fails, dilute the sauce with water or unseasoned stock, and if necessary re-thicken it with cornflour or arrowroot. It's not only a salty sauce that can require correction; sometimes we can be a little over-zealous with sugar, or cream or an acid. To right a too-sweet sauce, add salt or lemon juice; for an overly creamy sauce cut the fat with vinegar; for a too sharp sauce whisk some cold butter into the hot sauce, off the cooker.

SERVING PORTIONS

Some people like a lot of sauce, some people less. When it comes to how much you should serve, the rule of thumb is to dress a plate with an amount that looks good. You don't want to be stingy or flood the dish. You can always pass extra sauce around separately. As a guide for cooking purposes, 3 to 4 tablespoons (45–60 ml) would be ample per person for most sauces served as an accompaniment.

Salad Dressings

Salad dressings do not have the same well-documented history as sauces. What is known, however, is that the Romans used oil and vinegars to adorn their vegetables.

ONLY THE BEST

For a dressing you can be proud off, start with the best-quality oils and vinegars you can find since these really do form the bedrock of most dressings, especially vinaigrettes. If a recipe calls for extra-virgin olive oil, don't skimp and settle for olive oil that is less pure and bears only a semblance to the natural grassy flavour of extra-virgin. Similarly, when it comes to vinegars, invest in good-quality bottles, avoiding the cheap products that are often too sharp and acerbic, and lack any real depth of flavour.

EMULSIFY, EMULSIFY, EMULSIFY

The key to many dressings is to properly emulsify the fat and acid. But just what does this mean? In layman's terms, this refers to the technique of whisking or blending ingredients (that don't normally mix seamlessly) together so vigorously that the fat breaks down to tiny globules that are suspended evenly throughout the vinegar. Some recipes call for honey, mustard or egg yolks. These ingredients are 'emulsifiers' and help the other ingredients to come together. Another trick is to add the oil to the vinegar and other ingredients in a thin steady stream as you whisk or blend. There are plenty of dressings in this book that don't need to be emulsified. These come together much more easily and can even be stirred together in a bowl – many are in the Creamy Dressings chapter.

LAST-MINUTE DRESSING

The great thing about salad dressings is that they can be made well in advance. Often, you can keep them in the fridge stored in an airtight container for up to a week. What you absolutely can't do, however, is dress your salad and let it sit for hours or even many minutes before serving. Should you leave a dressed salad for any more than 15 minutes, it will start to wilt and become unappetisingly soggy. For a handy time-saver if you're entertaining, pour your dressing into the bottom of a salad bowl, then place the leaves over the top, being careful not to push them into the dressing. When your guests sit down to eat, simply toss and plate immediately.

Dips

As party, snack, picnic, lunch box and even dinner food, dips are wonderfully convenient. They can be made ahead, or at the very least prepared ahead then baked at the last minute if necessary; they're easily transportable; and they make very affordable entertaining fare. With an array of dunkers two or three dips can easily feed a large number of people. They're also easily customisable, so feel free to tinker with any of the recipes in the book, changing the flavours and ingredients to make them your own!

FRESH AND BALANCED FLAVOURS

Dips are often unjustly maligned as being unhealthy and hiding a multitude of sins. This is likely because it's not always easy to discern exactly what's in a dip. Especially if it's a heavy, bland-looking mass; the assumption is that it's packed with fattening fillers. The key to making even a creamy dip taste fresh is to counter the creamy elements with lots of herbs and spices. A great dip is always robustly flavoured and well-balanced. This means that even a tomato-based dip or salsa must not be overly sharp or acidic. Any harsh flavours should be tempered with a touch of sweetness.

PRESENTATION

A smooth dip or a pâté can sometimes struggle to look appetising even if it is thoroughly delicious. Showcase it in a way that highlights its best assets. Sprinkle a beige or brown dip liberally with fresh chopped herbs, or dust it with paprika for an eye-catching finish. If you're making a dip that has nuts in it, toast an extra portion of those same nuts and scatter them on top of the prepared dip. Drizzle a bright green, full-flavoured extra-virgin oil over a hummus or bean dip – it will add visual appeal and a zingy bite.

DIPPERS

Whether it's a platter of freshly-cut crudités or an array of warm breads, do your dips justice by having a good selection of dippers. But consider flavour pairings too. Don't offer a strong-tasting olive bread with a pungent dip. Instead opt for plain melba toast so the flavours don't fight with one another. Similarly, a delicate fish dip would benefit from being served with cucumber sticks, endives and julienned red pepper or bread sticks as opposed to heavily seasoned tortilla crisps.

When it comes to crudités, you might want to serve some vegetables raw, as well as some lightly blanched to offer some contrast. Crudités choices should be seasonal, too. When locally grown sugar snap peas are in season, for example, they are so sweet and crisp they are delicious eaten out of hand, but if you buy a pack of peas in the winter months, they will likely be imported and will benefit from quick cooking to heighten their flavours and sweetness.

Equipment

Getting a recipe just right rests partly on using the right equipment. Without a whisk, you'll have real trouble incorporating butter into a Hollandaise. Without a sharp knife, your chopped herbs will be unevenly cut and bruised, leaching their oils onto the chopping board.

Most of the recipes in this book call for equipment that you probably already have in your kitchen. If there's anything listed below that you're missing, it's worth making the additional purchases as they'll come in handy for preparing countless other dishes. Don't be tempted by cheap prices if it means compromising on quality. If you invest in sturdy, well-made items, they will last you for years.

WEIGHING SCALES

For maximum accuracy, especially when measuring out very small quantities, opt for digital scales. Select one that's easy to operate, read and clean, and ideally measures both wet and dry ingredients so you don't have to revert to measuring cups when it comes to liquids. When working with larger quantities, the more traditional mechanical scales that have either a rotating 'skirt' or a dial will get the job done.

LIQUID MEASURING CUPS

Here, the old-fashioned, classic design is best. A functional cup with a mess-free pouring spout, robust handle and calibrated measurements is just what you need for measuring liquids. Plastic cups are light and durable, but I prefer transparent glass ones that are easy to read. I also use a spririt measure to measure small measurements. It's primarily used when making cocktails, but I find it comes in useful when making small quantities of salad dressing.

MEASURING SPOONS

Don't rely on your cutlery for accurate measurements. The capacity of a dining tablespoon ranges anywhere from a generous teaspoon (about 7 ml) to a true tablespoon (15 ml). Similarly, a teaspoon for culinary purposes is always 5 ml, while a dining version can hold anything from 2.5 to 6 ml. For maximum versatility, opt for sets that have four measures, from ¼ teaspoon up to 1 tablespoon.

WHISKS

Whisks are vital for a lump-free, shiny and/or emulsified sauce or dressing. They are also essential for whipping air into cream and eggs for light, airy, voluminous mixtures. One medium-sized, stainless steel balloon whisk will do. When it comes to making smaller quantities of sauces or dressings, even a medium whisk can be difficult to manoeuvre into the corners of a small saucepan. With this in mind, invest in two or three different whisk sizes. For the smallest of quantities, I like to use the small coil whisks.

KNIVES

If you're short on space, just two knives – a large 20 cm (8-inch) kitchen knife, and a small 7.5 cm (3-inch) paring knife will see you through almost any recipe. For longevity, ease of use and cleanly cut fruit and vegetables, herbs and meats, you'll need very sharp and sturdy knives – so invest in quality. Spending a little bit more can make the difference between knives that last a couple of years and ones that endure for decades. Of course, maintenance is important, too. Use a sharpening steel at home to maintain a blade in good shape, and send your knives off to a professional grinder once a year to breathe new life into dull edges.

MIXING BOWLS

Have as many bowls as your kitchen can accommodate – you'll find countless uses for them, and there's nothing more annoying than having to rush back to the sink after every job to wash out one bowl so you can reuse it. At least four bowls, I think, are necessary, in a variety of sizes and depths. I like to have a series of smaller nesting bowls that fit snugly inside one another and another set of larger nesting bowls. Stainless steel and heavy-duty plastic bowls are the best and most versatile, although ceramic and glass bowls can be good – they just run the risk of being broken when the activity in the kitchen is fast-paced!

ZESTERS AND GRATERS

Box graters are good for softer cheeses like Cheddar, but can be tiresome to use for hard cheeses such as Parmesan and zesting lemons. For these jobs, opt for Microplane graters that produce fine flecks of zest or cheese with little effort.

PESTLE AND MORTAR

Before I turn to the blender, coffee grinder or food processor, I always consider whether I can get the job done with my pestle and mortar. Though it might take a little longer, it requires less clean up, and it's generally less hassle than having to navigate the electrical appliances. When selecting a pestle and mortar, choose one that's a good size for your kitchen, so you don't have to hide it in a cupboard somewhere; that's weighty and durable, preferably made of heavy stone or granite; and that has a non-reactive surface.

BLENDERS AND FOOD PROCESSORS

To properly prepare many of the recipes in this book, you'll need a blender or a food processor. Blenders purée in seconds, easily producing smooth dressings, sauces and dips. A hand blender is good for processing smaller amounts or for blending directly in the saucepan. Sometimes, when there are just a few ingredients in small amounts to blend, and you don't have a pestle and mortar, it can be useful to invest in a mini blender. A food processor can carry out the same duties as a blender, plus it chops, grates and mixes, depending on what blade or function you use. Choose a food processor that has a smaller bowl that can be nested inside a larger, roomier bowl so you can use it whether you're making a dip for ten or a dressing for four.

ELECTRIC HANDHELD MIXER

This is another must-have in my opinion. It quickly and efficiently turns egg whites into billowy meringues, and it blends with ease, whether the ingredients are in a bowl or in a saucepan over heat, to produce smooth, fluffy mixtures.

COOKING UTENSILS

When I'm preparing a cooked sauce or sautéing ingredients, I always reach for a wooden spoon. They are comfortable to use, never get too hot and are gentle on nonstick pans. I like to have a few in various sizes and shapes.

For other tasks, it's useful to have a ladle to spoon out liquids; a slotted spoon to remove solids while leaving any liquid or fat behind; and a skimmer to sift out impurities or skim fat from the surface of a sauce or stock. Spatulas, too, with their long handles and flexible, rubber heads, come in extremely handy. They are especially useful for scraping out the final remnants of a sauce or dip from a pan, mixing bowl, blender or food processor.

SIEVES

A fine mesh sieve can make the difference between an unappetising sauce riddled with lumps and a refined, satiny smooth one. If you have the space, it's good to have two or three sieves, in different sizes and with varying degrees of fineness. My collection includes metal sieves as well as non-reactive, nylon sieves ideal for delicately flavoured sauces since they don't transfer any flavours or odours.

POTS AND SAUCEPANS

You don't need a whole arsenal, but you do need a few heavy-based pots and saucepans of different sizes – a small, medium and large one at least, some high-sided. It's important to use an appropriately sized pan when making a sauce as it affects the rate at which ingredients cook or at which a sauce reduces. Choose good-quality, weighty, lidded stainless steel or cast-iron vessels that are well-balanced and that evenly distribute heat during cooking. I like saucepans with one long handle as it makes moving them easier, but some cooks prefer two-handled pots. When it comes to making homemade stock, you'll need a large, deep stockpot so you can make a sizable amount at a time.

FRYING PANS AND WOKS

Invest in good-quality frying pans that feel heavy and robust in your hand and that don't buckle over heat. I have a couple of stainless steel ones in two sizes – a medium and a large one; a 25 cm (10-inch) cast-iron pan that's my usual go-to whether I'm sautéing, searing or making a pan-sauce; and a nonstick frying pan that I use for toasting nuts, seeds and spices. I like pans that have sloping sides and a rolled edge that makes pouring out the contents a cinch. The handles are important too: opt for frying pans that have round handles that are tapered where you grip them so they are comfortable to use.

Ingredients

Oils

VEGETABLE OIL

Generic vegetable oil is made from a combination of oils that can include corn, rapeseed, peanut, soybean and grape seed oil. It is naturally free of cholesterol and trans fat and is refined to produce a versatile, clear and relatively neutral-tasting oil that's ideal for cooking.

RAPESEED OIL

A specific vegetable oil made from rapeseeds. A good source of monounsaturated fats, it's one of the healthiest oils on the shelf. Like other vegetable oils – soybean, grape seed and peanut, for example – it's quite neutral in flavour, with a light texture that makes it a good choice for light dressings, mayonnaise and pan sauces.

OLIVE OIL

A verdant, heart-healthy oil extracted from ripe olives. It can range in depth of flavour, spiciness and colour depending on the olives used, the grade of the oil, the region in which the olives are grown and the process used to extract the oil.

Extra-virgin olive oil is mechanically cold-pressed without the use of heat to produce the purest, most flavourful and aromatic olive oil. It should be reserved for dressings and other no-cook applications where its flavour can shine. When it comes to sautéing, opt for the lowest-grade variety labelled 'olive oil' or 'pure olive oil', since heat destroys the aromas and nuances of more expensive virgin oils.

NUT OILS

These bear the aromas and flavours of the nuts from which they are extracted and add a delicious, nutty taste to dressings. Walnut and hazelnut oils are perhaps the most commonly found, but search online or in specialist shops for varieties such as pistachio, pecan, pine nut, cashew and macadamia oil. They can be expensive so cut them with mild-flavoured olive oil to ensure a little goes a long way.

Vinegars

A splash of vinegar can do wonders for a sauce, balancing flavours, enhancing any fresh herbs and adding a refreshing, bright finish. In a dressing or vinaigrette, the acid is a bigger star. It brings an assertive, piquant note to counter the rich oils or creamy elements, and enlivens bitter leaves.

WINE VINEGARS

Made from red and white wine or even champagne, these carry the flavours of the wines they are made from. But they can vary greatly in quality depending on the brand, so don't settle for the cheapest bottles, which can often be mouth-puckeringly astringent. A good vinegar will have a balance of tartness and sweetness and a depth of flavour.

BALSAMIC VINEGAR

There's a distinct difference between an authentic, syrupy balsamic vinegar, which is made from Trebbiano grapes and is aged for a minimum of one year, and 'supermarket shelf' balsamic. The latter is often red wine vinegar combined with cooked grape juice and sometimes caramel colouring. It can often make a fine vinaigrette, but for a sublime dressing or a special occasion opt for the real deal.

CIDER VINEGAR

A golden-hued vinegar distilled from apples. Adds a touch of sweetness and piquancy to savoury sauces and is great in salad dressings where you want a bright, fruity tang.

SHERRY VINEGAR

A sharp, nutty and rich vinegar made from sherry – a fortified wine. It can be quite expensive due to the fact that it's aged and carefully blended. Use it when you want high acidity and complex flavours with just a hint of sweetness.

FRUIT VINEGARS

Fruit vinegars such as raspberry and strawberry are delicious in salad dressings that include berries or orchard fruit. Alternatively, combine with or use in place of red or white wine vinegar in a vinaigrette. Make sure you don't cook with them since the heat will destroy the flavour. Instead, stir a drop or two into a sauce once it's off the heat, or into a dip with a seasoning of salt and pepper.

Dairy

Whether it's thick cream, grated cheese, sour cream or butter, dairy products add richness and body.

CHEESE

HARD CHEESES

Parmesan, Gruyère, pecorino, Asiago and mature Cheddar are some of the hard cheeses included in recipes in this book. They all have their distinctive flavours, but as a rule, hard cheeses veer towards the nutty, sharp and salty end of the spectrum, becoming increasingly earthy and assertive as they age. When making a sauce or a dip where you want the cheese to melt completely, be sure to grate it finely.

FRESH GOAT'S CHEESE

A soft, unripened, mild and delicately tangy cheese made from fermented goat's milk, especially delicious in dips.

BLUE CHEESE

This catch-all descriptor refers to a host of strong, pungent cheeses with veins of blue running through them. The most common are: Roquefort, Gorgonzola, Maytag and Stilton. When a recipe calls for blue cheese and doesn't specify which one, choose your favourite. They add an assertive bite and complexity to cheese sauces, and go well with pasta.

CREAM CHEESE

A mild, creamy, spreadable cheese, cream cheese is used in dips and sauces. Bring to room temperature before using, and opt for full or reduced fat versions but not fat free – it may curdle or melt with a grainy finish.

MASCARPONE

While it's often referred to as a 'cheese', technically this is a rich, thickened cream. It's a little like sour cream but thicker with a more complex flavour, a little less tang and a slightly sweet finish. Deliciously versatile, you'll find it used in sweet recipes for a creamy finish but it's also used to enrich meat sauces. Because of its high fat content, it will not curdle over gentle heat.

RICOTTA

Made from whey that's leftover from the production of other cheeses, ricotta translates to 'recooked'. It is a soft fresh cheese that is thick and silky though slightly grainy in texture. It has a light, sweet and milky flavour. Great in dips and pasta sauces where it adds creaminess and body.

DOUBLE CREAM

Great for cooking, double cream is very rich and luscious with a fat content of 48 per cent. Because of this high fat content, it can be subjected to high heat without curdling (unlike single cream) making it ideal for thickening and adding a decadent, creamy finish to sauces. It not only withstands boiling, but it whips and freezes well.

CRÈME FRAÎCHE

France's more luxurious, unctuous version of sour cream; to be precise, it's twice as rich and twice as thick. It has a characteristic sharpness and texture. Like double cream, it's excellent for cooking since it won't curdle over heat.

SOUR CREAM

Made from single cream cultured with bacteria to produce its tangy flavour, sour cream can be used in dressings where a light creamy texture and piquancy is desired. It can also be used to finish a sauce, but stir it in at the end once the pan is off the heat and never let it boil, otherwise it will curdle.

GREEK YOGHURT

Like sour cream, never subject this pleasantly sour, fermented milk product to high heat or else it will separate. Instead stir it into cooked sauces, right at the end and pull off the heat immediately, or cook very gently at low heat. Greek yoghurt is thicker and often more intensively flavoured than regular yoghurt because it is strained. Use low-fat Greek yoghurt as a healthy alternative in no-cook dips and dressings when you're after a creamy texture without the guilt.

BUTTERMILK

Traditionally the leftover liquid from churned butter, this slightly acidic ingredient is today made by adding a bacterial culture to skim milk. It makes light dressings.

BUTTER

Use unsalted butter unless otherwise stated, and use cold butter unless the recipe calls for room temperature. I spend a little extra on good butter, especially if I think it's contributing flavour or whisked into a finished sauce.

Some sauces use clarified butter – butter that has been heated to separate the milk solids, which are removed before the clear liquid is used. To do this, melt the butter and let it simmer for about 10 minutes, so that the water evaporates and the milk solids coagulate and settle to the bottom of the pan. Remove from the heat and leave for 2 to 3 minutes. Skim any foam from the top, and pour the clarified butter into a measuring cup, leaving behind the coagulated solids. Leave to cool, until just warm.

EGGS

Eggs are used as a thickening base in a mayonnaise or a Hollandaise, or to create light, fluffy and viscous concoctions such as sabayon, fruit curds and custards. Add eggs to a heated mixture over indirect heat, such as in a bain-marie or a bowl placed over a pan of simmering water, otherwise the egg will overcook and scramble. I always opt for free-range, and when possible organic.

Herbs

Always use fresh herbs, unless specified by the recipe. Chop at the last minute to preserve their fragrance and add near the end of cooking, unless otherwise directed. In a pinch you can substitute dried for fresh using a ratio of 1 to 3, although it's preferable to use another fresh herb. Dried herbs lack the flavour of fresh and often go stale quickly.

FLAT-LEAF PARSLEY

The ultimate multipurpose herb, it has a bright, punchy verdant flavour that complements a plethora of ingredients.

ITALIAN BASIL

Aromatic, and flavoured with liquorice and clove, it pairs well with Mediterranean ingredients. Use a sharp knife to shred the leaves to avoid bruising them, or tear into pieces.

CHERVIL

A more delicately flavoured relative of parsley, chervil with its lacy, grass green leaves, has notes of liquorice and anise. Add right at the end of cooking or after you've taken the pan off the cooker, to maximise the herb's flavour.

CHIVES

Oniony, a little garlicky and mildly pungent, chives add flavour and colour to creamy sauces and dips.

DILL

Delicate, with an aromatic anise, fennel-like flavour that complements fish, seafood and white meats. Use it quickly after buying or cutting as it is highly perishable.

THYME

A sprig or two added at the beginning, or the chopped leaves of this woodsy, minty herb thrown in at the end of cooking, balances the aromatic flavours in the pan. Use judiciously so as not to overwhelm other ingredients.

ROSEMARY

A little goes a long way with this herb. It adds a warmth and aroma and stands up well to rich, bold flavours.

Spices

When using whole spices, toast them in a dry frying pan for a few minutes until fragrant and slightly darkened to bring out as much of their aromas and flavours as possible. Use a coffee grinder or a pestle and mortar to crush them to a fine powder if necessary. When a recipe calls for ready-ground spices, make sure they are fresh. Stale ground spices taste of little more than barely perfumed dust, so be sure to replace yours at least once a year.

STAR ANISE

A beautiful, star-shaped, reddish-brown spice, star anise is boldly flavoured with a highly perfumed scent and strong notes of fennel and liquorice. Especially popular in Far Eastern cuisines, use the whole spice to infuse sauces, removing it before serving.

CINNAMON

Sweet, woody and aromatic, cinnamon whether ground or whole, adds a spicy, tingly warmth to sweet and savoury sauces and dips. The ground spice adds more of a punch, whereas the rolled bark infuses a more subtle flavour. If using the whole spice, be sure to remove before serving.

CUMIN SEEDS

Used in Mexican, Indian, Southeast Asian and Middle Eastern cuisines, dark brown cumin seeds and ground cumin possess a nutty, peppery and pungent taste.

CORIANDER SEEDS

Often used paired with cumin, the round, brown seeds of the coriander plant add a warm, citrusy, piney flavour to dishes. Use it ground or whole as required.

GROUND CAYENNE

Though technically not a spice, I've included ground cayenne here since it's often treated as one. Cayenne is a very hot red chilli that's most often dried whole or ground into a very fine, vibrant red powder.

FENNEL SEEDS

These oblong, greenish-brown seeds have a striking resemblance in flavour to aniseed. They are used in Italian, Northern European and Indian cuisines.

GROUND TURMERIC

A relative of ginger, bright yellowy-orange turmeric is widely used in Asian cooking, adding a vibrant hue and an earthy, mustardy and even peppery flavour. While fresh turmeric is hard to find, the dried, ground powder is readily available in supermarkets.

BLACK PEPPER

As far as I'm concerned the only way to use black pepper is to grind it freshly when you want it since ready-ground pepper loses its potency very quickly. Have a pepper grinder or mill by your cooker and grind the peppercorns as finely or as coarsely as you like.

Condiments

WORCESTERSHIRE SAUCE

A few splashes of this spicy, tangy, salty sauce made from a multitude of ingredients including anchovies, vinegar and tamarind add a depth of flavour.

DIJON MUSTARD

Originally from Dijon in France, this mustard adds piquancy and spice to sauces and acts as an emulsifier in vinaigrettes, helping to prevent the oil and vinegar separating.

WHOLE-GRAIN MUSTARD

Prepared mustard containing whole mustard seeds, this pungent condiment adds an extra bite and warmth. As an alternative, you can use coarse or stone-ground mustard.

SOY SAUCE

A salty liquid made from fermented soybeans and roasted wheat or barley and salt. Used in Asian cooking, it lends a rich, meaty finish and boosts flavour.

TOMATO KETCHUP

This sweet tomato sauce is a common ingredient in several classic creamy dressings and piquant sauces, bringing colour, tang and a rich flavour to the plate.

PREPARED HORSERADISH

Pungent and fiery, horseradish adds a subtle kick. Fresh horseradish root is difficult to come by, so I rely on jarred prepared horseradish instead.

HOT SAUCE (TABASCO)

Every kitchen needs a hot, vinegary chilli sauce such as hot sauce. A drop or two livens up a dish, and it's just the thing to add bite without having to handle fresh chillies.

Sweeteners

WHITE SUGAR

A pinch of sugar is sometimes added to a savoury recipe to balance out other flavours. Use granulated white sugar unless otherwise stated. If you prefer, you can use 'golden' white sugar, which has a subtle caramel finish.

SOFT BROWN SUGAR

A semi-refined sugar with some molasses left in, it comes in light and dark varieties with the latter containing more molasses. Light brown has a delicate toffee flavour whereas dark brown is fudgy, spicier and warmer.

HONEY

The type of honey you use will impact the final flavour of the sweet or savoury sauce, dressing or dip you're making. If you're simply looking for sweetness without a heavy floral note, then it's best to go for a light-coloured runny honey that will be mild in flavour. If the honey is an important component and you want it to bring a distinctive flavour, opt for a dark, wildflower variety. As a general rule, the darker the honey, the more pungent and flavourful it will be.

GOLDEN SYRUP / CORN SYRUP

Though corn syrup and golden syrup are different – the former is made from cornflour and the latter from sugar cane or sugar beet juice, these liquids can be used interchangeably in recipes in this book.

Stocks

It's vital to use the best-quality stock you can find. Almost always this means making it yourself. The good news is that stocks can be frozen – so you can whip up a large batch and store it in useable portions.

It's not always easy, however, to set aside the best part of the day, or at the very least, a whole afternoon, to tend to a pot of bones! When it comes to beef stock, the next best solution is to buy fresh stock (found in the refrigerated section) since the shelf-stable beef stock products tend to be of a lesser quality to the long-life, pasteurised chicken or vegetable stocks available.

Chicken Stock

2 raw chicken carcasses, roughly broken up
2 medium onions, peeled and cut into wedges
2 medium carrots, peeled and roughly chopped
2 stalks celery, roughly chopped
2 medium leeks, green leaves removed and discarded, white parts roughly chopped
Small handful fresh parsley stalks
2 to 3 fresh thyme sprigs
1 bay leaf
6 to 8 whole black peppercorns

Place all the ingredients in a deep stockpot and cover with at least 2 litres of cold water – all the ingredients must be thoroughly submerged – and bring to a boil. Reduce the heat and let simmer. Skim off any scum and fat that floats on the surface. Continue to simmer gently, over low heat – you're looking for just a few bubbles rising to the surface, skimming every now and then as necessary, for 3 to 4 hours.

When the water evaporates and drops below the ingredients in the stock, add fresh cold water to cover. With each addition, bring the stock back up to a boil, skim and return to a gentle simmer.

When the stock is ready, pour through a fine sieve into a large container with a lid. For a clearer stock, don't press down on the ingredients when straining. Leave the stock to cool completely then chill overnight, covered, in the fridge. The following day, remove and discard any fat that has risen and solidified on the surface of the stock.

At this point, the stock can be refrigerated as is or frozen until needed. Alternatively, decant into a wide pan and simmer briskly over medium-high heat until reduced by half, skimming off any scum that rises to the surface, for a more concentrated liquid. Strain into a lidded container and leave to cool completely before freezing or refrigerating.

Variation: For a darker, richer chicken stock, before making the stock, roast the chicken carcasses in a hot oven at 220°C (425°F) for about 45 minutes to an hour until a deep golden-brown colour, turning occasionally. For extra flavour, cut the vegetables into even 2-cm (1-inch) dice and sauté in a little olive oil until golden brown before adding to the stockpot – be sure not to burn them or the final stock will be bitter.

Basic Vegetable Stock

2 large onions, peeled and quartered

3 carrots, peeled and roughly chopped

2 stalks celery, roughly chopped

2 leeks, green leaves removed and discarded,
   white parts roughly chopped

Small handful white or brown mushrooms,
   halved or quartered if large

Small handful fresh parsley stalks

2 to 3 fresh thyme sprigs

1 bay leaf

6 to 8 whole black peppercorns

Place all the ingredients in a medium stockpot and cover completely with at least 2 litres of cold water. Bring to a boil over medium-high heat, then lower the heat and simmer for 45 minutes, skimming off any foam occasionally. Strain the stock.

At this point, the stock can be cooled and refrigerated or frozen until needed. Alternatively, decant into a wide pan and simmer briskly over medium-high heat until reduced by half, skimming off any scum that rises to the surface, for a more concentrated liquid. Strain and leave to cool before freezing or refrigerating.

Variation: For a rich vegetable stock, first cut all the vegetables above into 2-cm (1-inch) chunks and sauté in a little olive oil and 1 teaspoon (about 5 ml) of tomato purée until a deep golden-brown colour. You may have to do this in batches. Proceed with the recipe above, making sure to remove and discard any burnt vegetable chunks, and cooking the stock for 1 hour.

Fish Stock

2 medium onions, roughly chopped

1 small bulb fennel, chopped

2 medium carrots, peeled and roughly chopped

1 medium leek, green leaves removed and discarded,
   white part roughly chopped

450 g fish bones and trimmings such as tails and heads
   of white fish (don't use oily fish such as salmon or mackerel),
   thoroughly washed and all blood rinsed off

1 bay leaf

Small handful parsley stalks

6 to 8 whole black peppercorns

Place all the ingredients in a medium stockpot and cover completely with at least 1 ½ litres of water. Bring to a boil over medium-high heat, then skim off and discard any scum that rises to the surface. Reduce the heat and simmer, skimming, occasionally, for 20 to 30 minutes only.

Strain the stock through a fine sieve. It can now be cooled and refrigerated or frozen until needed. Alternatively, decant into a wide pan and simmer briskly over medium-high heat until reduced by half, skimming off any scum that rises to the surface, for a more concentrated liquid. Strain stock into a container, and leave to cool completely before freezing or refrigerating.

Shellfish Stock

1 large onion, cut into wedges

2 medium carrots, roughly chopped

1 small bulb fennel, roughly chopped

Heads and shells from about 675 g prawns, and/or empty
   lobster or crab shells and claws, well-rinsed in cold water

1 bay leaf

Small handful parsley stalks

6 to 8 whole black peppercorns

Place all the ingredients in a large stockpot and cover completely with at least 2 litres of cold water. Bring to a boil over medium-high heat, then reduce the heat and simmer for 30 to 40 minutes, skimming off any scum that rises to the surface.

Strain the stock, discarding the solids. Wash out the stockpot and return the strained liquid to it. Bring the liquid back to a boil and simmer briskly until the stock has reduced by half. Strain stock into a container and leave to cool before freezing or refrigerating.

Variation: For a richer, bolder stock, cut all the vegetables into 1-inch (2 cm) pieces and sauté in a little olive oil until golden. Add the shells and cook for 3 to 4 minutes, stirring. Stir in 1 teaspoon (5 ml) tomato purée, and after a minute add the remaining ingredients and the cold water and finish the recipe as directed.

Rich Beef Stock

1 kg beef and/or veal marrow bones,
    trimmed of excess fat
2 tbsp (30 ml) vegetable or rapeseed oil
2 large onions, unpeeled and chopped
2 large carrots, peeled and chopped
2 stalks celery, chopped
1 medium bulb fennel, chopped
2 leeks, green leaves removed and discarded,
    white parts chopped
180 g brown mushrooms, chopped
2 tsp (10 ml) tomato purée
Small handful parsley stalks
2 sprigs thyme
1 bay leaf
6 to 8 whole black peppercorns

Preheat oven to 220°C (425°F). Place the bones in one or two roasting pans and roast for about an hour until a deeply golden brown, tossing every now and then to ensure they are coloured evenly all over.

Heat the oil in a large frying pan and add the vegetables. Sauté over medium heat until deeply golden and caramelised, about 8 to 10 minutes.

Add the tomato purée, and continue to cook, stirring, for a further minute.

Transfer the vegetables to a large stockpot with the beef bones, leaving behind any rendered fat in the roasting pan, and add the remaining ingredients. Cover completely with at least 2 ½ to 3 litres of cold water and bring to a boil over medium-high heat. Skim off any scum that rises to the surface, then reduce the heat and simmer gently – you only want a few bubbles rising to the surface, for 5 to 6 hours, skimming occasionally. When the water evaporates and drops below the ingredients in the stock, add enough fresh cold water to cover the ingredients. With each addition, bring the stock back up to a boil, skim and return to a gentle simmer.

When the stock is ready, pour through a fine sieve into a large container with a lid. For a clearer stock, don't press down on the ingredients when straining. Leave the stock to then cool completely then chill overnight, covered, in the fridge. The following day, remove and discard any fat that has risen and solidified on the surface of the stock.

At this point, the stock can be refrigerated as is or frozen until needed. Alternatively, decant into a wide pan and simmer briskly over medium-high heat until reduced by half, skimming off any scum that rises to the surface, for a more concentrated liquid. Strain stock into a lidded container and leave to cool completely before freezing or refrigerating.

Stock Storage Tips

When making stock, it's always wise to make twice as much as you'll think you'll need for the recipe at hand. The leftover stock can be easily frozen without impairing its flavour for up to 3 months.

For really easy storage, reduce a finished stock until it is nearly syrupy. Cool, and decant into ice cube trays. Freeze then remove the frozen cubes and keep in the freezer in a sealable bag. When using, simply dilute the cubes in just-boiled water as needed. When freezing, always make sure you label it with the date on which you made and froze the stock so you know when to use it by.

Pan Sauces and Gravies

It is difficult to give precise recipes for these types of sauces. Instead, what you need is a foolproof formula that you can adapt to virtually any roast, steak or sautéed meat preparation.

The foundation of a tasty pan sauce or gravy is the caramelised and crusty bits that are left at the bottom of a frying pan or a roasting tray after you've roasted a joint or a bird or pan-fried a piece of meat. Avoid using nonstick pans, as these don't yield good, if any, 'crusty' bits. Instead, opt for a well-seasoned cast-iron or stainless steel pan or frying pan.

The first step of the classic pan sauce is to pour off any excess fat after the meat has been cooked and removed from the pan so the finished sauce isn't overly fatty.

Now you need to de-glaze the pan by adding a liquid to carry the meat juices and dissolve and lift off any stuck-on bits of caramelised meats. Very often an alcohol of some sort, such as wine, brandy or sherry, but it could also be water, stock or double cream. Place the pan over a medium-high heat, and add the liquid. Once it comes to the boil, use a wooden spoon to scrape the bottom of the pan to dislodge any stubborn residue.

Allow the liquid in the pan to bubble away briskly for a minute. If you added an alcohol, make sure it cooks until reduced by at least half to boil away the harsh alcohol flavours. At this point, more stock or cream can be poured in and the sauce reduced to the desired consistency. Alternatively, cornflour, arrowroot or *beurre manié* (see page 6), can be added as thickeners. Finally, season to taste with salt and pepper. If desired, add mustard, vinegar or lemon juice for a touch of brightness.

For a traditional gravy, remove the cooked joint and set aside to rest. Pour off the fat, leaving behind about 2 tablespoons (30 ml). Place the roasting pan directly on the cooker on medium heat, and add 2 to 3 tablespoons (30 to 45 ml) plain flour. Using a wooden spoon, incorporate the flour into the fat and meat juices and scrape off all the caramelized bits from the bottom and corners of the pan.

Cook for about 2 minutes until the roux is a golden colour, then whisk in about 340 ml hot, rich chicken or beef stock. (Adjust the amount depending on how many people you're serving.) Bring to a boil, and simmer to reduce the gravy until it reaches your desired consistency. Season to taste with salt and pepper and a little mustard and a little vinegar or lemon juice, if desired. Strain gravy before serving. For variations, add some wine, port or sherry to the pan before adding the stock and bubble away until reduced by two-thirds before adding the stock. Additionally, a little double cream can be added in the final minutes of cooking, for an even richer, more luxurious gravy.

In both pan sauce and gravies, herbs can be added to flavour the sauce. Chopped, fresh soft herbs such as parsley and chervil should be added at the end to preserve their delicate flavours and keep their colour, whereas hardier herbs such as rosemary or thyme, can be added earlier.

EMULSIFIED SAUCES

1 Hollandaise

An indulgent accompaniment to a whole host of dishes from simple poached eggs to grilled lobster, there's no denying that a perfectly executed, homemade hollandaise is an irresistible treat. It is one of the five French mother sauces (see page 6).

INGREDIENTS

110 g unsalted butter
3 tbsp (45 ml) white wine vinegar
1 bay leaf
6 black peppercorns
1 tbsp (15 ml) water
2 large egg yolks
Pinch of cayenne pepper
½ tbsp (8 ml) fresh lemon juice, plus more to taste
Salt

MAKES 155 ml, which will serve 2 to 3 people.

Melt the butter in a small saucepan over medium heat. Cool until warm.

Put the vinegar, bay leaf, peppercorns and water in a small saucepan and bring to a boil. Simmer for a minute, until the liquid has reduced to about 1 tablespoon (15 ml). Cool slightly, then strain into a medium heatproof bowl. Cool to room temperature.

Place the bowl over a pan of simmering water, making sure the bottom of the bowl doesn't touch the water. Add the egg yolks to the bowl and whisk into the vinegar until well combined. Drizzle in the melted butter in a thin, steady stream, whisking constantly, until all of the butter is fully incorporated and the sauce is pale, fluffy and thick enough to leave a ribbon trail that stays for a couple of seconds. This can take up to 8 minutes.

Stir in the cayenne pepper, ½ tablespoon (8 ml) lemon juice and season to taste with salt, adding more lemon juice if desired. Remove from the heat and serve immediately. Alternatively, keep the bowl over the pan of barely simmering water for up to 40 minutes – stirring occasionally until ready to serve.

Serve with: fish, vegetables or eggs benedict (with muffins, poached eggs and ham).

HANDY TIPS

You can make hollandaise using a blender. Place the cooled, strained vinegar reduction in a blender with the yolks and cayenne. Blend briefly until mixed. With the motor running, pour the warm butter through the feeder tube in a very thin drizzle. Use all the butter; the sauce should be thick and fluffy. Add the lemon juice, and season to taste.

Variations

2 HOLLANDAISE WITH HERBS

Follow the recipe for **Easy Lemon Hollandaise** and stir in ½ tablespoon (8 ml) each of chopped fresh parsley, dill, chervil and chives.
Serve with: grilled prawns, fish fingers or with chopped, steamed spinach.

5 'MALTAISE'

Omit the lemon juice. Place the finely grated zest and juice of 1 medium-sized blood orange in a small saucepan, simmer until reduced to 2 to 3 tablespoons (30 to 45 ml), then stir into the finished sauce.
Serve with: steamed asparagus or broccoli.

3 CHAMPAGNE VINEGAR AND STRAWBERRY

Replace the white wine vinegar with champagne vinegar and stir in 70 g chopped and crushed ripe strawberries.
Serve with: baked or grilled fish, scallops or prawns.

6 WITH PRAWNS AND DILL

Omit the cayenne, and stir 70 g of chopped, cooked and peeled prawns; 1 tablespoon (15 ml) of chopped fresh dill and freshly cracked black pepper, to taste, into the completed sauce.
Serve with: poached or grilled fish.

4 WHOLE-GRAIN MUSTARD AND TARRAGON

Stir 1 ½ teaspoons (8 ml) whole-grain mustard and 1 tablespoon (15 ml) chopped fresh tarragon into the sauce.
Serve with: steak, burgers or as a dipping sauce for thick-cut chips.

7 EASY LEMON

Replace the vinegar reduction with 1 ½ tablespoons (23 ml) lemon juice, and stir in 1 teaspoon (5 ml) finely grated lemon zest and ½ to 1 tablespoon (8 to 15 ml) lemon juice to the finished sauce, to taste.
Serve with: eggs benedict, eggs florentine or cold poached salmon.

CREAMY 'MOUSSELINE'

Add ½ teaspoon (3 ml) of lightly crushed pink peppercorns to the finished sauce, if desired, then fold in 120 ml of softly whipped cream just before serving.
Serve with: poached fish, eggs or steamed vegetables.

WITH JALAPEÑO

Heat 1 tablespoon (15 ml) finely minced, seeded jalapeño pepper and half of a garlic clove, also minced, in the melted butter in the main recipe, over a very low heat, for 2 minutes. Proceed as for the **Easy Lemon Hollandaise**, using lime juice instead of lemon juice.
Serve with: grilled chicken, turkey burgers or meaty fish.

WITH TRUFFLE

Prepare the **Hollandaise** or **Easy Lemon Hollandaise**, then whisk 1 teaspoon (5 ml) Dijon mustard and ½ tablespoon (8 ml) finely chopped fresh or canned black truffles into the completed sauce. For extra flavour, stir in ¼ teaspoon (1 ml) truffle oil.
Serve with: grilled steak, roast chicken, scallops or poached eggs.

11 Beurre Blanc

There is little as impressive as presenting a platter of perfectly cooked seafood, accompanied with a perfectly cooked classic French white butter sauce, or *beurre blanc*, to a table of dinner-party guests. Since this sauce is almost all butter, don't scrimp, buy the best you can find, and always opt for unsalted butter. This way, you're in control of the seasoning from the get-go.

INGREDIENTS

2 small shallots, finely chopped
2 tbsp (30 ml) white wine vinegar
225 ml dry white wine
225 g very cold unsalted butter,
 cut into small cubes

2 tsp (10 ml) lemon juice
Salt and black pepper

MAKES 255 ml
Serves 4 to 6

Place the shallots, vinegar and white wine in a small saucepan and bring to the boil. Simmer for 10 to 12 minutes, or until only a tablespoon (15 ml) of liquid remains.

Remove the pan from the heat and whisk in three or four cubes of butter at a time until the sauce is thick, creamy and emulsified. If the sauce starts to cool and the butter is slow to melt into it, return to a low heat briefly. When all the butter is used up, whisk in the lemon juice and season to taste with salt and pepper.

Serve with: steamed, baked, poached and grilled fish, seafood and poultry dishes.

Handy Tips

To ensure the emulsion in the sauce holds, it's important to use very cold butter. To keep your cubed butter from softening in a warm kitchen, arrange the cubes in a single layer on a plate and place in the freezer while making the white wine and vinegar reduction.

Variations

12 GRAPEFRUIT AND DILL

Replace the lemon juice with the juice of half of a medium-sized grapefruit that has been reduced in a small saucepan over medium-high heat to about 2 tablespoons (30 ml). Stir 2 teaspoons (10 ml) finely grated grapefruit zest and 2 tablespoons (30 ml) chopped fresh dill into the finished sauce.
Serve with: poached fish or prawns or grilled asparagus and other green vegetables.

13 PINK CHAMPAGNE AND PINK PEPPERCORN

Replace the white wine and white wine vinegar in the main recipe with pink champagne and champagne vinegar. Stir ¼ teaspoon (1 ml) crushed pink peppercorns into the finished sauce.
Serve with: roasted chicken breasts.

14 BEURRE ROUGE

Replace the white wine vinegar with red wine vinegar and the white wine with red wine. For extra flavour, reduce 110 ml beef stock to a generous tablespoon (20 ml) and use it to finish the sauce.
Serve with: meaty fish like halibut or monkfish, or a simply cooked filet mignon or lamb chops.

COCONUT MILK AND CORIANDER

Replace the white wine vinegar with 180 ml of coconut milk and reduce the white wine to 120 ml. Simmer the reduction to 2 to 3 tablespoons (30 to 45 ml). Add 2 tablespoons (30 ml) finely chopped fresh coriander to the finished sauce.
Serve with: sautéed mixed vegetables, grilled courgette or grilled fish, especially if it has a spicy marinade.

'NANTAIS' HERB

Increase the white wine vinegar to 60 ml, and simmer the reduction to 1 ½ tablespoons (23 ml) of liquid. Complete the recipe, stirring in 1 tablespoon (15 ml) each of finely chopped fresh tarragon, chervil and parsley.
Serve with: salmon, smoked salmon, mackerel or sardines.

WITH CRAB

Add 140 g fresh lump crabmeat, picked over for shells, to the finished sauce. Season with a dash of hot sauce, ¼ teaspoon (1 ml) Worcestershire sauce and stir in 2 tablespoons (30 ml) finely chopped fresh chives.
Serve with: grilled lobster or prawns, spinach or other greens, or serve with steak for a 'surf and turf'.

WITH ROCKET

Purée 85 g rocket in the blender with 2 teaspoons (10 ml) lemon juice and a splash of water, if needed, and add to the finished sauce. Strain through a sieve before serving.
Serve with: poached or steamed chicken, roast spring lamb, or delicate white fish like sole.

WITH VANILLA

Add 1 split vanilla pod to the white wine and white wine vinegar mixture before making the reduction. Follow the recipe, removing the vanilla pod at the end, scraping out the beans and whisking them back into the sauce. Discard the pod.
Serve with: fish, shellfish, chicken or poached eggs.

WITH ESPRESSO

Dissolve 1 ½ teaspoons (8 ml) of espresso powder in 3 tablespoons (45 ml) of just-boiled water. Add the mixture to the white wine and white wine vinegar and complete as directed.
Serve with: lobster, scallops, sea bass or halibut.

21 Béarnaise

The hint of anise in this creamy sauce comes from a reduction of white wine vinegar and white wine steeped in shallots, bay leaves and tarragon.

INGREDIENTS

2 small shallots, minced

3 tbsp (45 ml) white wine vinegar

2 tbsp (30 ml) water or white wine

¾ tsp (4 ml) lightly crushed
   black peppercorns

3 sprigs fresh tarragon, plus
   1 tbsp (15 ml) finely chopped
   tarragon leaves, kept separately

210 g unsalted butter

3 large egg yolks

2 tbsp (30 ml) lemon juice

Salt

MAKES 240 ml

Serves 3 to 4

Place the shallots, vinegar, water or wine, peppercorns and tarragon in a heavy-based saucepan and simmer until 2 tablespoons (30 ml) of liquid remain. Remove from the cooker, strain and discard the solids. Set aside. Clarify the butter (see page 14). Cool until just warm.

Place the egg yolks and vinegar reduction in the top of a bain-marie or in a bowl set over a pan of simmering water, being sure the base does not touch the water. Whisk rapidly for up to 7 minutes, or until it is pale and creamy and leaves a ribbon trail when you lift the whisk. Remove the bowl from the heat. Add the butter in a thin, steady stream and whisk until the sauce is thick and shiny. Return the bowl to the heat every now and then for a few seconds. Stir in 1 tablespoon (15 ml) of the lemon juice, then adjust the seasoning with salt and the remaining juice. Stir in the tarragon leaves and serve, or keep warm over a pan of gently simmering water for up to 40 minutes, stirring occasionally.

Serve with: grilled meat or fish.

HANDY TIP

If the sauce 'splits' try one of these rescue remedies. Whisk together an egg yolk and 1 tablespoon (15 ml) of lemon juice or water. Slowly drizzle the broken sauce into this, whisking vigorously to create a fresh emulsion. Or, whisk one to two ice cubes into the broken sauce.

Variations

22 TOMATO AND BASIL 'CHORON' SAUCE

Stir 2 ½ tablespoons (38 ml) tomato purée, ½ teaspoon (3 ml) Worcestershire sauce, a pinch of sweet paprika and 2 tablespoons (30 ml) shredded basil into the finished sauce.

Serve with: grilled lamb kebabs or leg steaks, or chicken.

23 HORSERADISH AND CRÈME FRAÎCHE

Add 2 tablespoons (30 ml) crème fraîche, 2 tablespoons (30 ml) prepared horseradish, ½ teaspoon (3 ml) Dijon mustard and plenty of black pepper to the recipe. Replace the tarragon with 2 tablespoons (30 ml) chervil.

Serve with: beef or smoked mackerel.

For a sauce for roast beef, omit the béarnaise. Mix 2 tablespoons (30 ml) each freshly grated horseradish and crème fraîche with a pinch each of sugar and salt.

24 MINT 'PALOISE' SAUCE

Replace the tarragon sprigs with mint sprigs and add a pinch of sugar to the vinegar reduction. Stir chopped fresh mint leaves into the sauce in place of the chopped fresh tarragon leaves.

Serve with: roast lamb, grilled chicken or roast vegetables.

25 Beurre Noisette

This decadent sauce couldn't be easier to make; and it's perfect with a piece of pan-fried fish. *Beurre noisette* is essentially browned butter. The trick is to watch the butter in the pan like a hawk, take your eyes off of it for a moment and it's gone from hazelnut brown to burnt ebony, like a flash in the pan!

INGREDIENTS

MAKES 120 ml
Serves 2 to 3

110 g unsalted butter
1 tbsp (15 ml) lemon juice, plus more to taste
Salt
2 tbsp (30 ml) chopped fresh parsley leaves

Cut the butter into cubes and place in a small frying pan over medium heat. Once the butter is melted increase the heat to medium-high and continue to cook, swirling the pan, until the butter starts to foam and becomes a golden, nutty brown colour. Remove from the heat immediately, and stir in the lemon juice. Season to taste with salt, adding more lemon juice if desired. Finally, stir in the chopped parsley.

Serve with: sautéed fish or tossed through spaghetti or linguine.

HANDY TIP

To make a brown butter dessert sauce, omit the lemon juice and parsley, and strain the *beurre noisette* through a fine sieve. Heat 60 ml maple syrup in a small saucepan, and bring to a boil. Whisk in the sieved brown butter, add a small pinch of salt. Serve over ice cream or pound cake garnished with fruit.

Variations

26 WITH SAGE

Place 2 tablespoons (30 ml) finely shredded sage in a small heatproof bowl. Make the sauce, omitting the parsley, then pour the hot sauce over the sage. Cool until just warm, strain through a fine sieve, then discard the sage.
Serve with: mushroom or pumpkin ravioli, or combined with raw shredded kale or brussels sprouts with extra lemon juice for a refreshing salad.

27 WITH CRISPY BACON AND SHERRY VINEGAR

Cook 2 rashers of bacon, cut into small cubes, in a dry frying pan over medium heat, for 6 to 8 minutes, or until crisp. Remove from the pan and drain on kitchen paper. Make the sauce, replacing the lemon juice with a reduction made from 3 tablespoons (45 ml) sherry vinegar simmered with 1 tablespoon (15 ml) water until reduced to about 1 tablespoon (15 ml) of liquid. Stir in the bacon.
Serve with: blanched or steamed greens, or pork chops.

28 WITH SMOKED ALMOND AND ORANGE

Omit the parsley and add the finely grated zest and diced segments of half an orange and 1 tablespoon (15 ml) chopped smoked almonds into the finished sauce.
Serve with: grilled or sautéed salmon, pan-fried chicken breasts, or blanched or steamed green beans.

29 Romesco

This sauce recalls the flavours of the Mediterranean. It originates from the Northeast of Spain, where it's said local fishermen created it to accompany the catch of the day.

INGREDIENTS

1 thick-cut slice of white bread, cut into cubes
60 ml extra-virgin olive oil
30 g blanched slivered almonds, lightly toasted in a dry pan
160 ml drained roasted peppers from a jar
1 large garlic clove
½ tbsp (8 ml) red wine vinegar
½ tsp (3 g) smoked paprika
60 ml well-strained canned chopped tomatoes
Salt and black pepper

MAKES 240 ml
Serves 4

Preheat oven to 180°C (350°F). Place the bread in a small bowl. Drizzle with 1 tablespoon (15 ml) olive oil then toss well. Arrange the bread in a single layer on a baking sheet and cook until golden, about 15 minutes, turning once or twice. Leave to cool.

Transfer the bread to a blender or food processor, with all the other ingredients except the remaining olive oil. Process until smooth. With the motor running, pour in the remaining olive oil in a thin, steady stream. Transfer to a bowl and season with salt and pepper to taste. (Pictured left and opposite top.)

Serve with: roasted or grilled meats or poultry, or seafood – particularly fried calamari or herring.

HANDY TIP

To save time, use ready-made, supermarket-bought croutons. You'll need about 25 g.

30 RYE

Replace the white bread with a slice of dark rye bread.
Serve with: red meat and poultry, in sandwiches.

Variations

WITH AUBERGINE

Replace the peppers with 140 g diced aubergine
sautéed with 2 tablespoons (30 ml) olive oil, and the
paprika with 1 teaspoon (5 ml) cumin. Stir
2 tablespoons (30 ml) coriander into the sauce.
Serve with: crudités, grilled chicken or meat.

MISO AND CASHEW

Replace the almonds with cashew nuts. Add 1 teaspoon
(5 ml) soy sauce and 1 ½ tablespoons (23 ml) red miso
after the oil. Stir 2 tablespoons (30 ml) finely sliced
green onions (green part only) into the finished sauce.
(Pictured top.)
Serve with: Asian-style chicken or fish, tempura.

WITH FETA

Add 110 g finely crumbled feta cheese to the blender or
food processor after the oil. (Pictured centre.)
Serve with: crudités, sautéed or grilled chicken.

WITH RAISINS

Soak 2 tablespoons (30 ml) raisins in 1 tablespoon
(15 ml) brandy and 1 tablespoon (15 ml) boiling water
for 20 minutes. Drain, add to blender with the bread.
(Pictured bottom.)
Serve with: grilled or sautéed lamb, pork or steak.

WITH PINE NUTS

Replace the almonds with lightly toasted pine nuts.
Add 2 teaspoons (10 ml) fresh thyme leaves and a
small handful of fresh parsley leaves with the bread.
Serve with: steak, lamb chops, burgers or meatballs.

36 Tapenade

This dip hails from Provence in the south of France.

INGREDIENTS

250 g pitted black olives
2 garlic cloves, crushed
3 anchovies
2 tsp (10 g) capers, rinsed

1 to 2 tbsp (15 to 30 ml)
  olive oil
Black pepper
Squeeze of lemon juice

SERVES 4

Put the olives, garlic, anchovies, capers and oil in a food processor. Season with black pepper and process to a smooth purée. Add lemon juice to taste.

Serve with: hard-boiled quail's eggs, crudités or toast.

HANDY TIP

Some French cooks add a drop of brandy.

Variations

37 CREAMY

Stir the tapenade into 110 g cream cheese, then add lemon juice to taste.
Serve with: crudités, prawns or chicken.

38 WITH HERBS

Add ½ teaspoon (3 ml) chopped fresh marjoram.
Serve with: fish, prawns or roasted baby potatoes.

39 WITH LEMON AND TARRAGON

Add 2 tablespoons (30 ml) chopped fresh tarragon and the grated zest of 1 lemon with the lemon juice.
Serve with: simply cooked fish and seafood.

40 Mayonnaise

Made-from-scratch mayonnaise, named after the town of Mahon in Majorca, Spain, where it originated in the late 18th century, is worlds apart from supermarket iterations and infinitely superior too. Use the freshest eggs you can find – preferably organic and free range. You'll see that I call for mostly vegetable or rapeseed oil in the recipe; this is because the distinctive verdant taste of olive oil can be overpowering and so is best used almost as a flavouring.

INGREDIENTS

180 ml sunflower
    or rapeseed oil
6 tbsp (90 ml) olive oil
2 large egg yolks, at room
    temperature
1 tsp (5 ml) white wine
    vinegar
1 ½ tsp (8 ml) Dijon mustard
1 tbsp (15 ml) lemon juice
Salt and black pepper

MAKES 255 ml
Serves 4 to 6

Make sure all ingredients are at room temperature as this will help prevent the mayonnaise from splitting. Combine the two oils in a measuring cup. Set aside.

In a medium bowl, blender or food processor, combine the egg yolks, vinegar and mustard and add a pinch of salt and black pepper. Whisk the mixture vigorously by hand, or process for a few seconds until pale and frothy.

If using a machine, with the motor running, pour in the oil in a thin, steady stream until the mayonnaise starts to emulsify and thicken. When all the oil has been incorporated, transfer the mayonnaise to a bowl.

If making by hand, while whisking constantly, add a drop of the oil to the bowl with the egg yolk mixture. Continue adding drops and whisking until the sauce starts to emulsify. Now, add the remaining oil in a thin, steady stream, while continuing to whisk at a brisk pace until all of the oil has been added and the mayonnaise is thick and creamy.

Stir in the lemon juice, and season to taste with salt and pepper.

Serve with: grilled seafood and chicken, cold prawns or lobster.

HANDY TIPS

There's no hiding it, mayonnaise is unhealthy and disastrous for any diet. Still, there's some hope if you're watching your calories. For a lower fat, lighter version, use 1 whole egg instead of 2 egg yolks.

variations

 ### AVOCADO CORIANDER

Use 240 ml of extra-virgin olive oil (omit the vegetable/rapeseed oil), then beat the mashed-until-smooth flesh from 1 medium ripe avocado into the mayonnaise. When combined, add ½ tablespoon (8 ml) lime juice and 3 tablespoons (45 ml) chopped fresh coriander leaves.
Serve with: fish or chicken tacos, or as a dip for nachos.

 ### THOUSAND ISLAND

Stir 5 tablespoons (75 ml) tomato ketchup, 1 teaspoon (5 ml) red wine vinegar, 1 tablespoon (15 ml) prepared horseradish, 1 tablespoon (15 ml) honey and a quarter of a minced, seeded large red bell pepper into the mayonnaise. For a Bloody Mary Mayo add 2 tablespoons (30 ml) vodka. For a classic Marie Rose sauce to serve with prawn cocktail, omit the red bell pepper and horseradish.
Serve with: meat and veggie burgers, grilled steaks, or use to dress salads.

 ### SWEET ONION AND ROSEMARY

Cook 1 chopped medium sweet onion in 1 tablespoon (15 ml) olive oil over medium heat with a pinch of sugar and 1 ½ teaspoons (8 ml) finely chopped fresh rosemary leaves, stirring occasionally, for 20 minutes or until the onion is a dark golden colour. Cool completely. Process in a blender until smooth, then stir into the mayonnaise with 60 ml plain Greek yoghurt. Season to taste.
Serve with: cooked and cooled pasta with peas for a salad.

 ### BLUE CHEESE

Combine the mayonnaise with 85 g crumbled blue cheese and 1 tablespoon (15 ml) finely chopped fresh chives. Taste and adjust the seasoning.
Serve with: lamb chops, burgers or as a dip for grilled asparagus.

 ### CHILLI

Use 240 ml rapeseed or vegetable oil (omit the olive oil), then stir 1 tablespoon (15 ml) finely minced canned chipotle chillies, 1 teaspoon (5 ml) Worcestershire sauce and 1 small garlic clove, well crushed, into the sauce.
Serve with: chips, or spice-rubbed chicken.

 ### RED WINE BALSAMIC

Combine 180 ml red wine with 2 tablespoons (30 ml) balsamic vinegar and 1 tablespoon (15 ml) soft dark-brown sugar in a small saucepan and bring to a boil. Simmer until thick and syrupy (like maple syrup). Leave to cool completely. Stir into the mayonnaise and season with salt and plenty of freshly cracked black pepper.
Serve with: roast beef or ham sandwiches, or cold cuts.

'SAUCE INDIENNE' CURRY MAYO

Cook 1 finely minced small shallot in ½ tablespoon (8 ml) vegetable or rapeseed oil over medium heat until softened, then add 1 ½ tablespoons (23 ml) mild curry powder and cook for another 2 minutes. Leave to cool, then beat or whisk into the mayonnaise with 2 tablespoons (30 ml) chopped fresh coriander leaves.
Serve with: thick-cut chips, chicken or turkey burgers, prawns, lobster or meaty fish such as halibut or monkfish.

'GIBRICHE' SAUCE

Replace the 2 raw egg yolks with 4 cooked, cooled egg yolks that have been mashed until smooth. If the sauce is too thick, thin with a little water. Add 1 tablespoon (15 ml) each chopped, rinsed and drained capers, chopped fresh tarragon and dill to the finished mayonnaise.
Serve with: baked or grilled fish.

RÉMOULADE

Prepare the **Gibriche Sauce**, adding 1 teaspoon (5 ml) anchovy paste, 1 teaspoon (5 ml) finely grated onion and 1 finely minced garlic clove to the egg yolks, and replacing the tarragon with chopped fresh parsley leaves.
Serve with: grated celery root, mixed salads, cold meat, fish or seafood.

50 Aioli

This pungent, garlicky mayonnaise holds its own against the richest foods. For a sweeter, subtler flavour, roast the garlic cloves in a covered dish in a medium oven for 30 to 40 minutes, until soft and caramelized, then use in place of raw garlic.

INGREDIENTS

3 large garlic cloves
Salt
180 ml mild olive oil
85 ml rapeseed or
 vegetable oil
2 large egg yolks
½ tbsp (8 ml) lemon juice,
 plus more as needed
½ tsp (3 ml) smoked paprika
Black pepper

MAKES approximately
255 ml
Serves 4

Using a pestle and mortar or the flat side of a large knife against a board, mash or grind the garlic to a paste with a pinch of salt. Combine the oils in a measuring cup. Set aside. In a bowl, blender or food processor, combine the egg yolks, lemon juice, paprika and two-thirds of the garlic. Add a pinch of salt and black pepper and whisk the mixture vigorously by hand, or process for a few seconds until pale and frothy.

If using a machine, with the motor running, pour in the oil in a thin, steady stream until the mayonnaise starts to emulsify and thicken. When all the oil has been incorporated, transfer the mayonnaise to a bowl.

If making by hand, while whisking constantly, add a drop of the oil to the bowl with the egg yolk mixture. Continue adding drops and whisking until the sauce starts to emulsify. Now, add the remaining oil in a thin, steady stream, while continuing to whisk at a brisk pace until thick and creamy.

Taste and add lemon juice, salt, pepper and the rest of the garlic, if desired. (Pictured right.)

Serve with: pan-seared or roasted meats or poultry; crudités, steamed artichokes, or potato or courgette chips; crostini; or in a fish soup or stew.

HANDY TIPS

As with mayonnaise (see page 31), aioli runs the risk of separating. Avoid this happening by adding the oil in a thin, steady stream and by making sure all the ingredients are at room temperature.

Variations

51 SPICY ROUILLE

Toast ½ teaspoon (3 ml) cumin seeds and ½ teaspoon (3 ml) fennel seeds in a dry frying pan over medium-low heat, until fragrant. Grind to a rough powder with a large pinch of saffron and a scant ¼ teaspoon (1 ml) chilli flakes. Add to the blender with the egg yolks.
Serve with: spicy fish stews, grilled fish or prawns, mussels.

52 WITH PICKLED GINGER AND WASABI

Replace the paprika with 2 teaspoons (10 ml) wasabi powder. Stir 1 tablespoon (15 ml) finely chopped pickled ginger (from Asian supermarkets) into the finished sauce.
Serve with: sushi, shredded cabbage for an Asian-style slaw, or with grilled tuna, swordfish or mahi mahi.

LEMON THYME

Replace the vegetable/rapeseed oil mixture with 240 ml extra-virgin olive oil and use all the garlic. Stir the grated zest of one lemon, 2 teaspoons (10 ml) chopped fresh thyme leaves and 3 tablespoons (45 ml) crème fraîche into the finished aioli. Season with salt and pepper.
Serve with: grilled prawns or lobster, scallops or risotto.

PORCINI MUSHROOM

Rehydrate 10 g dried porcini in 60 ml of just-boiled water. Squeeze dry, chop finely, then sauté with 1 shallot, finely chopped. Add strained soaking liquid, cook until it has evaporated, season with salt and pepper. When cold stir into aioli with 1 tablespoon (15 ml) chopped chives.
Serve with: burgers, steak or roast beef.

GREEN OLIVE AND ANCHOVY

Replace vegetable/rapeseed oil mixture with 240 ml extra-virgin olive oil, and the paprika with cayenne pepper. Add 2 teaspoons (10 ml) anchovy paste and 1 teaspoon (5 ml) whole-grain mustard with the egg and garlic mixture. Stir 8 finely chopped pitted green olives into the aioli. (Pictured top.)
Serve with: spicy fish stews or soups, as a dip or on toast.

SMOKY PEPPER

Purée 170 g roasted jarred red and yellow peppers and stir into a batch of **Aioli** – made with 1 teaspoon (5 ml) smoked paprika. Stir in 2 tablespoons (30 ml) chopped fresh coriander leaves. (Pictured bottom.)
Serve with: crostini; grilled or roasted chicken; or chips.

57 Tahini sauce

Tahini, a paste made from hulled, ground sesame seeds, is used prolifically in Greek, Turkish and Middle Eastern cuisine. With its intensely creamy, nutty flavour, it's an essential ingredient in hummus, but it also makes a great base for sauces. Add a good amount of lemon juice as tahini is oily and rich and benefits from a tart counterpoint.

INGREDIENTS

1 large garlic clove (or 2 small)
Salt
60 ml tahini (sesame seed paste)
A pinch of ground coriander
A pinch of ground cumin

3 tbsp (45 ml) lemon juice
60 ml water
Black pepper

MAKES 285 ml
Serves 4 to 6

Mash the garlic with a sprinkling of salt using a pestle and mortar. Transfer to a small bowl and add the tahini and the spices. Whisk until smooth, then gradually blend in the lemon juice – the sauce will start to thicken at first, but will loosen again after 20 seconds or so. Once all the lemon juice has been incorporated, gradually whisk in the water, 1 tablespoon (15 ml) at a time, until you reach a creamy, pouring consistency. Season to taste with salt and pepper. (Pictured right and opposite top.)

Serve with: grilled or sautéed red meat, chicken or turkey, or steamed or roasted greens.

HANDY TIP

If you don't have a pestle and mortar, use the flat side of a large kitchen knife to mash your garlic by grinding it against a chopping board. Start by chopping the cloves roughly and sprinkling over some coarse salt, then mash until the desired consistency is reached. The salt helps in a number of ways, it will help to create an abrasive surface to break down the fibres in the garlic, and stop the garlic from slipping out from under the knife. Finally, salt also draws out moisture from the garlic cloves making it easier to crush to a pulp.

variations

WITH PARSLEY AND TOASTED SESAME

Stir 2 tablespoons (30 ml) chopped fresh parsley leaves and 2 teaspoons (10 ml) sesame seeds (lightly toasted in a dry frying pan until aromatic and golden then cooled) into the finished sauce.
Serve with: salads or vegetables, roast lamb or kebabs.

HONEY-MUSTARD

Follow the recipe for **Honey-Mint Tahini Sauce**, increasing the amount of honey to 2 teaspoons (10 ml) and adding 1 ½ teaspoons (8 ml) Dijon mustard to the garlic and tahini mixture.
Serve with: a ham or grilled vegetable sandwich, or as a dip for carrots, cherry tomatoes and cucumber.

WITH GINGER AND SOY SAUCE

Whisk 1 teaspoon (5 ml) finely grated ginger into the garlic and tahini mixture, then beat 2 tablespoons (30 ml) soy sauce and 1 tablespoon (15 ml) rice wine vinegar into the finished sauce.
Serve with: tofu, prawns, fish or an iceberg wedge.

YOGHURT

Follow the recipe for the **Honey-Mint Tahini Sauce**, blending in 3 tablespoons (45 ml) plain Greek yoghurt before adding the mint to the finished sauce.
Serve with: falafel, lamb or veggie burgers, lamb leg steaks or grilled pork chops.

WITH CHILLI

Add ¼ teaspoon (1 ml) paprika to the spices, and stir half a finely chopped, seeded, large red jalapeño chilli into the finished sauce. (Pictured centre.)
Serve with: roasted cauliflower or roast chicken.

HONEY-MINT

Whisk 1 teaspoon (5 ml) honey into the tahini and garlic mixture, then stir 2 tablespoons (30 g) shredded fresh mint leaves into the sauce. (Pictured bottom.)
Serve with: grated carrots, grilled aubergine or courgette.

64 garlic butter

Compound butters are perhaps the easiest and most convenient 'sauces' to prepare. These butter discs melt 'to order' on heated meat, fish or vegetables, or stir them into mashed potato or through pasta. Alternatively, melt the butter in the microwave or on the hob just before serving and drizzle as needed.

INGREDIENTS

2 large cloves garlic
Salt
120 g unsalted butter, softened
2 tbsp (30 ml) finely chopped fresh parsley leaves

2 tsp (10 ml) cognac (optional)
1 tbsp (15 ml) lemon juice
Black pepper

MAKES

120 ml

Mash the garlic with a pinch of salt using a pestle and mortar or the flat side of a large kitchen knife against a chopping board. Transfer to a small non-metallic bowl or to a food processor. Add the butter, parsley, cognac (if using) and lemon juice to the bowl or food processor with ¾ teaspoon (8 g) salt and ½ teaspoon (3 g) black pepper. Beat vigorously with a wooden spoon or process using the pulsing function until everything is combined. Wrap in cling film or greaseproof paper and form into a log. Twist the ends tightly and chill in the fridge for at least 20 minutes to firm up, or freeze until needed. The garlic butter will keep in the fridge for up to one week and two months in the freezer.

To use, remove from the fridge or freezer, leave to soften slightly, unwrap and cut the log of garlic butter into slices 1 cm (½-inch) thick.

Serve with: simply-cooked fish, meat and vegetables.

HANDY TIP

To make it easier to blend, make sure the butter is at room temperature. Whipping the butter a little on its own will help the ingredients to combine.

variations

65 WITH PRAWNS

Omit the cognac and add 85 g very finely minced, peeled, cooked prawns to the softened butter mixture along with ¼ teaspoon (1 ml) hot sauce and 1 tablespoon (15 ml) chopped fresh dill.
Serve with: grilled, baked or poached fish.

66 WATERCRESS LIME

Use the food processor method, replace the lemon juice with lime juice, omit the cognac and add ½ teaspoon (3 ml) finely grated lime zest and 70 g chopped fresh watercress leaves to the softened butter and garlic mixture.
Serve with: boiled baby potatoes, peas, grilled or sautéed chicken breasts or salmon steaks.

67 WITH HARISSA

Omit the cognac and add 1 tablespoon (15 ml) harissa paste (see page 100) to the softened butter mixture.
Serve with: roast or braised lamb, hot rice or couscous.

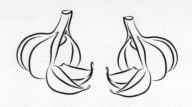

WITH PEA AND MINT

Use the food processor method, omit the cognac, mashed garlic and parsley and add 2 tablespoons (30 ml) cooked and cooled fresh peas or defrosted frozen peas and 2 tablespoons (30 ml) roughly chopped fresh mint leaves to the softened butter.
Serve with: tagliatelle or linguine pasta with lots of freshly grated Parmesan or soft goat's cheese, sautéed white fish, scallops or prawns.

WITH TOMATO AND THYME

Sauté half of a finely chopped shallot in olive oil until translucent, remove from the heat and cool completely. Combine all the ingredients, omitting the parsley and cognac, in a food processor or non-metallic bowl. Add the shallots with 2 teaspoons (10 ml) chopped fresh thyme leaves and 1 tablespoon (15 ml) sun-dried tomato pesto.
Serve with: steamed vegetables, steak or lamb chops.

WITH MAPLE BACON

Finely chop one thick-cut rasher of smoked bacon and cook in a small frying pan until crisp and all the fat has rendered. Drain on kitchen paper and reserve 1 teaspoon (5 ml) of the fat. When cool, combine all the ingredients, omitting the mashed garlic and the parsley and adding 1 ½ tablespoons (23 ml) maple syrup, the bacon and the reserved fat.
Serve with: corn bread or toasted muffins, pork chops, steamed or boiled carrots, mashed butternut squash.

WITH GOAT'S CHEESE AND CHIVE

Beat 85 g soft goat's cheese in a small non-metallic bowl until light and fluffy. Add the mashed garlic, softened butter, lemon juice, salt and black pepper together with 2 tablespoons (30 ml) finely chopped fresh chives and ½ teaspoon (3 ml) Dijon mustard.
Serve with: baked or mashed potatoes, roasted or grilled mushrooms.

THAI CURRY AND CORIANDER

Omit the parsley and add 3 tablespoons (45 ml) finely chopped fresh coriander leaves and 2 teaspoons (10 ml) Thai red curry paste to the softened butter.
Serve with: grilled, roasted or boiled sweetcorn, or egg or rice noodles.

WITH SWEETCORN

Place 85 g drained, canned sweetcorn in the food processor and blend until puréed. Add all the other ingredients plus 1 teaspoon (5 ml) honey and a quarter of a chopped, seeded red jalapeño chilli.
Serve with: blinis, tuna or swordfish steaks, or burgers.

CREAMY & CHEESY SAUCES

74 Béchamel

In the history of cooking, there are few things as impressively simple as béchamel sauce. You just need three ingredients, a saucepan, a wooden spoon, and a whisk, and you get a versatile sauce. This is one of the five French 'mother' sauces (see page 6), and it can be used on its own over fish or vegetables, or as a base for more complex sauces. It is also one of the staples in dishes like lasagne, moussaka and macaroni cheese.

INGREDIENTS

120 g unsalted butter
1 L whole milk
115 g plain flour
Salt and white pepper
Pinch of nutmeg

MAKES 1 L, which will serve 4 to 6 people enough for a large lasagne or moussaka for 6 to 8 people

Heat the milk in a small saucepan until it just begins to simmer. Remove from the cooker and set aside.

Melt the butter in another heavy-bottomed saucepan over medium heat, but do not let it go brown or burn. Add the flour and mix quickly with a wooden spoon until it is completely incorporated. Cook for 2 to 3 minutes, stirring continuously. Do not let it burn. This is called a roux, and it is often used to thicken sauces or stews.

Add a little milk of the hot to the saucepan and, using a whisk, mix it into the roux. Continue to add milk a little at a time, whisking continuously, until all the milk has been incorporated. Keep whisking until the sauce is simmering, reduce the heat and simmer for 3 to 4 minutes, stirring continuously. Season with salt, pepper, and a pinch of nutmeg. Remove from the heat, and use immediately.

Serve with: egg, vegetable and gratin dishes.

HANDY TIP

One main ingredient, not mentioned above, is patience! Do not try to add the milk too quickly as it may form lumps and you will not get a smooth sauce. You could use freshly ground black pepper, but white pepper will keep your sauce looking clean and white. If you need to keep your béchamel warm for a few minutes, butter a piece of greaseproof paper the same size as the saucepan, and gently lay it on top of the sauce to prevent a skin forming. Never leave it bubbling over heat.

Variations

75 CRÈME SAUCE

When the sauce is complete, remove from the heat and whisk in 240 ml double cream.
Serve with: Use as the base for many creamy pasta sauces.

78 WITH MUSHROOMS

Replace 240 ml of the milk with 240 ml mushroom stock (made by soaking 14 g dried wild mushrooms in just-boiled water for 10 minutes). Fry 60 g chopped wild mushrooms in a little butter with the drained and finely chopped rehydrated mushrooms. Set aside. Whisk 2 teaspoons (10 ml) finely chopped fresh thyme, 60 ml double cream into the finished sauce, then stir in the mushrooms.
Serve with: pasta, steak, or in a vegetarian lasagne.

76 WITH CHEDDAR CHEESE

Add 2 teaspoons (10 ml) whole-grain mustard and 1 teaspoon (5 ml) Worcestershire sauce with the last 480 ml of milk. Remove from heat and stir through 450 g shredded Cheddar cheese.
Serve with: pasta, or spooned over steamed or blanched greens and grilled until golden.

79 WITH GARLIC

Sweat 3 minced cloves of garlic gently in a little butter. Add the 1 L milk from the main recipe and heat gently. Remove from heat when warm, and make the sauce, keeping the garlic in the milk.
Serve with: grilled meat and baked mushrooms.

77 AURORE SAUCE

Add 120 ml tomato purée with the last 480 ml of milk.
Serve with: pasta.

80 NANTUA SAUCE

Stir 120 g butter, 120 g cream cheese and 450 g peeled, cooked and mashed prawns to the finished sauce and cook for 2 minutes.
Serve with: shellfish, especially lobster, or steamed vegetables.

81 MORNAY SAUCE

Enrich the sauce with 225 g shredded Gruyère cheese, 225 g shredded Emmenthal cheese and 120 g cream cheese. Stir until all the cheese is melted and fully incorporated into the sauce.
Serve with: vegetables, pasta, grilled or steamed fish.

82 SOUBISE SAUCE

Before starting to make the sauce, roughly chop 2 peeled white onions. Fry in a little olive oil and purée in a blender. Make the roux and whisk in 120 ml whole milk. Add onion purée and 120 ml beef stock. Season to taste.
Serve with: hot vegetables.

83 TOMATO SOUBISE SAUCE

Make the **Soubise Sauce**, but add 2 tablespoons (30 ml) tomato purée when completing the sauce.
Serve with: roasted Mediterranean vegetables.

84 Four-cheese sauce

This versatile sauce can be adapted in countless ways.

INGREDIENTS

420 ml whole milk
2 tbsp (30 ml) unsalted butter
½ medium onion, finely minced
1 bay leaf
1 large clove garlic, minced
1 ½ tbsp (23 ml) plain flour
55 g grated Gruyère cheese
55 g blue cheese, crumbled
55 g grated aged Cheddar cheese

28 g grated Parmesan cheese
60 ml double cream
Pinch nutmeg
Salt and black pepper

SERVES 4, enough for 340 g
dried macaroni or to make
macaroni cheese

Heat the milk in a small saucepan over medium heat until it starts to steam and small bubbles appear at the surface. Remove from the heat and cover to keep hot.

Melt the butter in a separate medium saucepan over medium heat. Add the onion and bay leaf and cook, stirring occasionally, until the onion is soft and translucent, about 5 minutes. Add the garlic and cook, stirring, for 30 seconds. Add the flour and cook, stirring, for 1 to 2 minutes. Gradually whisk in the hot milk, bring to a boil, then simmer gently for 5 minutes, whisking frequently, until thick. Lower the heat, discard the bay leaf. Add the cheeses and stir until smooth, bring to a very gentle simmer and stir in the cream. Whisk until combined. Remove from the heat, stir in the nutmeg, and season to taste. (Pictured right and opposite top.)

Serve with: pasta, steamed, blanched broccoli and cauliflower and grilled, or with spinach. For a Lobster Thermidor, fold in cooked lobster meat, return to the lobster shell and broil until bubbling and golden brown.

HANDY TIP

This is a great recipe to use up bits and pieces of cheese, just make sure to use 200 g in total.

variations

85 NACHO SAUCE

Replace half the Cheddar with Pepper Jack cheese, and add 1 teaspoon (5 ml) hot sauce and 200 ml supermarket-bought salsa to the finished sauce.
Serve with: crisps, or as a dip for nachos and crudités.

89 CHEDDAR-MUSTARD

Omit the blue, Parmesan and Gruyère cheeses, and use 200 g Cheddar in total. Once the cheese has melted into the sauce, stir in 1 tablespoon (15 ml) English or Dijon mustard.
Serve with: cooked spinach, pasta or pork dishes.

86 WITH BRUSSELS SPROUTS

Finely shred 170 g trimmed brussels sprouts and sauté in a little olive oil and butter until tender. Season to taste and combine with the finished sauce.
Serve with: short pasta such as rigatoni or farfalle, and gnocchi, or as a sauce with steak or pork.

90 WITH SMOKED CHEESE

Omit the Gruyère and blue cheeses and add 110 g grated smoked Gouda with the other cheeses.
Serve with: nachos and crisps, in pasta bakes, over polenta, or to make macaroni or cauliflower cheese.

87 WITH CRÈME FRAÎCHE AND CHIVE

Omit the double cream and stir 4 tablespoons (60 ml) crème fraîche, and 3 tablespoons (45 ml) finely chopped fresh chives into the finished sauce. (Pictured centre.)
Serve with: filled crêpes, steamed or blanched vegetables, chicken or ravioli.

88 WITH TOMATO AND BASIL

Whisk 5 tablespoons (75 ml) tomato purée into the sauce before adding the cheeses, then stir 3 tablespoons (45 ml) finely shredded fresh basil leaves into the finished sauce. (Pictured bottom.)
Serve with: Mediterranean vegetables, vegetable- or meat-filled pasta, in a seafood or vegetarian lasagne.

91 Saffron Cream Sauce

This recipe was inspired by the traditional French *Sauce Bâtarde*, a white sauce enriched with egg yolks.

INGREDIENTS

120 ml crème fraîche
2 large egg yolks
½ tbsp (8 ml) olive oil
1 tbsp (15 ml) unsalted butter
1 shallot, finely chopped
1 small clove garlic, minced
Pinch sweet paprika

2 tbsp (30 ml) cognac or brandy
Generous pinch saffron strands
60 ml dry white wine
200 ml hot fish or chicken stock
   (see pages 16 and 17)
Salt and black pepper

SERVES 4

Whisk together the crème fraîche and the egg yolks in a heatproof bowl until thoroughly blended. Set aside.

Heat the olive oil and butter in a medium saucepan over medium-low heat, add the shallot and garlic and cook, stirring, until the shallot is translucent and the garlic softened but not coloured. Stir in the paprika and cook for 30 seconds. Remove from the heat and add the cognac (or brandy). Using a long matchstick, ignite the alcohol. Let the flames die down, stir in the saffron and white wine. Return to the heat, bring to a boil, and simmer briskly until the liquid has almost disappeared, about 3 minutes. Add the stock, bring back to a boil and simmer for 2 minutes. Remove from the heat and leave to cool for a minute. Very slowly pour the hot mixture onto the crème fraîche, whisking until combined. Pour back into the pan, and return to a medium-low heat. Cook, stirring until the sauce is thick enough to coat the back of a spoon, 4 to 5 minutes. Remove from the heat and season with salt and pepper.

Serve with: seafood, chicken or green vegetables.

HANDY TIP

Take care when heating the sauce: if the heat is too high the egg will start to cook and the sauce will be lumpy.

Variations

92 WITH PRAWNS

Remove the shells from 110 g cooked small prawns (12 to 14). Sauté the shells in a small amount of olive oil until browned, about 5 minutes. Add 255 ml fish stock and simmer for 15 minutes. Strain, discard the shells and set aside the stock. Make the sauce using the stock and add the prawns, chopped if necessary, to the finished sauce.
Serve with: baked or poached fish or lobster.

93 WITH MUSSELS

Cook 16 mussels in a pot with 60 ml dry white wine until they open, 4 to 6 minutes. Transfer to a bowl, discarding any that won't open. Simmer liquid for 2 minutes until reduced to 120 ml. Strain. Make sauce replacing the wine with the mussel liquid and 120 ml fish stock. Add 2 tablespoons (30 ml) chopped chives and the mussels to the sauce.
Serve with: baked and poached fish.

94 WITH TOMATOES

Add the diced flesh of 2 small peeled and seeded plum tomatoes, and 1 tablespoon (15 ml) chopped fresh oregano to the finished sauce.
Serve with: chicken, veal or pork medallions, meaty fish, grilled king prawns or grilled lobster.

95 WITH ARTICHOKES

Thinly slice 110 g of cooked, well-drained artichoke hearts, and add to the sauce when you return it to the heat to thicken in the final step.
Serve with: veal, lamb cutlets or steaks, chicken or pork.

98 WITH GINGER

Add ½ teaspoon (3 ml) finely grated peeled ginger to the pan with the saffron and wine.
Serve with: chicken, turkey, vegetables, fish or shellfish.

96 WITH LEMON

Add 2 tablespoons (30 ml) fresh lemon juice and ½ teaspoon (3 ml) freshly grated lemon zest to the pan with the saffron and wine. Stir 2 tablespoons (30 ml) finely chopped fresh parsley leaves into the finished sauce.
Serve with: baked or pan-fried chicken, fish, prawns or sautéed scallops, steamed broccoli or cauliflower.

99 WITH CORIANDER

Stir 2 tablespoons (30 ml) finely chopped fresh coriander leaves into the finished **Saffron and Ginger Sauce**.
Serve with: fish, shellfish or chicken baked or poached Asian-style with garlic, ginger and green onions.

97 WITH GRAPES

Prepare the **Saffron and Lemon Cream Sauce** and add a small handful (about 10) peeled and halved, seedless green grapes to the sauce in the final minute of cooking.
Serve with: chicken, or pork chops or medallions.

100 WITH SPICES

Make the **Saffron and Ginger Sauce**, and add a generous pinch of ground cumin and a generous pinch of ground coriander to the pan with the sweet paprika. Season the finished sauce with a dash of hot sauce, if desired.
Serve with: steamed greens or roasted courgette, carrots and beetroot.

101 Cheese & Buttermilk Sauce

Buttermilk and yoghurt give this sauce a unique tart and complex flavour. Try it folded into *al dente* pasta for a macaroni cheese with bite. Don't be alarmed if it starts to curdle when you add the buttermilk; it will come together once you stir in the cheese.

INGREDIENTS

1 tbsp (15 ml) unsalted butter
1 tbsp (15 ml) all-purpose flour
160 ml buttermilk
70 g freshly grated aged
   Cheddar cheese
Dash Worcestershire sauce
2 tbsp (30 ml) Greek yoghurt, at
   room temperature

2 tsp (10 ml) finely chopped
   fresh marjoram
Salt

SERVES Serves 2 to 3 tossed
through 250 g of macaroni

Melt the butter in a small saucepan over medium heat. Stir in the flour and cook for 2 to 3 minutes until the mixture (or the roux) is a light golden or straw colour. Very gradually whisk in the buttermilk. Add ¼ teaspoon (1 ml) salt and cook, simmering gently, for 1 minute.

Reduce the heat to low and add the Cheddar and Worcestershire sauce. Stir until the cheese has completely melted and remove the sauce from the heat. Whisk in the yoghurt and marjoram. Season with salt to taste. (Pictured right.)

Serve with: short pasta such as macaroni or penne, or grilled or pan-fried chicken or pork.

HANDY TIP

If you don't have buttermilk, it's easy to make it yourself by adding 1 tablespoon (15 ml) lemon juice or white vinegar to 120 ml milk and letting it stand at room temperature for 10 minutes. Alternatively just use yoghurt thinned with a little milk or water.

variations

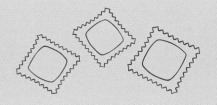

102 MOROCCAN-SPICED YOGHURT SAUCE

Add ½ teaspoon (3 g) ground cumin, ¼ teaspoon (1 g) ground coriander and a generous pinch of ground cayenne pepper to the pan with the flour.
Serve with: grilled courgette, roasted carrots, grilled mushrooms, or layered between slices of cooked aubergine.

105 WITH GARLIC AND YOGHURT

Add 1 large well-crushed garlic clove to pan with the flour in the main recipe. Omit the marjoram and stir in the thinly sliced green and light-green parts of 1 green onion to the finished sauce.
Serve with: steamed green vegetables, or spooned over blacked or grilled chicken.

103 WITH PARMESAN

Replace the Cheddar cheese with freshly grated Parmesan.
Serve with: pasta, ravioli or as an alternative to béchamel sauce in baked pasta dishes.

106 SMOKED GOUDA AND HERBS

Replace the Cheddar cheese with grated smoked Gouda, omit the marjoram and stir in 1 tablespoon (15 g) each of chopped fresh parsley leaves, chervil and chives.
Serve with: pasta, gnocchi, steak, veal, pork or chicken.

104 WITH SPINACH

Prepare the **Buttermilk Parmesan Sauce**, and stir 110 g finely chopped, cooked spinach, squeezed dry of any excess liquid, into the finished sauce. (Pictured left.)
Serve with: meaty fish like salmon, cod or halibut, cooked aubergine and mushrooms, filled crêpes, penne, macaroni or rigatoni or in pasta bakes.

107 BLUE CHEESE AND PEAR

Replace the Cheddar cheese with crumbled blue cheese and add the diced flesh of half of a small, firm but ripe peeled pear to the sauce with the yoghurt. (Pictured right.)
Serve with: gnocchi, cheese-filled ravioli or sliced steak and pork.

108 Roasted Garlic Asiago Cream Sauce

This sauce is the epitome of comfort food. A head might seem like a lot of garlic for one meal, but don't use less: roast garlic is buttery and sweet.

INGREDIENTS

1 head garlic
½ tbsp (8 ml) olive oil
1 tbsp (15 ml) cornflour
80 ml milk
255 ml double cream

55 g freshly grated Asiago cheese
Salt and black pepper

SERVES 4 tossed through 340 g of farfalle, fusilli or garganelli pasta
Makes about 310 ml

Preheat oven to 120°C (250°F). Peel off papery outer skin from the garlic, keeping head intact. Place in small casserole dish. Pour 2 tablespoons (30 ml) water over the top and drizzle with the olive oil. Cover with foil or a lid and bake until soft and mushy, 45 minutes to an hour. When cool enough to handle, squeeze the flesh from the skins, place in a bowl and mash with a fork to form a smooth paste. Combine the cornflour with enough cold water to form a smooth slurry, set aside.

In a saucepan, bring the milk and cream to a simmer over medium heat, stirring every now and then. Whisk in the cornflour and cook for 2 to 3 minutes. Lower heat, add the cheese, garlic, ¼ teaspoon (1 ml) salt and a pinch of black pepper. Whisk until the cheese melts and the sauce is smooth. Remove from the heat. (Pictured right.)

Serve with: pasta or grilled or roasted steak.

HANDY TIP

Adding cheese to simmering cream with some cornflour is the easiest, quickest way to make a cheese sauce.

Variations

109 'CAESAR' SAUCE

Add 3 to 4 drained and finely chopped anchovy fillets to the finished sauce.
Serve with: raw baby spinach or rocket, cooked greens or grilled portabello mushrooms.

110 WITH RED PEPPER

Finely chop or purée 85 g well-drained, jarred roasted red peppers. Set aside. Combine 2 teaspoons (10 ml) tomato purée into the roasted garlic paste before and add to the saucepan with the peppers.
Serve with: lamb, steak, pork or vegetables such as mashed potato.

111 WITH BACON

Cook 4 rashers of bacon until browned and crisp then drain on kitchen paper. Dice the bacon when cool and stir into the finished sauce with 1 ½ tablespoons (23 ml) chopped fresh parsley leaves. (Pictured top.)
Serve with: short pasta such as penne, macaroni or fusilli for pasta bakes topped with grated cheese; steamed and grilled greens.

112 WITH PEAS AND MARJORAM

Omit the roasted garlic and add 140 g of blanched fresh or defrosted frozen peas to the finished sauce. Heat gently until the peas are piping hot, then stir in 1 tablespoon (15 ml) finely chopped fresh marjoram. (Pictured bottom.)
Serve with: short pasta, cheese or meat ravioli, gnocchi or chicken.

113 WITH PEPPERONCINO

Add ½ to 1 teaspoon (3 to 5 g) dried chilli flakes to the saucepan with the cheese and garlic paste.
Serve with: short pasta such as penne, fusilli or macaroni, fresh tagliatelle or spinach fettuccine.

114 PECORINO AND CHIVE

Substitute Pecorino cheese for the Asiago, and stir 1 ½ tablespoons (23 g) chopped fresh chives into the finished sauce.
Serve with: roasted baby potatoes or chunks of roasted sweet potato, or use in lasagne.

115 Mushroom & Onion Sauce

Earthy mushrooms team up with slow-cooked onions and rich mascarpone in this decadent sauce. For a family dinner, use cremini and button mushrooms, but for a special meal splurge on wild mushrooms.

INGREDIENTS

1 tbsp (15 ml) olive oil
2 tbsp (30 ml) unsalted butter
1 medium onion, thinly sliced
1 clove garlic, minced
450 g mixed wild and cultivated mushrooms, cleaned and sliced or torn into small bite-sized pieces
Salt and black pepper
80 ml dry white wine
80 ml vegetable stock (see pages 17)
140 g mascarpone cheese
60 ml sour cream
3 tbsp (45 ml) chopped fresh chives

SERVES 4 tossed through 340 g of pappardelle, linguine or tagliatelle pasta

Heat the oil and butter in a frying pan over medium heat. Add the onion and cook, stirring, until translucent and golden, 10 to 12 minutes, add the garlic and cook for a further 1 minute. Add the mushrooms and season with ½ teaspoon (3 ml) salt and ¼ teaspoon (1 ml) pepper. Cook until the mushrooms are tender, stirring every now and then. Increase the heat to high and cook until the liquid has evaporated. Add the wine, increase the heat and bring to a boil. Simmer briskly for 2 to 3 minutes until most of the liquid evaporates. Add the stock and simmer for another 2 minutes. Add the mascarpone and sour cream and reduce the heat to low. Stir until the sauce is smooth and creamy. Remove from the heat and add the chives. Adjust the salt and pepper to taste.

Serve with: pasta, or grilled, pan-fried or roast chicken, or beef fillet medallions, pork tenderloin or chops.

HANDY TIP

This recipe makes for a creamy but chunky sauce with the mushrooms left in bite-sized pieces. If you prefer a finer sauce, mince the mushrooms.

Variations

116 WITH PAPRIKA

Add 1 tablespoon (15 ml) sweet paprika to the pan with the mushrooms, and omit the mustard.
Serve with: hot, buttered noodles or gnocchi.

117 WITH RED WINE

Substitute red wine for the white wine and replace the chives with 2 tablespoons (30 ml) chopped fresh parsley leaves.
Serve with: beef and venison steaks, roast beef and sautéed liver.

118 WITH WHITE KIDNEY BEANS

Add 140 g drained and rinsed canned white kidney beans with the vegetable stock.
Serve with: grilled sausages, roast chicken and rice.

119 WITH MIXED HERBS

Use 1 tablespoon (15 ml) of chives and combine with 1 tablespoon (15 ml) each of chopped fresh tarragon and parsley leaves.
Serve with: chicken, pork or turkey meatloaf, or pork and veal meatballs.

120 GOAT'S CHEESE

Stir 200 g soft mild goat's cheese into 3 tablespoons (45 ml) hot vegetable stock or water until smooth. Set aside. Replace the sour cream and mascarpone with the goat's cheese mixture. Omit the chives and replace with 3 tablespoons (45 ml) chopped fresh tarragon.
Serve with: fresh egg pasta and gnocchi.

121 WITH SHERRY

Replace the white wine with 60 ml dry sherry.
Serve with: pork medallions and chops, chicken escalope, and thinly sliced beef steak.

122 WITH ASPARAGUS AND MUSHROOM

Break off and discard the woody bottom sections of 340 g of asparagus (about 12 spears) and cook the spears in a pot of boiling, salted water for 5 minutes or until just tender. Cut each spear into 2-cm (1-inch) pieces and set aside. Stir in the asparagus with the vegetable stock.
Serve with: rice, pasta and noodles.

123 WITH MUSTARD AND THYME

Add 1 tablespoon (15 ml) chopped fresh thyme leaves to the pan with the mushrooms, omit the chopped chives and stir in 1 teaspoon (5 ml) Dijon mustard with the mascarpone and sour cream.
Serve with: buttered noodles, gnocchi or polenta, grilled, baked or sautéed chicken, or pan-fried pork or veal.

124 WITH TRUFFLE

Make the **Mushroom, Mustard and Thyme Sauce** and add 2 tablespoons (30 ml) finely chopped fresh or canned truffles to the sauce with the stock.
Serve with: baked, roast or grilled chicken, sautéed pork medallions, fresh egg pasta, mixed wild rice or polenta.

125 Mustard & Cider Sauce

Punchy whole-grain mustard and fruity cider make a perfect pairing in this sauce, with just enough cream for a smooth, rich finish.

INGREDIENTS

2 tbsp (30 ml) unsalted butter
1 small leek, white and light-green parts only, thinly sliced in half moons
1 sprig thyme
200 ml apple cider

60 ml double cream
1 tbsp (15 ml) whole-grain mustard
Salt and black pepper

SERVES 2

Heat the butter in a small frying pan over medium heat. Add the leek and thyme and cook, stirring, until the leek is tender and cooked through, about 6 minutes. Add the cider to the pan, bring to a boil and simmer briskly until the liquid has reduced by half. Add the cream and mustard, then simmer for a couple of minutes to thicken slightly. Remove the thyme sprig from the sauce, and season to taste with salt and pepper. Garnish with fresh thyme. (Pictured right.)

Serve with: pork steaks, medallions or chops.

HANDY TIP

Apple cider comes in several varieties; you can get dry, sweet and medium cider. Changing up the type you use will give you slightly different flavours. For a less sweet sauce, go for a dry cider.

variations

126 WITH MAPLE SYRUP

Add 2 tablespoons (30 ml) maple syrup to the pan with the cream and mustard.
Serve with: chicken or pork sausages, meatballs, or veal, pork or turkey meatloaf.

Pear, mustard and cider sauce is perfect with roast pork

127 WITH GINGER

Substitute the same quantity of ginger ale for the apple cider, and add ¼ teaspoon (1 ml) freshly grated peeled ginger to the pan with the leeks.
Serve with: chicken, steamed or blanched bok choy, or buttered savoy cabbage.

130 WITH ROSEMARY

Omit the thyme sprig and add 1 teaspoon (5 ml) finely chopped fresh rosemary leaves to the pan with the leeks.
Serve with: buttered cabbage, sautéed brussels sprouts, roasted fennel, or chicken, pork or veal.

128 WITH FENNEL AND ANISE

Lightly toast ½ teaspoon (3 ml) fennel seeds in a dry pan until fragrant. Roughly crush and set aside. Follow the main recipe, adding the fennel and 1 tablespoon (15 ml) Pernod (or ouzo or Sambuca) with the cream and mustard.
Serve with: sausages, or firm white fish such as cod or haddock or sautéed scallops.

131 WITH BALSAMIC VINEGAR AND RAISINS

Soak 28 g raisins in a small amount of just-boiled water for 15 minutes until plump; drain and set aside. Add 2 teaspoons (10 ml) balsamic vinegar to the pan with the cider. Stir 1 teaspoon (5 ml) honey and the reserved raisins into the sauce with the cream and mustard. (Pictured below right.)
Serve with: pork or chicken dishes, pork, veal or beef sausages, or buttered red cabbage.

129 WITH PEAR

Use pear cider in place of the apple cider and add the diced flesh of half a peeled and cored pear to the pan with the cream and mustard. (Pictured right.)
Serve with: pork, veal or chicken dishes.

132 Leek & Parmesan Sauce

We're always looking to up our vegetable intake, and here's a great-tasting sauce that incorporates an antioxidant-loaded green that's also full of flavour. Don't forget the fresh lemon zest at the end – it cuts through the rich cream for a bright, refreshing finish.

INGREDIENTS

1 tbsp (15 ml) olive oil
1 tbsp (15 ml) unsalted butter
2 small leeks, white and light-green parts only, sliced into thin half moons
Salt and black pepper
1 clove garlic, thinly sliced
3 tbsp (45 ml) dry white wine
140 ml double cream

2 tsp (10 ml) chopped fresh oregano
45 g freshly grated Parmesan cheese
¼ tsp (1 ml) finely grated lemon zest

SERVES 2 tossed with 170 g of uncooked pasta

Heat the olive oil and butter in a large frying pan over medium heat. Add the leeks with ½ teaspoon (3 ml) salt and ¼ teaspoon (1 ml) black pepper and cook, stirring every now and then, until tender, about 6 to 8 minutes. Add the garlic and cook for another 2 minutes. Add the wine and bring to a boil. Simmer briskly until the wine has almost completely disappeared. Add the cream and simmer gently for a minute or two until the sauce has thickened slightly. Stir in the oregano, Parmesan cheese and lemon zest. Adjust the seasoning.

Serve with: pasta, chicken or pork.

HANDY TIP

It's important to wash leeks thoroughly as soil and grit can lodge deeply within their many layers. Trim the root end and the dark green top then cut it in half lengthwise. Hold it, root-end-up, under cold running water and make sure the water runs between all the layers.

Variations

133 WITH HERBS

Reduce the oregano to 1 teaspoon (5 ml) and stir in 1 teaspoon (5 ml) finely chopped fresh parsley leaves and 1 teaspoon (5 ml) finely chopped fresh tarragon with the oregano.
Serve with: steamed or blanched vegetables, chicken, meaty fish or pork.

134 WITH MUSTARD AND CHIVES

Omit the oregano and stir 1 ½ teaspoons (8 ml) Dijon mustard and 2 tablespoons (30 ml) finely chopped fresh chives into the finished sauce.
Serve with: pork dishes, grilled or pan-fried chicken or meaty fish such as monkfish, halibut or cod.

135 WITH WALNUT AND GORGONZOLA

Lightly toast 55 g roughly chopped walnut halves in a dry frying pan. Set aside. Make the sauce, substituting crumbled gorgonzola for the Parmesan cheese. Mix in the walnuts just before serving.
Serve with: pasta, or grilled or pan-fried chicken or steak.

136 WITH MUSHROOMS

Soak 7 g dried wild mushrooms in a small amount of just-boiled water for 15 to 20 minutes or until softened. Squeeze any excess liquid from the mushrooms and finely chop. Add to the pan with the garlic, and add 3 tablespoons (45 ml) of the mushroom soaking liquid to the pan with the white wine. (Pictured top.)
Serve with: pappardelle or tagliatelle pasta, steak, venison medallions or pork chops.

137 WITH PANCETTA

Cook 55 g diced pancetta in a small amount of olive oil in a large frying pan until golden brown and crisp. Transfer to a plate lined with kitchen paper. Discard all but 1 tablespoon (15 ml) of fat from the pan, then use the same pan and the remaining fat to prepare the sauce, omitting the olive oil. Add the pancetta to the finished sauce. (Pictured bottom.)
Serve with: steak, pork or chicken dishes.

138 WITH RIESLING AND SAFFRON

Add a small pinch of saffron strands to the cooked leek mixture and cook for a minute, stirring. Continue with the recipe, but use Riesling wine, omit the Parmesan cheese and oregano and stir in 2 tablespoons (30 ml) finely chopped parsley instead.
Serve with: chicken, scallops or prawns.

139 Butternut Squash & Mascarpone Sauce

Cooked and blended into a purée, butternut squash – a nutritious, vitamin-packed vegetable – turns into a creamy sauce. For a healthier version, feel free to leave out the mascarpone – the sauce will be just as delicious.

INGREDIENTS

340 g peeled butternut squash, cut into 2-cm (1-inch) cubes
1 ½ tbsp (23 ml) olive oil
½ tsp (3 ml) dried thyme
Pinch dried chilli flakes
Salt and black pepper
3 whole garlic cloves, skin on
3 tbsp (45 ml) mascarpone cheese

180 ml hot vegetable stock (see page 17), or water

SERVES 4, with pasta. Enough for 675 g of ravioli or 340 g of penne or other short pasta.

Preheat oven to 190°C (375°F). Place squash in a bowl with the oil, thyme and chilli flakes and season generously with salt and pepper. Mix well, then transfer to a baking sheet with the garlic. Roast until the squash is tender, 30 to 35 minutes, tossing halfway through. When cool enough to handle, discard the skin from the garlic. Transfer the hot squash and garlic to a food processor or blender and blend until smooth. Add the mascarpone and process for 30 seconds or until smooth. Drizzle in the hot stock or water, blending all the time, until you have a thick pouring consistency – you might not need all the liquid. Season with salt and pepper.

Serve with: short pasta like penne or macaroni, ravioli or other filled pasta or layered with sheets of lasagne.

HANDY TIP

As an alternative to butternut squash, try using pumpkin or sweet potato.

Variations

140 WITH SUN-DRIED TOMATOES

Soak 45 g sun-dried tomatoes (not packed in oil) in just-boiled water for 20 to 30 minutes until softened. Squeeze out the excess water and roughly chop. Add to the blender with the squash.
Serve with: cheese ravioli or other pasta, sautéed pork or chicken.

141 WITH ITALIAN HERBS

Replace the thyme with dried oregano, then stir 1 tablespoon (15 ml) freshly grated Parmesan cheese and 2 tablespoons (30 ml) shredded fresh basil leaves into the finished sauce.
Serve with: pasta, gnocchi, grilled chicken or pork.

142 WITH CURRY

Sauté half a medium onion, finely minced, in 1 tablespoon (15 ml) olive oil until translucent. Add 1 tablespoon (15 ml) Thai red curry paste and cook, stirring, for 3 to 4 minutes. Remove from the heat, and add the onion mixture to the cooked butternut squash in the food processor (omit the thyme). Add 1 tablespoon (15 ml) finely chopped fresh coriander leaves to the sauce.
Serve with: grilled or pan-fried chicken, pork or steak.

Mexican Spiced Butternut Squash Sauce is perfect as a filling for burritos

143 WITH BASIL PESTO

Whisk 3 tablespoons (45 ml) jarred basil pesto into the finished sauce.
Serve with: linguine, spaghetti, cheese or meat-filled ravioli, or roast pork.

146 WITH PIMENTO

Make the **Mexican Spiced Butternut Squash Sauce** and stir 2 tablespoons (30 ml) packed finely minced drained jarred red sliced pimentos into the finished sauce.
Serve with: meaty fish such as halibut or monkfish, or chicken or pork dishes.

144 WITH MEXICAN SPICES

Follow the main recipe omitting the dried thyme and tossing 1 ½ teaspoons (8 ml) ground Mexican spice blend with the butternut squash before roasting.
Serve with: cheese ravioli or gnocchi, or use with rice as a stuffing for bell peppers or burritos.

147 WITH BLUE CHEESE

Prepare the main recipe until the point that you blend the butternut squash and garlic. Leave the purée in the blender. Combine the mascarpone cheese with 55 g crumbled blue cheese in a small saucepan. Heat gently and whisk until smooth. Add to the purée and blend briefly to combine. Thin with stock or water as in the main recipe.
Serve with: cooked broccoli or cauliflower, or penne or macaroni for a pasta bake.

145 WITH SAUSAGE AND SPICES

Remove the skin from 3 links of hot or sweet Italian-style sausages. Break up the meat into small chunks then sauté, stirring to break up the meat, in a small amount of olive oil until well browned. Drain on kitchen paper and set aside. Stir into the finished **Mexican Spiced Butternut Squash Sauce**.
Serve with: pasta, risotto rice or baked potatoes.

148 WITH CHEESE AND SPINACH

Prepare the **Butternut Squash and Blue Cheese Sauce** and add 110 g finely chopped steamed or blanched spinach squeezed dry of any excess liquid, to the finished sauce.
Serve with: grilled or pan-fried meat or poultry, or as an alternative sauce for macaroni cheese.

PESTOS & HERB SAUCES

149 Pesto

Packed with fresh basil and rounded out with pine nuts, Parmesan cheese and extra-virgin olive oil, this classic is one of the most popular go-to sauces for pasta, but it's also incredibly versatile and has a range of other uses. Pesto originates from the city of Genoa in northern Italy, and since it was traditionally made by hand in large, sturdy marble mortars with wooden pestles, it comes from the word *pestare*, meaning to pound.

INGREDIENTS

2 small garlic cloves (or
   1 large), roughly chopped
45 g pine nuts
Salt
45 g fresh basil leaves, stems
   removed
120–160 ml extra-virgin
   olive oil
55 g freshly grated Parmesan
   cheese

MAKES about 255 ml,
enough for 450 g (1 lb)
uncooked pasta

Place all the garlic and pine nuts with a pinch of salt in the bowl of a food processor and chop until fine. Add the basil leaves, process until finely minced. Slowly pour the olive oil into the feeder tube of the processor with the motor running, until the sauce is thick and smooth.

Add the cheese and process briefly to incorporate into the pesto. Adjust the salt to taste.

Serve with: linguine or spaghetti, use as a dip for crudités, a topping for pizzas, or spread over chicken breasts or firm white fish fillets and roast.

HANDY TIP

For a really vibrant green pesto, first blanch the basil leaves in boiling water for 10 to 15 seconds then plunge into a large bowl of iced water. Drain, squeeze out all the water, then use to make the pesto. This will set the colour in the basil leaves and stop the pesto from turning a dull shade of green.

Variations

150 WITH ASPARAGUS AND MINT

Cook 6 to 8 trimmed asparagus spears in boiling, salted water until tender. Drain and rinse under cold running water then roughly chop. Add to the food processor with the garlic and nuts, and replace half the basil with fresh mint leaves.
Serve with: pasta or gnocchi, mashed potato or crushed baby potatoes, or salmon, haddock, halibut or scallops.

153 WITH LEMON

Add the finely grated zest of 1 small lemon with the basil, and 1 tablespoon (15 ml) fresh lemon juice with the oil.
Serve with: spaghetti and linguine, short pasta such as penne and fusilli, seafood or chicken.

151 MIXED HERB

Replace the basil with 45 g of chopped, mixed fresh herbs, such as chervil, parsley, chives, tarragon and thyme.
Serve with: fish, or to top bruschetta or crostini.

154 PARSLEY AND HAZELNUT

Replace the basil with the same amount of fresh parsley leaves and the pine nuts with the same amount of roughly chopped, peeled hazelnuts.
Serve with: chicken or seafood, kebabs, noodles or bread.

152 WALNUT

Lightly toast 55 g walnut halves in a dry frying pan or medium oven, leave to cool then roughly chop. Replace the pine nuts with the walnuts and 2 tablespoons (30 ml) of the extra-virgin olive oil with walnut oil.
Serve with: chicken, turkey or pizzas.

155 ROCKET AND PISTACHIO

Replace the basil with baby rocket leaves, and substitute the pine nuts for 55 g pistachios.
Serve with: pasta, chicken, fish, prawns or scallops.

156 SUNFLOWER SEED, LEMON AND BASIL

Replace the pine nuts with 55 g of sunflower seeds and add
½ teaspoon (3 ml) finely grated lemon zest with the basil.
If the finished pesto is too thick, blend in a little more
extra-virgin olive oil.
Serve with: wholewheat pasta, chicken, fish or as a spread
for sandwiches.

157 CASHEW NUT AND CORIANDER

Replace the pine nuts with 55 g cashew nuts lightly toasted
in a dry frying pan and allowed to cool. Substitute fresh
coriander leaves for the basil.
Serve with: chicken, turkey, pasta, pizzas, burgers or as
a spread for sandwiches.

158 PISTOU

Replace the Parmesan cheese with freshly grated Gouda,
omit the pine nuts and add the chopped flesh of 1 small
seeded and skinned plum tomato with the rest of the
ingredients.
Serve with: wholewheat pasta, multigrain bread, chicken,
or as a spread for sandwiches.

159 Sun-dried Tomato Pesto

This bold take on the classic basil pesto is a great way to use sun-dried tomatoes. A little goes a long way with this full-flavoured sauce, especially if you use it to dress pasta. If it looks a little dry, add some cooking water as you toss the pasta in the pesto.

INGREDIENTS

70 g sun-dried tomato halves
2 small garlic cloves (or 1 large), roughly chopped
2 tbsp (30 ml) freshly grated Parmesan cheese
2 tbsp (30 ml) freshly grated Asiago cheese
2 tbsp (30 ml) pine nuts

2 tsp (10 ml) chopped fresh oregano leaves
160 ml extra-virgin olive oil
1 tsp (5 ml) red wine vinegar
¼ tsp (1 ml) crushed chilli flakes
Salt

SERVES 4
Makes about 310 ml

Place the sun-dried tomatoes in a small bowl. Cover with just-boiled water and let soak until soft, about 15 to 20 minutes. Using a slotted spoon, transfer the tomatoes to a food processor or blender, reserving the liquid. Add 60 ml of the soaking liquid along with the rest of the ingredients and ¼ teaspoon (1 ml) salt. Process until smooth, adding a little more of the tomato soaking liquid, a tablespoon at a time, if the pesto is too thick for your liking. Adjust the seasoning to taste. (Pictured right.)

Serve with: chicken, fish or steak, as a dip for crudités. Toss through steamed or boiled baby potatoes, or mixed greens, or use as a topping for crostini.

HANDY TIP

To make your pesto last longer, decant it into a jar, wipe the rim clean, then pour a thin layer of extra-virgin olive oil over the surface to seal it. Stored like this, the pesto will keep in the fridge for about 10 days.

Variations

160 WITH FETA

Replace the Asiago cheese with 2 tablespoons (30 ml) finely crumbled feta. Stir 2 tablespoons (30 ml) finely chopped fresh parsley leaves into the finished pesto.
Serve with: crudités, fish, chicken or pork, steamed greens, or stir into vegetable soups.

164 WITH WALNUTS

Replace the pine nuts with 45 g lightly toasted walnut halves.
Serve with: toast or crackers with soft goat's cheese, creamy soups, grilled Mediterranean vegetables, or as a sandwich spread.

161 WITH CHIPOTLE CHILLI

Add 1 canned chipotle chilli in adobo sauce, or 2 teaspoons (10 ml) chipotle chilli paste, to the food processor with the rest of the ingredients.
Serve with: new potatoes, broccoli, courgette, quinoa, couscous or soft polenta, chicken or turkey burgers.

165 WITH ANCHOVY AND CAPERS

Add 2 anchovy fillets in oil, drained, and 1 tablespoon (15 ml) chopped rinsed and drained jarred capers to the food processor with the rest of the ingredients.
Serve with: all kinds of fish or as a dip for crudités.

162 WITH OLIVES

Add 2 ½ tablespoons (38 ml) chopped pitted Kalamata olives to the blender. (Pictured top.)
Serve with: crostini or sandwiches, or spread thickly on fish and chicken and bake or broil.

163 WITH BROCCOLI RAAB

Cook 110 g broccoli raab or rapini in boiling, salted water until very soft. Drain, rinse under cold water, then roughly chop, and add to the rest of the ingredients with 1 teaspoon (5 ml) fresh thyme leaves. (Pictured bottom.)
Serve with: hot pasta, gnocchi or cheese ravioli.

166 Sweet Pea Pesto

With their sweet, buttery flavour, peas make a great alternative to basil in pesto. While it's a perfect use for in-season peas, you can use frozen too for a quick mid-week supper any time of the year. Sharp, tangy pecorino cheese works especially well here, but you can use whatever hard cheese you have on hand.

INGREDIENTS

280 g fresh or frozen peas, defrosted

1 small clove garlic, roughly chopped

28 g freshly grated pecorino cheese

Pinch of white sugar

28 g roughly chopped, peeled hazelnuts

80 ml extra-virgin olive oil

Salt and black pepper

MAKES 225 ml, enough to serve with 450 g uncooked pasta

Cook the peas in a saucepan of lightly salted boiling water for 2 to 3 minutes until just tender. Drain, refresh under cold running water, and drain again. Place all the ingredients except the olive oil in the small bowl of a food processor or blender with ¼ teaspoon (1 ml) salt and a generous pinch of pepper. Blend until you have a fine purée. Slowly pour the oil through the feeder tube, with the motor running, and process until the pesto is thick and smooth. Adjust the seasoning.

Serve with: pasta, as a spread for crostini and a sauce for fish and chicken dishes.

HANDY TIP

To skin hazelnuts, roast in a 200°C (400°F) oven for 5 minutes until browned. Tip into a sieve and shake. Pick out the nuts and discard the skins.

Variations

167 WITH MINT

Add 3 tablespoons (45 ml) roughly chopped mint leaves to the food processor with the rest of the ingredients.
Serve with: fish or crab cakes, or a fish finger sandwich.

168 ROAST GARLIC

Replace the fresh garlic with roasted garlic pulp: wrap 6 to 8 large, unpeeled cloves of garlic in foil with 1 teaspoon (5 ml) olive oil and 1 teaspoon (5 ml) water and bake in a 150°C (300°F) oven for 35 to 45 minutes until soft and golden brown. When cool enough to handle, squeeze the cloves from the skins and mash.
Serve with: fish, lamb or pork, mashed or crushed potatoes, or roasted baby carrots.

169 WITH ORANGE

Add 1 teaspoon (5 ml) finely grated orange zest and 1 tablespoon (15 ml) orange juice to the food processor with the rest of the ingredients.
Serve with: puréed or roasted carrots, lamb, or as a dip for crudités (combined with yoghurt if desired).

170 · WITH TARRAGON

Add 3 tablespoons (45 ml) roughly chopped fresh tarragon leaves to the food processor with the rest of the ingredients.
Serve with: fish, toast, as a sandwich filling with cooked prawns or crabmeat.

173 · ZESTY RICOTTA

Prepare the **Pea and Cream Cheese Pesto**, replace the cream cheese with ricotta and add 1 teaspoon (5 ml) lemon zest and 2 teaspoons (10 ml) lemon juice.
Serve with: pasta, creamy soups, risotto, chicken or lamb.

171 · WITH BASIL AND TOMATOES

Soak 2 tablespoons (30 ml) chopped sun-dried tomatoes in a little just-boiled water until soft. Add the strained softened tomatoes plus 15 g basil leaves with the rest of the ingredients.
Serve with: hot steamed or blanched vegetables, pasta, cheese ravioli or lamb chops.

174 · TOASTED ALMOND

Replace the hazelnuts with 45 g slivered almonds, lightly toasted in a dry frying pan and cooled to room temperature.
Serve with: pasta, gnocchi, as a topping for crostini, or stir through crème fraîche as a dip.

172 · WITH CREAM CHEESE

Replace the pecorino cheese with 3 tablespoons (45 ml) cream cheese. Stir in 2 tablespoons (30 ml) finely chopped fresh chives to the finished pesto.
Serve with: baked or mashed potato, sweet potato, or as a stuffing for chicken breasts.

175 · PISTACHIO AND THYME

Prepare the **Pea and Toasted Almond Pesto**, but replace the almonds with shelled, unsalted, roasted pistachios, and add 2 teaspoons (10 ml) chopped fresh thyme leaves to the blender.
Serve with: lamb.

176 Cashew Nut & Coriander Pesto

With its tangy, sweet and salty flavours, this exotic riff on the classic Italian pesto bears the hallmarks of a typical Southeast Asian condiment.

INGREDIENTS

28 g coriander leaves

55 g roasted unsalted cashew nuts

1 small clove garlic, roughly chopped

¼ tsp (1 ml) finely grated peeled ginger

2 tsp (10 ml) soft dark-brown sugar

1 ½ tbsp (23 ml) soy sauce, plus more as needed

3 tbsp (45 ml) vegetable or peanut oil

2 tbsp (30 ml) lime juice

MAKES about 160 ml, enough for 225 g uncooked rice or egg noodles

In a food processor or blender, combine all the ingredients except the oil. Process until you have a smooth paste. Slowly pour in the oil through the feeder tube, with the motor running, until the sauce becomes thick and creamy. Incorporate the lime juice. Add more soy sauce to taste.

Serve with: egg or rice noodles or with grilled or barbecued chicken, pork and beef.

HANDY TIP

You can easily make pesto using a pestle and mortar. First pound the coriander, cashews and garlic until you have a rough paste. Add the sugar and soy sauce and keep grinding until the mixture becomes smoother. Add the oil, a little at a time, incorporating each addition before drizzling in more. Stir in the lime juice.

Variations

177 THAI BASIL

Replace the coriander with sweet Thai basil and the soy sauce with fish sauce.

Serve with: cold rice noodles, grilled or pan-fried chicken or pork, Thai-style fish or crab cakes.

178 PEANUT AND SESAME

Replace the cashews with roasted, unsalted peanuts and add 1 teaspoon (5 ml) toasted sesame oil.

Serve with: crudités, as a marinade or sauce for chicken, pork or prawns.

179 WITH CHILLI

Seed and roughly chop 1 medium red or green chilli and add with the coriander leaves and peanut mixture.

Serve with: steamed or baked fish, shellfish and chicken, or with mayonnaise as a dressing for Asian-style noodle or pasta salads.

180 Mint sauce

Mint and lamb is a match made in heaven; the sweet, herbaceous flavours in the sauce cut through the rich, unctuous meat and pick up on the verdant notes in young lamb fed on succulent pastures.

INGREDIENTS

MAKES about 120 ml.
Serves 4

28 g fresh mint leaves, stems removed and discarded and leaves roughly chopped
2 tbsp (30 ml) white sugar
2 ½ tbsp (38 ml) white wine vinegar or malt vinegar, plus more as needed

Place the mint leaves, sugar and vinegar in blender and blend until you have a finely minced, pulpy paste. Add 3 tablespoons (45 ml) of boiling water. Leave to stand for 5 minutes for the sugar to dissolve, then blend for about 10 seconds. Transfer to a small bowl or jar and leave to infuse for at least 1 hour before serving.

Serve with: lamb, goose or duck, white fish or salmon.

HANDY TIP

To make half the quantity, use half the ingredients and prepare in a pestle and mortar instead of a blender. Grind the chopped mint with the sugar until you have a paste, then add the vinegar gradually. Finally, stir in the hot water.

variations

181 BALSAMIC MINT

Replace the white wine or malt vinegar with balsamic vinegar.
Serve with: lamb, roast beef or meat cold cuts, or drizzle over roasted or boiled carrots and baby potatoes.

182 RASPBERRY MINT

Replace the wine or malt vinegar with raspberry vinegar and add 6 to 8 crushed raspberries to the finished sauce.
Serve with: cold poached or roast chicken, hot roast duck, goose or lamb.

183 WITH PARSLEY AND LIME

Replace half the mint leaves with fresh parsley leaves and the malt vinegar with fresh lime juice.
Serve with: spicy lamb koftas or kebabs, Moroccan-style spiced roast lamb, or lamb sandwiches.

184 Gremolata

This zesty Italian mix is more a topping than a sauce.

INGREDIENTS

1 medium lemon
2 garlic cloves, minced

60 ml finely chopped parsley leaves

SERVES 2 to 4

Use a vegetable peeler to remove wide strips of peel from the lemon; mince with a sharp knife. Combine with the parsley and garlic; leave to infuse for at least 30 minutes or up to 6 hours (covered and refrigerated).

Serve with: steak, pork or lamb, or combine with olive oil and drizzle over potatoes and greens.

HANDY TIP

When removing the lemon peel, be careful to remove as little of the bitter, white pith as possible.

Variations

185 ORANGE

Replace the lemon peel with the minced peel of 1 orange.
Serve with: fish, roasted Mediterranean vegetables or carrots combined with olive oil.

186 MIXED HERB

Use 1 tablespoon (15 ml) parsley combined with 1 tablespoon (15 ml) each fresh tarragon, thyme, oregano and chervil.
Serve with: chicken, fish, or combine with olive oil as a dip.

187 WITH BACON

Cook 1 strip of bacon in a frying pan with a drizzle of oil until crisp and browned. Drain on a kitchen paper then crumble finely. Add to the gremolata.
Serve with: sautéed prawns, scallops or salads.

188 Classic chimichurri

Barbecued beef, the staple of Argentinean cooking, is rarely served without a side of this fresh herb-filled sauce. There's a common misconception that chimichurri is a chilli-based condiment, but in fact the Argentines shy away from spicy foods and you'll find the local chimichurri will include just a pinch of dried chilli flakes – more for flavour than heat.

INGREDIENTS

1½ tbsp (23 ml) fresh
  parsley leaves
½ tbsp (8 g) coriander leaves
120–160 ml extra-virgin olive oil
80 ml red wine vinegar
2 large garlic cloves, minced

½ tsp (3 ml) dried chilli flakes
1 tsp (5 ml) dried oregano
Salt

SERVES 4 as a condiment

Place all the ingredients (except the salt) in the small bowl of a food processor and blend until you have a purée. Season to taste with salt. Transfer to a bowl and cover with cling film or pack into a jar with a screw-top lid. Leave to infuse in the fridge for at least 3 to 4 hours, or up to 2 days before using.

Serve with: barbecued or grilled meat, especially steak, peppers and mushrooms.

HANDY TIP

This fresh-tasting verdant sauce doubles as a delicious marinade for steak and chicken. Simply place the meat in a sealable bag, pour over the marinade, close up the bag and leave in the fridge, turning once or twice, for at least 2 hours and up to 8 hours before grilling, barbecuing or pan-frying.

Variations

189 WITH CUMIN

Replace the oregano with 1 ½ teaspoons (8 ml) cumin seeds, which have been toasted in a dry frying pan until fragrant and then cooled and ground to a rough powder.
Serve with: lamb chops, cutlets, meatballs or burgers, warm roasted or grilled vegetable salads.

190 WITH LEMON AND MIXED HERBS

Use 45 g fresh mixed herbs such as parsley, mint, coriander, basil and chervil. Stir the juice of half a lemon and grated zest of 1 lemon into the finished sauce.
Serve with: fish and shellfish, or blanched green beans and sugar snap peas.

191 WITH ROASTED JALAPEÑO

Cook 1 or 2 jalapeño chillies under a hot grill, 15 cm (6 inches) from the heating element, for 4 to 5 minutes until roasted and blackened in spots on all sides. Chop and add to the food processor with the other ingredients.
Serve with: barbecued steak, chicken or pork, burgers, or slow-cooked meat cuts like brisket.

192 WITH RED PEPPER

Stir 3 tablespoons (45 ml) finely chopped jarred roasted red peppers into the finished sauce.
Serve with: sardines, mackerel or salmon, chicken or steak.

193 BASIL

Omit the coriander leaves, reduce the parsley to 14 g and add 14 g fresh basil leaves.
Serve with: roasted courgette, aubergine and red peppers, chicken, fish such as salmon, halibut or sea bass.

194 SUN-DRIED TOMATO

Soak 28 g sun-dried tomatoes in a small amount of just-boiled water for 20 minutes until soft and plump. Squeeze dry and finely chop. Stir into **Basil Chimichurri.**
Serve with: salmon, pork, chicken, pasta or potato salad.

195 WITH FRESH TOMATOES

Peel, seed and finely chop 3 plum tomatoes and stir into the finished sauce.
Serve with: grilled or roasted beef and chicken, mozzarella or goat's cheese salad.

196 WITH GREEN TOMATOES

Make the **Fresh Tomato Chimichurri,** replacing the plum tomatoes with green tomatoes or tomatillos, and red wine vinegar with white wine vinegar.
Serve with: grilled meats, mushrooms and sweetcorn.

197 BALSAMIC VINEGAR

Replace the red wine vinegar with balsamic vinegar.
Serve with: steak, lamb, grilled mushrooms or peppers.

198 English Parsley Sauce

The French may have invented the béchamel sauce, but the English made it their own by infusing it with parsley. Unlike most other recipes that call for this herb, this one uses both the peppery stalks – which infuse the milk – and the sweeter, milder leaves – which are added just before serving to keep their colour.

INGREDIENTS

6 to 8 parsley stalks
320 ml whole milk
¼ small onion
4 to 6 black peppercorns
1 bay leaf
2 tablespoons (30 ml) unsalted butter

2 tablespoons (30 ml) all-purpose flour
60 ml finely chopped fresh parsley leaves
1 tsp (5 ml) lemon juice
1 tbsp (15 ml) single cream
Salt and black pepper

SERVES 4

Roughly chop the parsley stalks and place in a small saucepan with the milk, onion, peppercorns and bay leaf. Scald the milk by bringing it to a very gentle simmer over medium-low heat. Remove from the heat and leave to infuse for 10 to 20 minutes. Strain, discarding the solids.

Melt the butter in a heavy-based saucepan over medium-low heat. Stir in the flour and cook for 1 to 2 minutes until the roux is a very light beige colour. Slowly whisk in the milk, a little at a time. Increase the heat and bring to a boil, continuing to whisk all the time. Cook, simmering gently, for 3 to 5 minutes until thickened. Remove from the heat, stir in the parsley leaves, lemon juice and cream, and season to taste with salt and pepper. Serve immediately.

Serve with: salmon, roast, smoked or cured ham, or spinach, broccoli or cauliflower.

HANDY TIP

When scalding the milk, it's important to see small bubbles before pulling the saucepan off the heat. This step breaks down the proteins in the milk and helps to make the finished sauce thick, smooth and velvety.

Variations

199 WITH DILL AND CAPERS

Reduce the chopped parsley to 2 tablespoons (30 ml) and stir in 2 tablespoons (30 ml) finely chopped dill leaves and 1 ½ tablespoons (23 ml) finely chopped drained and rinsed capers to the sauce with the fresh parsley leaves.
Serve with: steamed, poached or baked fish, fish cakes.

200 WITH CHIVE AND CRÈME FRAÎCHE

Use 180–240 ml milk and omit the cream. Reduce the chopped parsley to 2 tablespoons (30 ml) and stir 60 ml crème fraîche and 2 tablespoons (30 ml) finely chopped fresh chives into the finished sauce.
Serve with: fish, chicken or ham, or filled crêpes.

201 WITH CHEDDAR

Stir 85 g shredded aged Cheddar cheese and 1 teaspoon (5 ml) Dijon mustard into the finished sauce. Thin with a little extra hot milk if the sauce is too thick.
Serve with: buttered noodles, sautéed chicken or pork escalopes or cutlets, or vegetables.

202 coriander & coconut chutney

Creamy, sweet coconut and punchy, herbaceous coriander make a great combination in this no-cook chutney that's often served in Indian cuisine as a palate freshener and soothing palliative to accompany pungent, spicy curries.

INGREDIENTS

55 g fresh coriander leaves on stalks, roughly chopped
1 clove garlic, roughly chopped
85 g unsweetened shredded coconut, preferably fresh

1 ½ tbsp (23 ml) lemon juice
¼ teaspoon (1 ml) salt
2 tsp (10 ml) soft brown sugar
80 ml coconut milk

SERVES 4 as a condiment. Makes 200 ml

Place all the ingredients in a blender or the small bowl of a food processor and purée until smooth. Adjust the seasoning to taste.

Serve with: tandoori spiced grilled chicken, fish or prawns, Indian curries or samosas.

HANDY TIP

If you can't find fresh coconut, use desiccated coconut, which is stocked in the baking aisle of most supermarkets.

variations

203 WITH GREEN CHILLI

Add 1 small green chilli, seeded or with the seeds left in (depending on how much heat you like) to the blender or food processor with the rest of the ingredients.
Serve with: grilled, barbecued or sautéed chicken, prawns, lamb kebabs, burgers.

204 WITH SPICES

Roast ½ teaspoon (3 ml) caraway seeds and ½ teaspoon (3 ml) mustard seeds in a dry frying pan until darkened (but not burnt) and fragrant. Leave to cool, then grind to a rough powder. Add to the food processor with the rest of the ingredients.
Serve with: grilled, pan-fried or barbecued steak, lamb, pork, chicken or fish kebabs.

205 WITH PEANUTS

Replace the desiccated coconut with 110 g roasted, salted peanuts.
Serve with: grilled or barbecued chicken or pork, canapés.

Add an extra dimension to curries and Asian canapés with this herby chutney

206 WITH GINGER

Add a roughly chopped peeled 1.25 cm (½ in) knob of ginger with the rest of the ingredients.
Serve with: fish or chicken curries, or Asian-style canapés.

209 WITH YOGHURT

Replace the coconut milk with plain yoghurt.
Serve with: lightly spiced fish, chicken, lamb, seafood and curries.

207 WITH TAMARIND

Add 2 teaspoons (10 ml) tamarind paste to the **Coriander, Coconut and Ginger Chutney**, omitting the lemon juice and increasing the brown sugar to 1 tablespoon (15 ml).
Serve with: lamb, chicken or turkey kebabs, koftas, burgers or Asian-style canapés.

210 WITH MINT AND YOGHURT

Make the **Coriander, Coconut and Yoghurt Chutney** and replace the coriander with 55 g fresh mint leaves, stems discarded.
Serve with: Indian dishes such as curries, tandoori meat, chicken or seafood, Indian and Asian finger foods such as samosas.

208 WITH ROASTED COCONUT AND LIME

Replace the lemon juice with lime juice. Roast the desiccated coconut in a dry frying pan until browned and fragrant, cool to room temperature, before using.
Serve with: Asian-style grilled or barbecued meat and fish.

211 WITH POMEGRANATE

Make the **Coriander, Coconut and Yoghurt Chutney**, replacing the lemon juice with 3 tablespoons (45 ml) unsweetened pomegranate juice and reducing the coconut milk to 70 ml. Stir the seeds of half of a small pomegranate into the finished chutney.
Serve with: grilled, roast or sautéed chicken or fish, canapés.

STOCK-BASED SAUCES

212 Bacon & Mushroom Sauce

Earthy mushrooms and meaty bacon are an ideal pairing. This sauce uses fresh and dried shiitake, but you can mix and match the mushrooms you use.

INGREDIENTS

14 g dried shiitake
   mushrooms
1 tablespoon (15 ml) olive oil
3 rashers of bacon, diced
1 shallot, minced
140 g fresh shiitake
   mushrooms, caps sliced
   and stems discarded
255 ml beef or rich chicken
   stock (see pages 16 and 18)
1 tsp (5 ml) cornflour
   combined with 1 tbsp
   (15 ml) cold water
Salt and black pepper

SERVES 4 as a sauce, or
3 if tossed through noodles
[110 g dried noodles per
person]

Place the dried mushrooms in a bowl and pour over 180 ml of just-boiled water: leave to soak for 20 minutes or until soft. Remove from the liquid, squeezing the excess back into the bowl. Slice the caps and discard the mushroom stems. Strain and reserve the liquid.

Meanwhile, heat the oil in a frying pan over medium heat. Add the bacon and cook, stirring occasionally, until most of the fat renders and the bacon is crisp, 5 to 7 minutes. Remove and drain on kitchen paper. Pour off all but 2 tablespoons (30 ml) of fat from the pan. Add the shallot and sauté until soft, 2 to 3 minutes. Add the sliced, rehydrated and fresh mushroom caps and cook, stirring every now and then, until tender, about 5 minutes. Add the stock and mushroom liquid. Bring to the boil and simmer for 10 minutes. Stir in the cornflour mixture, and simmer for 2 to 3 minutes more, until the sauce is thickened. Return the bacon to the pan and season to taste with salt and pepper.

Serve with: meat or poultry, or toss through noodles.

HANDY TIP

For a vegetarian version, omit the bacon and use vegetable stock with a dash of Worcestershire and soy sauces.

variations

WITH WHOLE-GRAIN MUSTARD

Omit the bacon and add 2 teaspoons (10 ml) chopped fresh oregano with the mushrooms. Stir 1 tablespoon (15 ml) whole-grain mustard into the finished sauce.
Serve with: chicken or beef.

MIXED MUSHROOM AND ROSEMARY

Replace the dried shiitake mushrooms with dried mixed wild mushrooms, and use a combination of fresh shiitake, cremini and button mushrooms. Add 1 teaspoon (5 ml) finely chopped fresh rosemary leaves with the mushrooms.
Serve with: roast chicken, sautéed turkey breasts, steamed broccoli or chopped, cooked spinach.

WITH GORGONZOLA

Stir 110 g crumbled gorgonzola cheese into the finished hot sauce until the cheese melts.
Serve with: gnocchi or filled pasta, or reduce until very thick and use as a sauce on pizza bases or as a topping for crostini.

WITH FIVE-SPICE

Omit the bacon and add ¼ teaspoon (1 ml) five-spice powder with the mushrooms. Add 2 teaspoons (10 ml) soy sauce to the pan with the stock and mushroom-soaking liquid. Stir 2 thinly sliced green onions (green and light-green parts only) into the finished sauce. (Pictured centre.)
Serve with: sautéed chicken or pork medallions.

CREMINI MUSHROOM AND THYME

Omit the dried mushrooms, and use fresh cremini or brown mushrooms instead of shiitake. Add 2 teaspoons (10 ml) chopped fresh thyme leaves with the mushrooms, and 2 teaspoons (10 ml) Worcestershire sauce with the stock and mushroom-soaking liquid.
Serve with: chicken or lamb chops, or use with long grain rice as a stuffing for red peppers, courgette or aubergine.

PEPPERY MIXED MUSHROOM

Follow the recipe for the **Mixed Mushroom and Rosemary Sauce**, stirring ½ teaspoon (3 ml) roughly crushed pink or black peppercorns into the finished sauce. (Pictured bottom.)
Serve with: steak, roast beef or venison dishes.

219 chicken Velouté

The unctuous velouté is one of the classical five French mother sauces (see page 6). It can be made from chicken, fish, beef or veal stock. It begins with a roux – a cooked flour and butter paste, to which stock is added until a thick, velvety sauce forms.

INGREDIENTS

55 g unsalted butter
55 g plain flour
About 1 L hot chicken stock (see page 16)
Salt and black pepper

MAKES about 500 ml.
Serves 8, enough to accompany a large roast chicken, or a medium roast turkey

Melt the butter in a saucepan, add the flour and cook, stirring, over medium-low heat, until the mixture or roux is a light straw colour. Gradually add one-quarter of the stock, using a wooden spoon to stir out any lumps. Switch to a whisk and pour in the rest of the stock more quickly, whisking constantly. Bring to a boil over medium-high heat, making sure to skim off any scum that rises to the surface.

Reduce the heat to low, and simmer until the sauce is reduced by a third to a half (depending on how thick you like it), and is a satiny, creamy pouring consistency (similar to double cream), about 6 to 12 minutes. Strain, then season to taste.

Serve with: poultry and light meat dishes, tossed through spaghetti or linguine with chicken.

HANDY TIP

This sauce is great for a dinner party or Sunday lunch for a crowd as it can be made ahead and kept warm, or cooled and chilled in the fridge. Simply reheat gently on the hob until piping hot when ready to serve. To avoid it forming a skin on the surface, place a piece of cling film directly on top of the sauce.

Variations

220 WITH CARROT AND CUMIN

Stir ½ teaspoon (3 ml) ground cumin and ¼ teaspoon (1 ml) ground turmeric into the roux. Whisk 3 tablespoons (45 ml) crème fraîche and 120 ml carrot purée into the finished sauce.
Serve with: lamb dishes or use as an alternative to béchamel in lasagne and other baked pasta dishes.

221 WITH APPLE AND MUSTARD

Sauté 1 peeled, cored and diced Granny Smith apple in a little butter until golden and tender. Set aside. Stir 2 rounded teaspoons (10 ml) Dijon mustard, 2 tablespoons (30 ml) finely chopped fresh chives and the apple sauté into the finished sauce.
Serve with: pork chops or medallions, or roast beef.

222 WHITE WINE AND SAFFRON

Sweat 2 finely chopped shallots in 1 tablespoon (15 ml) unsalted butter. Pour in 80 ml white wine and simmer until syrupy. Add 3 tablespoons (45 ml) butter. When melted add 3 tablespoons (45 g) plain flour and follow the main recipe. Soak a generous pinch of saffron strands in 2 tablespoons (30 ml) hot stock and add to the finished sauce.
Serve with: fish or shellfish, or with chicken dishes.

This rich and creamy velouté makes a plain roast chicken a weekday treat

LEMON AND WHITE WINE

Make the **White Wine and Saffron Velouté**, but replace the saffron with 2 teaspoons (10 ml) finely grated lemon zest, and add 2 tablespoons (30 ml) lemon juice to the finished sauce.
Serve with: delicate white fish or poached chicken.

SPINACH PARMESAN

Prepare the recipe for the **Creamy Herb Velouté** but don't add the fresh herbs at the end. Instead, stir in 140 g defrosted frozen spinach, squeezed dry and chopped very finely and 3 tablespoons (45 ml) freshly grated Parmesan cheese. Heat through until piping hot and then thin with a little hot water or stock if the sauce is too thick.
Serve with: steak, roast lamb or beef, or stuffed cannelloni shells.

CREAMY HERB

Sweat 2 chopped shallots and ½ teaspoon (3 ml) chopped fresh thyme leaves in 1 tablespoon (15 ml) unsalted butter until soft and translucent. Add 3 more tablespoons (45 ml) unsalted butter. When melted add 55 g plain flour and proceed with the main recipe. Add 80–120 ml double cream to the finished sauce and simmer for 2 to 3 minutes until thick. Stir in 1 tablespoon (15 ml) each chopped fresh parsley, tarragon and chervil, and season.
Serve with: roast or pan-fried chicken, turkey or pork.

TRUFFLE

Make the **Creamy Herb Velouté** but omit the fresh parsley and tarragon and stir 1 tablespoon (15 ml) white truffle oil and 2 tablespoons (30 ml) chopped fresh chives into the finished sauce. Grate fresh black truffle (to taste) into the velouté before serving.
Serve with: baked or grilled chicken, gnocchi.

WITH GINGER AND LEMONGRASS

Place 180 ml double cream in a saucepan with the bottom 7 cm (3 inches) of a stalk of lemongrass and a peeled 2 cm (1-inch) knob of ginger that have been pounded with a pestle. Simmer until the cream has reduced by one third. Make the **Creamy Herb Velouté** but use the strained, infused cream and replace the herbs with 2 tablespoons (30 ml) chopped fresh coriander leaves.
Serve with: Asian-style grilled fish and meat, or noodles.

'AURORA' TOMATO

Make the **Chicken** or **Creamy Herb Velouté** and add 3 tablespoons (45 ml) tomato purée and ¼ teaspoon (1 ml) sugar to the finished sauce. Simmer for a minute and stir in 2 tablespoons (30 ml) shredded fresh basil leaves. Season with plenty of cracked, fresh black pepper.
Serve with: baked cod or halibut, poached lobster, pork medallions or chicken escalopes or cutlets.

229 Beef Jus

Jus essentially means 'juices' and at its most basic this sauce is a reduction of beef and vegetable juices. Based on the classic *espagnole*, one of the five French mother sauces (see page 6), but simpler to make, it is perfect for entertaining as it can be made in advance.

INGREDIENTS

2 tbsp (30 ml) olive oil

300 g beef trimmings or chicken wings, chopped into small pieces

1 medium onion, cut into small dice

1 carrot, cut into small dice

1 rib celery, cut into small dice

8 cremini or brown mushrooms, chopped

1 garlic clove, crushed

1 sprig thyme

2 parsley stalks

1 bay leaf

2 tsp (10 ml) tomato purée

1 ½ tbsp (23 ml) plain flour

1 L beef stock (see page 18)

Salt and black pepper

SERVES 4 to 6, about 360 ml

Heat the oil in a frying pan over medium heat. Add the beef trimmings or chicken wings, and cook, stirring occasionally, until a rich dark brown. Lower the heat and add all the vegetables, except the garlic and cook until softened, about 10 minutes. Add the garlic and cook until the vegetables are lightly browned.

Add the thyme, parsley, bay leaf, tomato purée and flour, and cook, stirring, until the vegetables are a darker brown colour. Add 255 ml water to the frying pan, bring to the boil and simmer for 5 minutes. Transfer to a saucepan, and add the stock. Bring to a boil and skim off any scum that rises to the surface. Reduce the heat, and simmer for 45 minutes, or until the liquid reduces by at least two-thirds, skimming as necessary. Strain through a fine sieve. For a thicker consistency, return the sauce to a clean pan and simmer for another 5 minutes. Season with salt and pepper.

Serve with: beef, lamb and game dishes.

HANDY TIP

To achieve the ideal, clear, glossy sauce, skim off as much of the scum as you can and, when you sieve the sauce, don't press down on the vegetables.

Variations

230 WITH THYME

Add 2 teaspoons (10 ml) finely chopped fresh thyme leaves to the finished sauce.
Serve with: roast chicken or roast pork loin.

231 MARSALA AND WILD MUSHROOM

Soak 14 g mixed dried wild mushrooms in 120 ml just-boiled water for 20 minutes or until soft. Remove from the water, squeezing the excess back into the bowl, and chop. Strain and reserve the liquid. Make the **Beef Jus**, adding the mushroom-soaking liquid with the stock. Stir the mushrooms and 1 tablespoon (15 ml) chopped fresh parsley leaves into the finished sauce, and simmer for 5 minutes.
Serve with: roast chicken, turkey or Cornish hens.

232 CARAMELISED RED ONION

Thinly slice 1 medium red onion, and cook in 1 tablespoon (15 ml) butter, 1 tablespoon (15 ml) olive oil and 1 teaspoon (5 ml) white sugar for 20 to 25 minutes until dark golden and caramelised. Add to the finished sauce, and whisk in 1 tablespoon (15 ml) cold butter just before serving.
Serve with: pepper-crusted steak, or pulled pork or chicken.

The classic French Beef Jus with Red Wine is the perfect accompaniment to meat and game dishes

SAUCE 'ROBERT'

Heat 85 ml white wine and 2 tablespoons (30 ml) white wine vinegar in a small saucepan and reduce by half. Add to the finished sauce with 1 tablespoon (15 ml) Dijon mustard and 2 tablespoons (30 ml) chopped fresh chives.
Serve with: roast pork or grilled pork chops.

WITH BALSAMIC VINEGAR

Make the **Beef and Red Wine Jus.** Add 3 tablespoons (45 ml) balsamic vinegar to the red wine and aromatics before reducing. Stir ½ teaspoon (3 ml) soft light-brown sugar into the finished sauce.
Serve with: steak, venison medallions or calves' liver.

WITH TOMATO AND ROSEMARY

Add 180 ml tomato purée with the stock. Stir 2 teaspoons (10 ml) finely chopped fresh rosemary leaves into the finished sauce.
Serve with: vegetables, egg noodles or grilled meats.

RED CURRANT 'POIVRADE' GRAVY

Make the **Beef and Red Wine Jus**, but combine the red wine with 3 tablespoons (45 ml) red wine vinegar before reducing. Add 1 ½ tablespoons (45 ml) red currant jelly, and ½ teaspoon (3 ml) crushed black peppercorns to the finished sauce. Just before serving whisk 1 tablespoon (15 ml) cold butter into the sauce. Do not reheat the sauce once the butter has been added.
Serve with: lamb, steak or roast beef.

WITH RED WINE

In a saucepan simmer 250 ml red wine, 5 black peppercorns and 1 roughly chopped shallot until reduced by half. Strain and stir into the finished sauce. Return to the saucepan, bring to a boil and simmer very gently for 5 minutes.
Serve with: roast beef, sliced hanger or flank steak.

WITH PORT AND STAR ANISE

Make the **Red Currant 'Poivrade' Gravy.** Add 1 whole star anise to the red wine and aromatics before reducing. Stir in 55 ml of port to the finished sauce. Remove the star anise before serving.
Serve with: sautéed pork tenderloin, sirloin strips or seared duck breasts.

239 marsala sauce

This sauce derives much of its complexity from marsala, a fortified sweet Italian wine. If you can't find it, substitute with Madeira, sherry or port.

INGREDIENTS

180 ml marsala wine
1 ½ tbsp (23 ml) olive oil
2 shallots, finely chopped
1 clove garlic, minced
1 ½ tbsp (23 ml) plain flour

400 ml hot beef stock (see page 18)
Salt and black pepper

SERVES 4

Bring the marsala to a boil in a saucepan, simmer until reduced by half. Heat the oil in a frying pan, cook the shallots, stirring, until translucent. Add the garlic and cook for a further minute. Stir in the flour, then after 2 minutes, slowly add the marsala, whisking to beat out any lumps. Simmer for 2 to 3 minutes. Whisk in the stock and simmer until the sauce thickens to coat the back of a spoon. Season to taste with salt and pepper.

Serve with: beef or pork dishes.

HANDY TIP

Shallots can be tricky to peel. To ease the process, soak in just-boiled water for 2 to 3 minutes until the outer skins soften and start to pull back. Rinse in cold water, slice off top and root ends and squeeze the shallots out of their skins.

variations

240 WITH GRAPES

Stir 12 to 15 halved large black seedless grapes into the finished sauce with ½ tablespoon (8 ml) shredded fresh sage leaves. Simmer for 2 minutes.
Serve with: duck, venison or steak.

241 WITH CREAM AND DIJON MUSTARD

Add 120 ml double cream and 1 tablespoon (15 ml) Dijon mustard to the sauce after it's been simmering for 5 minutes in the final step. Simmer until it coats the back of a spoon.
Serve with: chicken or pork.

242 WITH MUSTARD AND PORT

Follow the **Dijon and Cream Marsala Sauce.** Replace the marsala with port and whisk in 1½ tablespoons (23 ml) whole-grain mustard instead of the Dijon mustard.
Serve with: roasted strip, flank or hanger steak.

243 chocolate & chilli Mole

Mole comes from the word 'molli' meaning 'concoction'. Legend has it that the first mole was served at a convent in the Mexican town of Puebla de Los Angeles as a dish for a visiting dignitary. Today, every home has its own version.

INGREDIENTS

2 tbsp (30 ml) ground dried ancho chilli
140 g whole blanched almonds
55 g diced green plantain
1 tsp (5 ml) ground cinnamon
1 clove garlic
2 soft corn tortillas (homemade or supermarket-bought), torn into pieces
2 tbsp (30 ml) roasted pumpkin seeds

½ (93 g) disc Mexican chocolate or 28 g semisweet chocolate
480 ml chicken stock (see page 16)
120 ml chopped canned tomatoes, with juice
Salt to taste

MAKES about 480 ml

In a blender or food processor, grind the chilli powder, almonds, plantain, cinnamon, garlic, tortilla pieces, pumpkin seeds and chocolate with 240 ml of the chicken stock until puréed but grainy. Pour into a saucepan, add the remaining chicken stock and tomatoes, and simmer, stirring, over medium heat, until the chocolate melts. Season with salt.

Serve with: poultry.

HANDY TIP

The sauce will keep, chilled, for up to 3 days.

variations

244 YELLOW MOLE

Process 15 roasted, stemmed, deveined, and seeded guajillo or Amarillo chillies; 1 (368 g) can tomatillos with liquid; 2 cloves minced garlic; ½ teaspoon (3 ml) ground cumin; ½ teaspoon (3 ml) dried oregano; and ½ teaspoon (3 ml) ground cinnamon, in a food processor until smooth. Season with salt and pepper. Bring to a boil, then simmer for 15 minutes.
Serve with: chicken, turkey or roast vegetables.

245 GREEN MOLE

Purée 2 (368 g) cans tomatillos, 240 ml finely chopped onion, 60 ml toasted almonds, 1 tablespoon (15 ml) freshly chopped coriander, and 3 tablespoons (45 ml) diced green chillies in a food processor. Season to taste.
Serve with: chicken, turkey or pork.

246 DOCTORED-UP MOLE

Use a supermarket-bought mole and doctor with smoked chipotle sauce, honey and chopped garlic and coriander, to taste.
Serve with: poultry or beef.

247 Green Peppercorn Sauce

No *steak frites* is complete without this classic French sauce. Green peppercorns are from the same plant as black, but are harvested before they ripen. They are milder and less pungent than black.

INGREDIENTS

1 tbsp (15 ml) olive oil
1 shallot, finely minced
120 ml red wine
1 tbsp (15 ml) red wine vinegar
3 tbsp (45 ml) cognac or brandy
255 ml beef stock (see page 18)
140 ml double cream
2 tbsp (30 ml) green peppercorns

in brine, well-rinsed and drained
1 tsp (5 ml) chopped fresh thyme leaves
Salt and black pepper

MAKES 170 ml
Serves 2 to 3

Heat the oil in a saucepan over medium heat and add the shallot. Cook, stirring, until soft. Add the red wine, vinegar and cognac and bring to a boil. Once the liquid has reduced by at least half, add the stock, return to the boil, then simmer briskly for 15 minutes or until reduced by about two-thirds. Add the cream, bring back to a boil and simmer for 8 to 10 minutes or until the sauce has a velvety pouring consistency (like single cream). Stir in the green peppercorns and thyme leaves and season to taste. (Pictured opposite top.)

Serve with: sirloin, rib eye or filet mignon, lamb steaks, pork medallions, or roast beef or venison.

Handy Tip

For added flavour, if you're serving this sauce with steak or other sautéed meat, make it in the pan used to cook the meat. Reduce the red wine, vinegar, brandy and stock. Cook the meat in a frying pan and transfer to a plate to rest, then sauté the shallots in the same frying pan. Pour in the wine mixture, scraping the pan with a wooden spoon to loosen any stuck-on meat residue, and bring to the boil. Add the cream and continue as directed.

Variations

248 WITH GARLIC

Slice off the top third of a head of garlic. Place in a baking dish, drizzle with olive oil, then cover with a lid or foil. Bake for 45 minutes at 180°C (350°F) until soft. Once cool, squeeze cloves from their skins, mash and whisk into the sauce with 1 teaspoon (5 ml) Dijon mustard. Replace thyme with 2 tablespoons (30 ml) chopped fresh parsley leaves.
Serve with: steak, roast meats or beef, pork or turkey meatballs.

249 WITH CORIANDER

Toast ¾ teaspoon (4 ml) coriander seeds in a small dry frying pan until fragrant, remove from the pan and crush roughly. Add 1 finely minced garlic clove to the pan with the shallots. Add the crushed coriander seeds to the finished sauce.
Serve with: pan-fried or grilled spice-rubbed chicken, venison or beef steaks or medallions, roast pork loin.

250 PEPPERCORN AND TARRAGON

Make the **Pink Peppercorn Sauce,** but replace the pink peppercorns with black peppercorns, and replace the rosemary with 1 tablespoon (15 ml) finely chopped fresh tarragon.
Serve with: chicken dishes, meaty fish like monkfish or halibut, or prawns with rice or buttered noodles.

PORT AND BLACK PEPPERCORN

Replace the brandy with 4 tablespoons (60 ml) port, and the green peppercorns with 1 ½ teaspoons (8 ml) crushed black peppercorns. Stir 2 teaspoons (10 ml) red currant jelly into the finished sauce. (Pictured top.)
Serve with: duck, goose, roast beef or sautéed sirloin steak strips.

PINK PEPPERCORN

Replace the red wine and red wine vinegar with white wine and white wine vinegar, and the beef stock with chicken stock. Replace the green peppercorns with 1 ½ teaspoons (8 ml) coarsely crushed pink peppercorns, and the thyme with ½ teaspoon (3 ml) finely chopped fresh rosemary leaves. (Pictured centre.)
Serve with: chicken, turkey and pork dishes.

BLACK PEPPERCORN AND CRANBERRY

Make the **Port and Black Peppercorn Sauce** but replace the red wine vinegar with balsamic vinegar and the red currant jelly with 1 tablespoon (15 ml) cranberry sauce. Omit the cream. (Pictured bottom.)
Serve with: beef dishes, or roast turkey or duck.

254 Rich Vegetable Gravy

This rich vegetarian sauce rivals any meat-based gravy in terms of taste and complexity. Don't rush the browning of the vegetables; you want them to caramelise to add lots of deep flavours to the sauce.

INGREDIENTS

2 tbsp (30 ml) olive oil
1 medium onion, finely chopped
85 g carrots, chopped
55 g fennel, chopped
55 g celery, chopped
2 cloves garlic, minced
140 g brown mushrooms, chopped
1 medium tomato, chopped
1 tbsp (15 ml) tomato purée

1 sprig fresh thyme
850 ml vegetable stock (see page 17)
1 tbsp (15 ml) Worcestershire sauce
255 ml dry white wine
1 tbsp (15 ml) cornflour

MAKES about 450 ml
Serves up to 8 with a nut roast

Heat the oil in a frying pan over medium heat and cook onion, carrots, fennel, celery and garlic, stirring occasionally, until golden brown. Add the mushrooms, increase heat to medium-high, and cook, stirring, until the mushrooms are browned. Stir in the tomato, tomato purée and thyme and cook, covered, for 5 minutes. Whisk in the stock and Worcestershire sauce and simmer for 15 minutes. Add the wine, bring to the boil and simmer briskly for 25 to 30 more minutes. Strain through a fine sieve, pressing to extract as much liquid as possible. Transfer to a saucepan and simmer gently. Combine the cornflour with a little cold water to make a smooth paste. Whisk into the sauce and cook for 2 to 3 minutes until thickened slightly.

Serve with: any vegetarian dishes, especially roast stuffed squash, stuffed bell peppers or nut roasts.

HANDY TIP

Use a small amount of this sauce to add flavour to a braise or soup. Omit the cornflour and reduce for an additional 10 minutes, cool, pour into ice cube trays and freeze. Add a cube to a dish you're preparing.

Variations

255 WITH ANISE AND TARRAGON

Add 1 star anise to the frying pan with the carrots, onion and celery mixture. Stir 2 tablespoons (30 ml) chopped fresh tarragon into the finished sauce.
Serve with: vegetable kebabs, bean burgers, a wild rice and roast vegetable pilaf.

256 BUTTERNUT SQUASH

Sauté 280 g diced butternut squash with 2 tablespoons (30 ml) butter, ½ tablespoon (8 ml) olive oil and ½ teaspoon (3 ml) sugar until tender. Add the squash with the stock. Continue with the main recipe, but omit the cornflour and add 2 tablespoons (30 ml) each shredded sage leaves and double cream.
Serve with: vegetable tarts or cooked vegetables.

257 MUSHROOM

Sauté 1 medium onion, thinly sliced, in 1 tablespoon (15 ml) butter, ½ tablespoon (8 ml) olive oil, a pinch of sugar and ½ tsp (3 ml) chopped thyme leaves until soft. Push to one side. Add 1 tablespoon (15 ml) butter and sauté 110 g sliced mushrooms until tender. Add to the finished gravy and simmer for 1 minute.
Serve with: steak, roast beef or wide egg noodles.

258 RIESLING, PEAR AND MARJORAM

Add 255 ml pear juice with the stock. Simmer for 15 minutes before adding 240 ml Riesling as the white wine. Stir 2 tablespoons (30 ml) chopped fresh marjoram into the finished sauce.
Serve with: roast pork, chicken, turkey or vegetables.

Take your time to make a deeply flavoured gravy to serve with many vegetarian dishes

CREAMY VEGETABLE

Add 120 ml double cream to the finished gravy, bring back to a boil, then simmer for 5 minutes. Stir in 1 tablespoon (15 ml) each chopped fresh parsley, chervil and tarragon leaves before serving. (Pictured left.)
Serve with: nut roasts, roasted butternut squash, wilted greens, roast chicken or turkey.

ROSEMARY-THYME

Stir 2 teaspoons (10 ml) each chopped fresh thyme and rosemary leaves into the strained sauce when it goes back onto the heat. (Pictured right.)
Serve with: roasted, stuffed aubergine and courgette, or grilled portabello mushrooms.

261 Yellow Pepper Sauce

Serve an extra helping of vegetables into a family meal by blending it into a delicious sauce. This freezes well, so make a few batches at once, freeze what you don't use, then defrost when needed.

INGREDIENTS

1 ½ tbsp (23 ml) olive oil

1 tbsp (15 ml) butter

½ medium onion, finely chopped

1 clove garlic, minced

Pinch ground cumin

Pinch ground fennel

Pinch ground turmeric

1 medium yellow bell pepper, seeded and chopped

140 ml hot chicken or vegetable stock (see pages 16 and 17), plus more as needed

Salt and black pepper

SERVES 2 to 3

In a frying pan, sauté the onion, garlic and ground spices in the butter and oil until the onion is translucent. Add the peppers and cook for 5 minutes, stirring occasionally. Stir in the stock and simmer for 10 minutes or until vegetables are very tender. Cool, then transfer to a blender and purée until smooth. Pour into a saucepan and reheat gently. If too thick, whisk in more stock, ½ tablespoon (8 ml) at a time. Season to taste.

Serve with: grilled or baked fish or chicken, or roast pork.

HANDY TIP

I use yellow pepper in this sauce because I love its bright colour, which is enhanced by a pinch of turmeric. You can use a red pepper instead: omit the turmeric and add ½ teaspoon (8 ml) of tomato purée with the diced pepper. Avoid green peppers, as they aren't sweet enough.

Variations

262 WITH ROAST SWEETCORN

Brush 1 small ear of sweetcorn with olive oil and roast in a hot oven until tender and charred in places. Cut off the corn, collecting the juice. Add to the blender with the rest of the ingredients. When reheating, stir in ¼ teaspoon (1 ml) white wine vinegar and ½ teaspoon (3 ml) sugar.
Serve with: grilled or barbecued tuna or swordfish steaks, lobster tails, or spice-rubbed chicken breasts.

263 WITH GINGER

Add 2 teaspoons (10 ml) finely grated, peeled fresh ginger to the pan with the peppers and stir 2 finely chopped green onions (the green and light-green parts only) into the finished sauce.
Serve with: Asian-style fish or chicken, or roast pork tenderloin or chops.

264 WITH FENNEL

Add 110 g diced trimmed fennel to the frying pan with the yellow pepper. Stir 1 tablespoon (15 ml) of fennel fronds, chopped, or 1 tablespoon (15 ml) chopped chives into the finished sauce.
Serve with: steamed mussels or mixed grilled seafood.

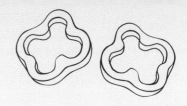

ZAATAR AND MARJORAM

Replace the cumin, fennel and turmeric with 1 teaspoon (5 ml) zaatar (a Middle Eastern spice blend), added to the frying pan with the onion. Stir 1 ½ teaspoons (8 ml) finely chopped marjoram into the finished sauce.
Serve with: grilled or pan-fried chicken, pork or steak.

WITH CURRY AND CORIANDER

Omit the cumin, fennel and turmeric and add 1 ½ teaspoons (8 ml) mild curry powder and ¼ teaspoon (1 ml) finely minced peeled ginger to the pan with the onion. Add 1 to 2 tablespoons (15 to 30 ml) finely chopped fresh coriander leaves to the finished sauce.
Serve with: rice, grilled or sautéed chicken, pork or fish.

WITH THAI BASIL AND LEMONGRASS

Omit the cumin, fennel and turmeric and replace with the bruised bulb of a stick of lemongrass, and add to the frying pan with the onion. Stir 1 tablespoon (15 ml) finely shredded Thai basil leaves into the finished sauce. Remove the lemongrass from the sauce before serving.
Serve with: fish, seafood, chicken or pork.

SPICY RED PEPPER

Replace the yellow pepper with a red one and add half a finely chopped jalapeño chilli and 1 teaspoon (5 ml) tomato purée with the peppers. Stir ¼ teaspoon (1 ml) sugar and hot sauce, to taste, into the finished sauce.
Serve with: roasted and grilled meat or poultry, or aubergine, courgette or butternut squash.

CREAMY YELLOW PEPPER AND BASIL

Stir 2 ½ tablespoons (38 ml) mascarpone cheese and 2 tablespoons (30 ml) shredded fresh basil leaves into the finished sauce.
Serve with: grilled or sautéed prawns or squid, or with chicken dishes.

RED PEPPER AND TOMATO

Make the **Spicy Red Pepper Sauce** but add 80 ml canned tomato sauce to the pan with the stock. Simmer gently for 10 to 12 minutes until thickened considerably before blending.
Serve with: sliced flank or hanger steak, or penne or rigatoni pasta with plenty of freshly grated Parmesan cheese.

271 Prawn Bisque Sauce

This adaptation of a classic French soup is one of my favourite sauces to accompany seafood. To serve it as a soup, dilute it with unseasoned stock.

INGREDIENTS

110 g shell-on cooked and cleaned prawns (about 8)
1 tbsp (15 ml) vegetable or rapeseed oil
½ tsp (3 ml) tomato purée
1 small shallot, chopped
½ tbsp (8 ml) brandy

250 ml fish stock (see page 17)
80 ml double cream
Dash Hot sauce
Salt and black pepper

MAKES about 120 ml
Serves 2 to 3 as a sauce

Peel the prawns, and reserve the shells and meat separately. Heat the oil in a saucepan, add the shells and cook, stirring, until golden brown. Stir in the tomato purée then add the shallots and brandy and cook until the brandy has almost disappeared. Add the stock, bring to a boil, then simmer gently for 15 minutes. Strain through a fine sieve and set aside.

Meanwhile roughly chop a third of the reserved prawn meat, using the remaining prawn for another dish. Combine the reserved prawn shell stock and the cream in a clean saucepan. Bring to a boil, then simmer briskly for 6 to 8 minutes (or up to 12 minutes for a thicker sauce to accompany pasta). Stir in the chopped prawn meat and hot sauce. Season to taste and serve.

Serve with: grilled seafood, baked, steamed or pan-fried fish, pasta.

HANDY TIP

You can make this sauce using prawn shells alone, without the meat, since all the flavour comes from the shells. I always buy prawns with the shells on, then, freeze the shells and when I have enough I'll make a rich shellfish stock – or this sauce!

Variations

272 WITH CURRY

Add 1 teaspoon (5 ml) curry powder and a pinch of ground turmeric to the prawn shells before adding the fish stock. Stir 1 tablespoon (15 ml) chopped fresh coriander leaves into the finished sauce.
Serve with: grilled lobster, or beef medallions for a 'surf and turf'.

273 WITH ASPARAGUS

Cut off the spears of 85 g fine asparagus, then finely slice the tender stems. Sauté in 1 tablespoon (15 ml) butter with ½ minced garlic clove and a pinch of salt and stir into the finished sauce.
Serve with: prawns, lobster or crab ravioli, or grilled or baked fish or seafood.

274 WITH LEMON DILL

Stir ½ teaspoon (3 ml) finely grated lemon zest, 2 tablespoons (30 ml) lemon juice and 2 tablespoons (30 ml) chopped fresh dill into the finished sauce.
Serve with: delicate baked, grilled or pan-fried fish or seafood.

275 Bouillabaisse Sauce

This sauce is inspired by bouillabaisse, a hearty Provençal fish stew laced with tomatoes, fennel seeds, saffron and herbs, and imbued with a rich fish stock.

INGREDIENTS

1 ½ tbsp (23 ml) olive oil
½ medium onion, chopped
1 small leek, white part only, sliced
1 clove garlic, chopped
¼ medium green pepper, seeded and chopped
2 whole tomatoes from a can of whole peeled tomatoes, chopped

285 ml fish stock (see page 17)
2 tbsp (30 ml) dry white wine
Pinch saffron stems (optional)
1 bay leaf
½ tsp (3 ml) fennel seeds
1 fresh sprig thyme
Salt and black pepper

MAKES 185 ml
Serves 3 to 4

Heat the oil in a saucepan. Add the onion, leeks and garlic. Cook, stirring, over medium heat until soft. Add the tomatoes, and cook, stirring, for 3 to 5 minutes. Add the fish stock, wine, saffron (if using), bay leaf, fennel seeds, thyme, ¼ teaspoon (1 ml) salt and a pinch of pepper. Bring to the boil and simmer briskly for 10 minutes.

Remove from the heat; discard the bay leaf and thyme. Leave to cool for 5 minutes, then transfer to a blender. Blend until smooth, then strain through a fine sieve. Rinse out the saucepan, and return the sauce. Bring to a boil and simmer briskly for 3 minutes. Season to taste.

Serve with: grilled salmon or monkfish, or steamed mussels or clams.

HANDY TIP

This sauce is quite thin. I like to spoon 120 ml in a shallow bowl then top with a fillet of cooked fish. If you prefer a heavier sauce, thicken with a little cornflour dissolved in some cold water, and simmer for 1 minute.

Variations

WITH CLAMS

Replace the fish stock with clam juice. Stir 60 ml canned chopped clams and 2 tablespoons (30 ml) chopped fresh parsley into the finished sauce.
Serve with: baked cod or halibut.

THAI-STYLE

Add 1 tablespoon Thai red curry paste to the onion-and-leek mixture as it cooks. Stir 2 tablespoons (30 ml) unsweetened coconut cream into the finished sauce.
Serve with: grilled lobster, sautéed scallops or prawns, or baked white fish fillets.

WITH VODKA

Add 2 tablespoons (30 ml) vodka to the finished sauce, then bring to a boil, reduce the heat, and simmer for 20 seconds. Stir in 2 tablespoons (30 ml) chopped fresh parsley and remove from the heat.
Serve with: meaty white fish or seafood pasta.

279 Fish Velouté

A modern velouté uses double cream rather than a roux to thicken the sauce.

INGREDIENTS

1 ½ tbsp (23 ml) butter
2 shallots
2 tbsp (30 g) minced fresh fennel
1 sprig thyme
140 ml dry white wine
285 ml hot fish stock (see page 17)
140 ml double cream

2 tbsp (30 ml) chopped fresh chives
Salt and black pepper

SERVES 4

Melt the butter in a saucepan over medium heat. Cook the shallot, fennel and thyme, stirring, until softened and translucent. Pour in the wine and simmer until a couple tablespoons (about 30 ml) are left and the liquid is syrupy.

Pour in the stock, bring to the boil and simmer briskly until reduced by a third. Pour in the cream, and simmer for 8 to 10 minutes, until thickened. Strain through a fine sieve, or simply remove the thyme. Stir in the chives, then season to taste.

Serve with: fish and shellfish.

HANDY TIP

To make a chicken velouté using this method, replace the fish stock with chicken and the chives with chopped fresh parsley leaves.

Variations

280 WITH CAVIAR

Stir 3 tablespoons (45 ml) black caviar into the finished sauce.
Serve with: poached eggs, lobster or scallops.

281 WITH HERBS AND MUSHROOMS

Add 110 g chopped button mushrooms with the shallots, and stir 1 tablespoon (15 ml) each of chopped fresh parsley and dill into the finished sauce.
Serve with: fish dishes, or as a soup thinned down with a fish or seafood stock.

282 WITH MUSTARD AND CAPERS

Stir 1 ½ tablespoons (23 ml) chopped rinsed capers and 1 teaspoon (5 ml) Dijon mustard into the finished sauce.
Serve with: salmon or halibut fish cakes, baked or pan-fried sole.

283 Pea & Mint Sauce

Make this verdant, brightly coloured sauce when peas are in season and at their best. Or, if you wish to evoke the freshness of spring and enliven and jazz up a winter or autumn meal, use frozen.

INGREDIENTS

170 ml vegetable stock (see page 17)
85 g fresh or frozen peas
1 small clove garlic, chopped
¼ tsp (1 ml) granulated sugar
Small handful whole fresh mint leaves, about 12 to 15
2 tbsp (30 ml) double cream

1 tbsp (15 ml) unsalted butter
1 tbsp (15 ml) lemon juice
Salt and black pepper

MAKES about 300 ml
Enough for 4 if serving as a sauce, or 2 to 3 servings of filled pasta

Bring the stock to a boil in a saucepan. Add the peas and cook until tender, about 5 minutes. Transfer to a blender, add the garlic, sugar and mint leaves and blend until completely smooth.

Rinse out the saucepan, then strain the sauce through a fine sieve if desired and return it to the pan. Bring to a boil, then lower the heat until the sauce is barely simmering. Whisk in the cream, butter and lemon juice then season to taste. Serve immediately.

Serve with: fish, asparagus, or ravioli or tortellini.

HANDY TIP

If you're using frozen peas, there's no need to defrost them first. They quickly warm up in the stock.

Variations

284 WATERCRESS

Replace the peas with chopped watercress and cook for just 30 seconds before transferring to the blender.
Serve with: poached chicken or baked fish.

285 WITH PANCETTA

Cook 28 g finely diced pancetta in a dry frying pan, stirring every now and then, until crisp and all the fat has rendered. Drain on kitchen paper. Add to the finished sauce with 2 tablespoons (30 ml) mascarpone cheese and 1 tablespoon (15 ml) freshly grated Parmesan.
Serve with: penne or fusilli pasta, or in a risotto.

286 WITH PERNOD

Sauté 1 minced shallot in a little butter until translucent, add 2 tablespoons (30 ml) Pernod (or ouzo or Sambuca) and bring to a boil. Simmer until the liquid is reduced to 1 tablespoon (15 ml), set aside. Add to the blender with the peas. Stir 1 tablespoon (15 ml) finely chopped fresh mint leaves into the strained sauce.
Serve with: fish, lobster, prawns or scallops, or simply cooked chicken.

CHILLI & BARBECUE SAUCES

287 Lemongrass, Ginger & Chilli Dipping Sauce

This versatile condiment is a refreshing and gutsy dipping sauce for Asian-style canapés.

INGREDIENTS

½ tbsp (8 ml) cornflour
3 red jalapeño chillies, seeded, and finely minced
2 cloves garlic, finely minced
Juice of 1 lime
1 tsp (5 ml) peeled, finely grated ginger
1 stalk lemongrass, tender bottom 7.5 cm (3 inches) of the bulb finely minced
3 tbsp (45 ml) rice vinegar
1 tbsp (15 ml) fish sauce, plus more as needed
110 g granulated sugar

MAKES about 255 ml

Combine the cornflour with 1 tablespoon (15 ml) cold water and stir until smooth. Set aside. Place the chillies, garlic, lime juice, ginger, lemongrass, rice vinegar, fish sauce and sugar in a saucepan with 180 ml water. Bring to the boil, then simmer for 10 minutes. Whisk in the cornflour mixture and simmer for 3 to 4 minutes until thickened. Cool completely before using. Lasts up to 2 weeks in the fridge.

Serve with: satay, spring rolls, fried fish cakes, or prawns.

HANDY TIP

As an alternative, use jarred, minced lemongrass.

288 WITH SESAME

Toast 1 tablespoon (15 ml) sesame seeds in frying pan until golden brown. When cool, stir into the finished sauce with 1 teaspoon (5 ml) toasted sesame oil.
Serve with: Thai-style crab cakes, tofu or vegetables.

290 WITH CREAM CHEESE

Make half the quantity of the sauce and add 160 g whipped cream cheese and 2 tablespoons (30 ml) shredded Thai basil.
Serve with: salads, potatoes, prawns, chicken or fish.

289 WITH CORIANDER

Add 3 tablespoons (45 ml) finely chopped coriander leaves.
Serve with: chicken, prawns or tofu, or with yoghurt as a salad dressing.

291 WITH FENNEL SEEDS

Stir in 2 teaspoons (10 ml) cooled, toasted fennel seeds.
Serve with: burgers, hot dogs, steak, chicken or prawns.

Variations

292 CHILLI, GREEN ONION AND LIME MAYO

Stir 2 to 3 tablespoons (30 to 45 ml) of the sauce into
120 ml mayonnaise, then stir in 1 finely sliced spring onion
(green and light-green parts only), 1 teaspoon (5 ml) finely
grated lime zest and 2 teaspoons (10 ml) lime juice.
Serve with: sandwiches, wraps, burgers, fried calamari or
lightly battered or breaded prawns, fish or chicken fingers.

293 WITH PEANUTS

Add 85 g finely chopped salted, roasted peanuts to the
finished sauce.
Serve with: spring rolls, Thai crab cakes, satay, or grilled
prawns or scallops.

294 STIR-FRY SAUCE

Combine 3 tablespoons (45 ml) of the finished sauce with
2 tablespoons (30 ml) oyster sauce, 1 tablespoon (15 ml)
soy sauce, 2 teaspoons (10 ml) chilli bean paste (optional),
2 tablespoons (30 ml) water and ½ tablespoon (8 ml)
cornflour. Stir until smooth. Add toward the end of stir-
fries, and cook for 2 to 3 minutes until slightly thickened.
Serve with: chicken, beef, tofu or vegetable stir-fries.

295 WITH PINEAPPLE AND MINT

Add 85 g finely diced fresh or canned pineapple and
2 tablespoons (30 ml) finely chopped fresh mint leaves to
the finished sauce.
Serve with: chicken, pork or seafood.

296 WITH PINEAPPLE AND COCONUT

Toast 85 g freshly grated or supermarket-bought desiccated
coconut in a frying pan until lightly golden. Set aside.
Make the **Chilli, Pineapple and Mint Dipping Sauce**
omitting the mint and adding the toasted coconut with
the pineapple.
Serve with: chicken, pork or beef meatballs or kebabs,
fried chicken.

297 Pineapple-chilli sauce

This is a fiery take on the ever-popular sweet-and-sour sauce found in Chinese restaurants the world over.

INGREDIENTS

1 tbsp (15 ml) cornflour
160 ml pineapple juice
55 ml chicken stock (see pages 16)
3 tbsp (45 ml) light-brown sugar
1 ½ tbsp (23 ml) mirin (sweetened rice wine)
3 tbsp (45 ml) rice vinegar
3 tbsp (45 ml) ketchup
1 long red chilli, seeded and minced

1 tbsp (15 ml) soy sauce, plus more as needed
2 spring onions, green and light-green parts only, thinly sliced
70 g fresh or canned pineapple chunks, finely diced

MAKES about 400 ml

Mix the cornflour with 1 tablespoon (15 ml) cold water in a small bowl and stir until smooth. Set aside.

In a saucepan, combine the remaining ingredients except the green onions and pineapple. Bring to a boil over medium heat, stirring to dissolve the sugar. Simmer for 2 to 3 minutes. Whisk in the cornflour slurry and cook for 2 minutes until thick and glossy. Remove from the heat. Stir in the green onions, pineapple, and add more soy sauce to taste.

Serve with: pan-fried fish, lightly battered fish fingers, pork or chicken strips, as a stir-fry sauce for chicken or pork.

HANDY TIP

If you want a really spicy sauce add 1 teaspoon (5 ml) of hot sauce.

Variations

298 WITH CUCUMBER

Stir half of a small cucumber, peeled, seeded and diced into the sauce with the green onions.
Serve with: battered or lightly breaded fish, steamed or grilled prawns.

299 WITH MANGO

Replace the pineapple with 85 g diced fresh, peeled mango.
Serve with: fish fillets, chicken escalopes or cutlets, lightly battered or pan-fried pork cutlets.

300 BLOOD ORANGE

Substitute blood orange juice for the pineapple juice, increase the brown sugar to 4 tablespoons (60 ml), stir 1 teaspoon (5 ml) finely grated orange zest into the finished sauce with the spring onions, and omit the pineapple.
Serve with: lamb, duck or chicken either as a stir-fry sauce or as a sauce accompaniment.

301 Harissa

This addictive North African condiment is packed with chillies and coriander, caraway, fennel and cumin seeds, making for a deeply aromatic blend that packs a spice punch to anything you serve it with.

INGREDIENTS

1 tbsp (15 ml) coriander seeds
1 ½ tbsp (23 ml) cumin seeds
½ tbsp (8 ml) fennel seeds
½ tbsp (8 ml) caraway seeds
8 large garlic cloves, roughly chopped
8 large red chillies, such as Fresno or jalapeño, seeded, if desired for a milder sauce, and roughly chopped
1 tbsp (15 ml) tomato purée

4 canned whole plum tomatoes, drained and roughly chopped
60 ml vegetable or rapeseed oil
1 tsp (5 ml) malt vinegar
Salt

MAKES just more than 255 ml
Lasts for 2 weeks in the fridge or 3 months in the freezer

Toast the coriander, cumin, fennel and caraway seeds in a small dry frying pan over medium heat, stirring, for a couple of minutes until fragrant. Remove from the heat and leave to cool for a few minutes. Transfer into a coffee grinder or pestle and mortar and grind to a fine powder. Tip into a small bowl, and set aside.

Place the garlic, onion, chillies, tomato purée, plum tomatoes and olive oil in a blender and process to a fine paste. Transfer the paste into a medium saucepan and bring to a boil over medium heat. Cook, simmering for about 15 minutes until the mixture becomes very thick, stirring every now and then to prevent it from catching and burning on the bottom of the pan. Stir in the spices, vinegar and ½ teaspoon (3 ml) salt, then remove from heat immediately. Serve at room temperature.

Serve with: Moroccan dishes such as stews, spicy stews such as tagines or couscous, grilled meats or fish, or as a dip for flatbreads.

HANDY TIP

To serve as a dip, thin with extra-virgin olive oil.

Variations

302 SWEET AND SOUR

Increase the malt vinegar to 1 tablespoon (15 ml) and stir 2 tablespoons (30 ml) soft dark-brown sugar into the finished sauce while still hot.
Serve with: grilled and roasted red meats, duck and goose, or spread sparingly onto crostini and top with soft goat's cheese.

303 WITH MINT

Stir 3 tablespoons (45 ml) chopped fresh mint leaves into the finished sauce.
Serve with: grilled fish or prawns, roasted vegetables such as carrots, aubergine, baby potatoes and courgette.

304 WITH ROASTED RED PEPPER

Add 125 g drained, jarred roasted red peppers to the blender with the rest of the ingredients. Stir through hummus or baba ghanoush. (Pictured right.)
Serve with: chicken, red meat, stews or curries.

305 WITH YOGHURT

Stir 1 to 2 tablespoons (15 to 30 ml) of the **Harissa** into 180 ml thick Greek yoghurt with 2 tablespoons (30 ml) finely chopped fresh coriander leaves and 1 tablespoon (15 ml) finely chopped fresh parsley leaves. Season with salt to taste. (Pictured far right.)
Serve with: rice, crudités, chicken, lamb or kebabs.

306 WITH TOMATO

Cook 1 small chopped onion in 2 tablespoons (30 ml) olive oil until translucent. Add 2 tablespoons (30 ml) **Harissa** with 1 (400 g) can well-drained chopped tomatoes, and 1 cinnamon stick to the pan. Simmer, stirring, until the tomatoes have broken down. Add ½ teaspoon (3 ml) sugar and 3 tablespoons (45 ml) chopped coriander leaves. Remove the cinnamon and season with salt.

Serve with: grilled fish, chicken or red meat.

307 WITH SPINACH AND YOGHURT

Sauté 170 g baby spinach leaves with 1 small clove garlic, minced, in a little olive oil and a pinch of salt and black pepper until wilted. When cool, squeeze out excess liquid and chop finely. Make the **Harissa and Yoghurt Sauce** omitting the herbs and adding the spinach and ½ teaspoon (3 ml) dried mint to the finished sauce.

Serve with: pitta bread as a dip, grilled fish or prawns, dolloped into grilled chicken or steak wrap sandwiches.

308 Southwestern Roasted Green Chilli Sauce

This rich, unctuous sauce is typical of the rustic, pungent 'green' condiments you'll find in New Mexico, Arizona and Texas.

INGREDIENTS

1 tbsp (15 ml) olive oil
½ medium onion
2 large cloves garlic, minced
½ small green pepper, finely minced
Salt
½ tsp (3 ml) ground cumin
¼ tsp (1 ml) ground coriander
½ tbsp (8 ml) plain flour
120–160 ml hot vegetable stock, (see page 17)
110 g canned roasted diced green chillies
½ tsp (3 ml) dried thyme

SERVES 4
Makes 255 ml

Heat the oil in heavy-based saucepan over medium heat. Add the onion and cook, stirring, for 3 to 4 minutes. Add the garlic and bell pepper with ¼ teaspoon (1 ml) salt and cook until the pepper is softened. Stir in the spices followed by the flour. Cook, stirring, for 1 minute, then add the stock, and bring to the boil, stirring, and cook until thickened. Add the green chillies and thyme and simmer for 3 to 4 minutes more. Remove from the heat, and adjust the salt to taste. Let the sauce cool for a couple of minutes, transfer to a blender and process to make a chunky purée.

Serve with: Mexican dishes such as enchiladas, burritos or tamales, eggs, steak, pork or chicken.

Handy Tip

To roast fresh chillies, skewer them onto a long-handled fork and hold over a gas flame, or place on a baking sheet under a hot grill. Turn frequently until they are blistered and blackened all over. Put in a plastic bag, close it and let them steam for 10 minutes. Remove the skins, stems and seeds using gloved hands under cold, running water.

Variations

309 WITH SWEETCORN

Roast 1 large ear sweetcorn under a hot grill, turning every few minutes until blistered. When cool enough to handle, slice off the kernels and discard cob. Add the kernels to the finished sauce.
Serve with: grits, over polenta or rice, or with spice-rubbed grilled chicken, pork or steak.

310 WITH BLACK BEAN

Stir 60 ml drained and rinsed canned black beans into the sauce with the green chillies.
Serve with: rice, enchiladas, tamales and other Mexican dishes.

311 RED PEPPER AND CORIANDER

Use red bell pepper instead of green, and stir 2 tablespoons (30 ml) chopped fresh coriander leaves into the finished sauce.
Serve with: meaty, firm fish, grilled or pan-fried prawns, chicken or pork.

312 Honey-Mustard Barbecue Sauce

There are few culinary pairings that go so impeccably together as honey and mustard.

INGREDIENTS

1 tbsp (15 ml) vegetable or rapeseed oil

½ medium onion, finely minced

1 large garlic clove, finely minced

180 ml prepared yellow mustard

160 ml dark honey

2 tbsp (30 ml) soft light-brown sugar

160 ml cider vinegar

2 tbsp (30 ml) tomato ketchup

1 tsp (5 ml) Worcestershire sauce

Salt

MAKES about 400 ml

Heat the oil in a saucepan and cook the onion over medium heat for 4 to 5 minutes until translucent. Add the garlic and cook for a further 30 seconds.

Add the remaining ingredients and whisk to combine thoroughly. Bring to a boil. Reduce the heat slightly, and simmer for 8 to 10 minutes, stirring every now and then, until thickened. Season with salt to taste.

Serve with: barbecued or grilled pork or chicken, grilled corn on the cob, as a dressing for potato salad.

HANDY TIP

Because of its high sugar content, this sauce gets incredibly hot when cooking. Be sure to cool to warm or even room temperature before using.

Variations

313 MAPLE SYRUP

Replace the honey with maple syrup.
Serve with: chicken kebabs or burgers, pork chops, corn on the cob or roasted sweet potato chunks.

314 DOUBLE MUSTARD

Reduce the prepared yellow mustard to 120 ml and add 3 tablespoons (45 ml) whole-grain mustard.
Serve with: burgers, sausages or barbecued chicken or pork dishes, roast or boiled baby potatoes.

315 WITH SPICED APRICOTS

Soak 85 g Turkish dried apricots in just-boiled water for 20 minutes until soft. Drain, purée in a blender, then mix with ½ teaspoon (3 ml) ground cumin and ¼ teaspoon (1 ml) each allspice and ground cayenne pepper and use in place of the ketchup and brown sugar.
Serve with: grilled and barbecued lamb, pork tenderloin or cutlets, or pulled pork.

316 Spicy Tomato Barbecue Sauce

Barbecue sauces need a base – tomato, vinegar, or mustard – as well as a sweet and sour element, spices and seasonings. This one has just the right amount of each component and is a real winner.

INGREDIENTS

1 tbsp (15 ml) chilli powder
1 tsp (5 ml) finely ground black pepper
2 tsp (10 ml) salt
1 tsp (5 ml) ground allspice
1 tsp (5 ml) garlic powder
1 tsp (5 ml) dry mustard
¼ tsp (1 ml) chipotle powder

120 g soft dark-brown sugar
4 tbsp (60 ml) white wine vinegar
2 tbsp (30 ml) Worcestershire sauce
1 tsp (5 ml) liquid smoke
480 ml tomato ketchup

SERVES 6 to 8

Combine the dry ingredients in a saucepan. Add the liquid ingredients, except the ketchup. Stir well until all are incorporated. Stir in the ketchup. Bring the mixture slowly to a boil, reduce the heat, and simmer gently for 20 minutes, stirring occasionally. (Be careful when boiling ketchup as it pops and spits.) Let cool. Store in the fridge before use. (Pictured opposite top.)

Serve with: all barbecued meats.

HANDY TIP

Just 1 teaspoon (5 ml) liquid smoke brings the perfect amount of smokiness to the sauce. This 'magic' ingredient is made by capturing and condensing smoke passed through wood chips in a combustion chamber.

Variations

317 WITH RED WINE AND BALSAMIC VINEGAR

Place 70 ml red wine in a saucepan with 6 peppercorns and 1 bay leaf. Simmer briskly until the liquid is reduced by half. Strain, and set aside. Replace the white wine vinegar with 80 ml balsamic vinegar and add the wine with the other ingredients.
Serve with: grilled or barbecued lamb, beef steaks or ribs and chicken, grilled or barbecued mushrooms.

318 WITH BOURBON

Add 100 ml bourbon to the saucepan with the rest of the liquid ingredients.
Serve with: sticky pork or beef ribs, pulled pork or chicken, burgers.

319 WITH TOMATO, SOY AND GINGER

Reduce the salt to ½ teaspoon (3 ml), adding 2 tablespoons (30 ml) soy sauce, 2 teaspoons (10 ml) sesame oil and 2 teaspoons (10 ml) finely grated peeled ginger to the saucepan with the liquid ingredients. Add more soy sauce to the finished sauce to taste if necessary.
Serve with: Asian-style ribs, soy-garlic marinated steak, pork chops or chicken kebabs.

320   WITH CURRY

Omit the liquid smoke and allspice and add 1 tablespoon (15 ml) mild curry powder with the rest of the dry ingredients.
Serve with: spice-rubbed ribs, steaks or grilled chicken, or tandoori-style chicken or lamb.

321   JAMAICAN JERK

Omit the chilli powder, allspice and dry mustard and replace with 2 tablespoons (30 ml) Jamaican jerk seasoning powder. (Pictured centre.)
Serve with: pulled pork or chicken wings or barbecued thighs and drumsticks.

322   WITH RASPBERRY AND CHIPOTLE

Add 250 g seedless raspberry jam and 1 teaspoon (5 ml) chipotle powder to the finished sauce in the pan. Simmer over medium heat, stirring well, until combined. Cook for 2 minutes over low heat. (Pictured bottom.)
Serve with: grilled or barbecued steak, other beef cuts, braised and shredded duck, beef or venison.

323 Hoisin Barbecue Sauce

This sauce is inspired by the dark, rich, uniquely sweet and deeply flavoured sauce that coats *Char Siu*, the Cantonese barbecued pork dish. This is a great addition to your summertime barbecue repertoire.

INGREDIENTS

2 tsp (10 ml) vegetable or rapeseed oil

2 spring onions, white and light-green parts only, finely minced

2 garlic cloves, minced

120 ml hoisin sauce

1 tbsp (15 ml) soy sauce, plus more as needed

3 tbsp (45 ml) sake or dry sherry

2 tbsp (30 ml) sweet chilli sauce

2 tbsp (30 ml) rice vinegar

1 tbsp (15 ml) honey

1 tsp (5 ml) toasted sesame oil

MAKES about 255 ml

Heat the vegetable oil in a small saucepan over low heat and cook the green onion for 1 minute, stirring, until translucent and cooked through. Add the garlic and cook for another 30 seconds. Add all the remaining ingredients, increase the heat to medium and bring to the boil. Simmer for 3 to 5 minutes or until thickened to your desired consistency. Serve as it is, or transfer to a blender and process for 15 to 20 seconds until very smooth. Taste, and add more soy sauce if necessary. Leave to cool before using.

Serve with: grilled, barbecued or roast pork, lamb steaks or chops, steak, or as a stir-fry sauce for red meats or pork.

HANDY TIP

Hoisin sauce is a sweet, pungent Chinese dipping condiment and cooking ingredient used as a component in a plethora of sauces. It's made from a combination of fermented soybean paste, soy sauce, garlic, spices and plums.

Variations

324 WITH GINGER

Add 1 tablespoon (15 ml) finely chopped peeled fresh ginger to the saucepan with the garlic.
Serve with: chicken or pork, portabello mushrooms, or use as a marinade for pork.

325 WITH FIVE-SPICE

Omit the sesame oil and stir ½ teaspoon (3 ml) five-spice powder into the saucepan with the hoisin sauce, soy, sake and the remaining ingredients.
Serve with: pulled pork or chicken, grilled or pan-fried tofu, or as a marinade for steaks, lamb kebabs or steaks or pork chops or ribs.

326 WITH ALE

Replace the sake with 140 ml ale, and cook the sauce for 15 minutes, or until thick.
Serve with: grilled or barbecued red meats or pork, burgers or sausages, or as a marinade.

327 WITH WASABI

Stir 1 tablespoon (15 ml) wasabi paste into the finished sauce.
Serve with: Asian-style pulled pork or chicken sandwiches, as a dip for meatballs, or chicken, beef or lamb kebabs.

Give barbecued meats an Asian twist with a hoisin barbecue sauce

328 WITH PEANUT BUTTER

Stir 3 tablespoons (45 ml) smooth peanut butter into the pan with the hoisin sauce and remaining ingredients. If the sauce is too thick after simmering for 3 to 5 minutes, stir in hot chicken stock or just-boiled water, 1 tablespoon (15 ml) at a time. (Pictured left.)
Serve with: sliced flank steak, grilled or barbecued pork chops or cutlets, shredded cabbage for an Asian-style coleslaw, or use as a dipping sauce.

329 WITH GINGER AND TANGERINE

Make the **Ginger Hoisin Barbecue Sauce** and add 80 ml fresh or bottled (unsweetened) tangerine juice to the saucepan with the hoisin sauce, soy, sake and the remaining ingredients. Cook the sauce for an additional 3 to 5 minutes, or until thickened to the desired consistency. (Pictured right.)
Serve with: duck, lamb or roast goose, use as a marinade or glaze for ribs, pork chops and cutlets, or as a stir-fry sauce for red meats.

330 Old-fashioned Barbecue Sauce

The not-so secret ingredient in this finger-licking sauce is cola – it brings a caramelly sweetness and rich colour to the sauce.

INGREDIENTS

1 tbsp (15 ml) cornflour
1 tbsp (15 ml) olive oil
½ medium onion, finely minced
2 garlic cloves, finely minced
2 (750 ml) cans cola
280 ml strained tomatoes
2 tbsp (30 ml) tomato purée

2 tbsp (30 ml) molasses
3 tbsp (45 ml) cider vinegar
60 ml soft dark-brown sugar
½ tsp (3 ml) sweet paprika
½ tsp (3 ml) mustard powder
60 ml Worcestershire sauce
Salt

MAKES 480 ml

In a bowl, combine the cornflour with 1 tablespoon (15 ml) water and stir until smooth. Set aside.

Heat the oil in a saucepan over medium-high heat and cook the onion, stirring, until soft. Add the garlic and cook for a further 1 minute. Add the remaining ingredients and stir until the sugar has dissolved. Then bring to the boil and simmer for 20 minutes or until reduced by about half. Season with salt to taste. Leave to cool to room temperature before using.

Serve with: all barbecued meats.

HANDY TIP

Don't substitute diet coca-cola – the artificial sweeteners leave an unpleasant chemical aftertaste.

331 WITH ROOT BEER

Replace the cola with root beer.
Serve with: pork, burgers, chicken or turkey.

Variations

332 WITH BOURBON

Make the **Ginger Beer Barbecue Sauce**, adding 70 ml bourbon to the onion and garlic. Simmer until reduced by two-thirds before adding the remaining ingredients.
Serve with: ribs, brisket or pulled pork or chicken.

333 WITH COFFEE

Reduce the cola to 500 ml and add 180 ml freshly made espresso coffee with the other ingredients.
Serve with: steaks, brisket, beef ribs or pork.

334 WITH STOUT BEER

Increase the strained tomatoes to 425 ml, reduce the coca-cola to 110 ml and add 280 ml stout beer. (Pictured top.)
Serve with: barbecued or grilled steak, ribs or lamb.

335 HOT 'N' SPICY

Add 1 to 2 chipotle chillies, finely minced, from a can of chipotle chillies in adobo sauce, and 2 teaspoons (10 ml) of the sauce with the rest of the ingredients.
Serve with: spice-rubbed barbecued pork tenderloin, spare ribs or beef, lamb steaks, burgers, or chicken.

336 CHILLI-CHOCOLATE

Stir 55 g finely chopped 80% dark chocolate into the **Hot 'n' Spicy Barbecue Sauce** while hot. (Pictured bottom.)
Serve with: chicken, beef, pork or enchiladas.

337 Piri Piri Sauce

This tangy chilli sauce is one of the most well-known culinary exports out of Portugal.

INGREDIENTS

6 to 8 large red chillies, such as fresno or jalapeño, seeded, if desired, and roughly chopped
60 ml lemon juice
2 tsp (10 ml) malt or white wine vinegar
2 tsp (10 ml) soft dark-brown sugar
5 tbsp (75 ml) extra-virgin olive oil
2 large garlic cloves, roughly chopped
½ tsp (3 ml) finely grated peeled fresh ginger
½ tbsp (8 ml) paprika
1 tsp (5 ml) dried oregano
½ tsp (3 ml) salt

MAKES 240 ml
Lasts for up to 1 month in the fridge in a covered container

Combine all the ingredients in a blender and process until you have a smooth purée. Stir well before using – this sauce has a tendency to separate.

Serve with: poultry, barbecued foods, poached and scrambled eggs.

HANDY TIP

This sauce is best made a few days in advance. Refrigerate in a covered jar or container for 2 to 4 days then stir well before serving.

Variations

338 WITH LEMON

Stir the finely grated zest of 1 lemon into the finished sauce.
Serve with: chicken, chicken or turkey burgers, fish.

339 WITH ROASTED CHILLIES

In batches, roast 10 large red chillies over an open flame using a gas cooker, or under a hot grill, until the skins are blistered and blackened in spots. Peel, remove the stems, remove the seeds if desired, then roughly chop and use in place of the fresh chillies.
Serve with: grilled steak, lamb, chicken, burgers or sausages.

340 WITH MIXED HERBS

Omit the dried oregano and add 2 tablespoons (30 ml) each fresh parsley and coriander leaves, and 1 tablespoon (15 ml) fresh oregano to the blender with the rest of the ingredients. This sauce only keeps in the fridge for up to one week.
Serve with: firm fish like salmon, swordfish or tuna, or oily fish like mackerel and sardines.

KETCHUPS & TOMATO SAUCES

341 Classic Tomato Sauce

This is the basic tomato sauce from which so many favourites are created. As with all recipes that rely on the quality of a few ingredients for the best results, this sauce needs good olive oil and the sweetest tomatoes. If you wish, offer freshly grated Parmesan cheese at the table.

INGREDIENTS

1 medium-sized onion, peeled and finely chopped
1 large carrot, scraped and finely chopped
1 large stalk celery, finely chopped
60 ml extra-virgin olive oil
450 g skinned and seeded fresh tomatoes, or 400 g canned tomatoes, with juice
Sea salt and freshly ground black pepper

MAKES enough sauce for 450 g uncooked pasta

Heat the oil in a heavy-based saucepan, and add onion, carrot and celery. Cook, stirring, until onion is transparent and the vegetables soft. Stir in tomatoes. Cover and simmer for 30 minutes, stirring regularly. Season with salt and pepper.

Serve with: pasta.

HANDY TIP

When draining the cooked pasta to serve with this sauce, save a cupful of the cooking water as the Italians do. Use it to thin down the sauce, if necessary, when tossing it with the pasta.

342 WITH GARLIC

Replace the onion, carrot and celery with 1 or 2 peeled cloves of garlic (crushed for maximum flavour, or left whole for mild). Fry the garlic slowly in oil until pungent, then continue with the recipe.
Serve with: pasta or polenta, fish or chicken, or pizzas.

343 WITH MOZZARELLA

Prepare the sauce. Once off the heat add a ball of mozzarella, cubed, and let melt before serving.
Serve with: short pasta such as rigatoni, penne or fusilli.

344 WITH ANCHOVIES

Drain and finely chop 55 g anchovy fillets packed in oil. Add to the sauce 10 minutes before the end of the cooking time.
Serve with: spaghetti, linguine or other long pasta.

345 WITH CRABMEAT

Add 200 g cooked jumbo lump crabmeat to the finished sauce and heat until crab is piping hot, then stir in 2 tablespoons (30 ml) chopped fresh chives.
Serve with: pasta such as spaghetti, linguine or fettuccine.

Variations

346 WITH PANCETTA

Fry 110 to 170 g pancetta, cubed, in a dry frying pan until browned and crisp, drain well then stir into the sauce with a handful of grated Parmesan cheese.
Serve with: linguine, fettuccine or pappardelle pasta.

349 WITH RICOTTA

Stir 2 to 3 tablespoons (30 to 45 ml) of ricotta and a handful of grated Parmesan cheese into the finished sauce.
Serve with: pasta with roasted vegetables, grilled or pan-fried prawns or chicken, or gnocchi.

347 WITH MASCARPONE

Stir in 2 to 3 tablespoons (30 to 45 ml) of mascarpone to make a deliciously creamy sauce.
Serve with: grilled, pan-fried or baked chicken, or pasta with prawns, chicken or roasted vegetables.

350 WITH RICOTTA AND TUNA

Add 170 g drained canned tuna to the **Tomato and Ricotta Sauce** 5 minutes before the end of the cooking time, stirring occasionally but being careful not to break up the tuna chunks too much.
Serve with: a pasta bake with béchamel sauce using large pasta shells, cannelloni tubes or lasagne sheets.

348 WITH SMOKED SALMON

Stir 200 g thinly sliced ribbons of smoked salmon into the finished **Mascarpone and Tomato Sauce**.
Serve with: short pasta tubes such as rigatoni and penne, or with other pasta shapes such as farfalle.

351 Tomato & Fish Sauce

Use a fish that can withstand a long cooking time without losing all its flavour and texture, such as swordfish, as well as some white fish, which will flake better. This gives you two separate textures within the same dish.

INGREDIENTS

3 tbsp (45 ml) olive oil

2 cloves garlic, thinly sliced

2 or 3 tbsp (30 to 45 ml) chopped fresh flat-leaf parsley

¼ dried red chilli

1 swordfish steak, cubed

2 cod fillets, cubed

2 to 3 tbsp (30 to 45 ml) dry white wine

300 ml strained tomatoes

Sea salt and black pepper

MAKES sauce for 450 g uncooked pasta

Heat the olive oil in a frying pan, add the garlic, parsley and chilli, and cook gently for 5 minutes. Discard the chilli. Add the fish and fry for 3 minutes, stirring gently, before adding the wine. Stir for 2 minutes, boiling off the alcohol, then add the strained tomatoes. Stir, season, cover and simmer for 15 minutes or until the sauce is thick and glossy.

Serve with: pasta and a garnish of chopped fresh mint.

HANDY TIP

Don't worry about keeping the cubes of fish entirely intact when making this sauce. They are supposed to break down somewhat as this will help the sauce thicken and all the flavours meld together.

variations

352 WITH SCALLOPS

Replace the swordfish and cod with 8 large scallops, cut into quarters. Simmer in the sauce for 5 minutes.
Serve with: penne or macaroni.

353 EXTRA SPICY

Increase the amount of chilli by as much as 1 whole dried red chilli, or equivalent chilli powder.
Serve with: spaghetti or fettuccine.

354 WITH MUSSELS

Add 12 cooked and shelled mussels to the sauce about halfway through the simmering stage.
Serve with: spaghetti or linguine.

355 Roast Tomato & Ricotta Sauce

Roasting tomatoes intensifies their flavour and sweetens them. This complex sauce is both rich in tomatoes and deliciously creamy.

INGREDIENTS

1 kg plum tomatoes, cored and halved lengthwise

3 tbsp (45 ml) olive oil

3 sprigs thyme

Salt and black pepper

1 medium onion, finely chopped

5 tbsp (75 ml) dry white wine

170 g whole-milk ricotta cheese

SERVES 4 tossed through 340 g pasta

Preheat the oven to 210°C (415°F). Place the tomatoes, cut sides up, in a single layer on a baking tray. Drizzle with 2 tablespoons (30 ml) of the olive oil and add the thyme. Sprinkle generously with salt and pepper. Roast on a high shelf in the oven for 1 hour, until the tomatoes are tender and shrunken. When cool enough to handle, discard the thyme, peel the tomatoes and chop the flesh.

Cook the onion in the remaining oil, stirring, until translucent. Add the wine and simmer until the liquid has almost completely evaporated. Add the chopped tomatoes and simmer, stirring occasionally, for 15 minutes until you have a very thick sauce. Stir in the ricotta until thoroughly combined with the tomatoes. Cook for a few minutes and season to taste with salt and pepper. Serve immediately. (Pictured opposite top.)

Serve with: short pasta such as penne, fusilli or rigatoni.

HANDY TIP

If you're preparing this recipe for someone who is lactose intolerant but who can eat goat's cheese (as many people with this condition can), replace the ricotta with a soft, unripened goat's cheese such as *fromage blanc*.

Variations

356 WITH CAULIFLOWER

Roast the trimmed florets of half a small head of cauliflower, drizzled with olive oil and seasoned with salt, pepper and dried chilli flakes, until tender and browned. Add to the tomato sauce before the ricotta.
Serve with: steak, sautéed or grilled chicken, or use in pasta bakes with short pasta.

357 WITH KALAMATA OLIVE AND FETA

Stir 3 tablespoons (45 ml) chopped, pitted kalamata olives into the thickened tomato sauce and replace the ricotta cheese with 110 g crumbled feta.
Serve with: gnocchi, short pasta or soft polenta.

358 WITH SAUSAGE

Remove and crumble the meat from 2 or 3 spicy Italian-style sausages. Cook in a little olive oil until browned and cooked through, breaking up the meat as much as possible. Drain on kitchen paper and add to the tomato sauce before stirring in the ricotta.
Serve with: tagliatelle, pappardelle or fettuccine.

359 WITH WHITE BEANS

Stir 140 g drained, rinsed canned white beans into the
thickened tomato sauce before stirring in the ricotta.
Serve with: short pasta tubes, gnocchi or soft polenta.

360 WITH AUBERGINE

Sauté a small or half a medium-sized diced aubergine in
a little olive oil until tender. Season well with salt and
pepper and set aside. Add to the thickened tomato sauce
(before the cheese has been added), then simmer for
a couple of minutes before stirring in the ricotta and
completing the recipe. (Pictured centre.)
Serve with: short pasta such as penne or rigatoni, or
pasta shells.

361 CLAM 'DIAVOLO' SAUCE

Replace the ricotta with 2 (182 g) cans of chopped
clams with their juice and a generous pinch of dried
chilli flakes. Simmer for 5 to 10 minutes until the
mixture is thickened, then stir 2 tablespoons (30 ml)
chopped fresh parsley leaves into the sauce before
serving. (Pictured bottom.)
Serve with: spaghetti, linguine or fettuccine.

362 'No cook' Sugo Vacanza

This is the traditional, simple, raw tomato sauce Italians make in the summer, when it is much too hot to spend time in the kitchen.

INGREDIENTS

8 large, ripe tomatoes, peeled and seeded
1 clove garlic, crushed or mashed
2 tbsp (30 ml) finely chopped fresh flat-leaf parsley
9 leaves fresh basil, torn
Sea salt and black pepper
120 ml extra-virgin olive oil, plus extra as needed

MAKES sauce for about 450 g uncooked spaghetti

Chop tomatoes roughly and put them in a bowl with the garlic, parsley, basil, salt and pepper. Stir in the oil and let stand, covered, for at least an hour, preferably not in the fridge. (Pictured top.)

Serve with: hot, al dente spaghetti, adding more oil if required.

HANDY TIP

Tearing the basil rather than shredding it using a knife helps keep all the aromatic, flavourful oils in the leaf and, therefore, the sauce. If you do want to shred basil, use your sharpest knife and firm, decisive movements to cut the leaves cleanly. Blunt or jagged cuts will make the oils leach out onto the cutting board rather than being preserved in the leaves.

Variations

363 WITH RICOTTA

Add 3 tablespoons (45 ml) ricotta to the sauce and pasta when you toss them together.
Serve with: hot spaghetti.

364 WITH BLACK OLIVES

Add a handful of coarsely chopped pitted black olives to the sauce before letting it stand.
Serve with: hot pasta.

365 WITH CAPERS

Replace the basil with a generous tablespoonful of rinsed and dried capers, coarsely chopped.
Serve with: hot pasta.

366 WITH PESTO

Replace the fresh basil leaves with 2 to 3 tablespoons (30 to 45 ml) basil pesto, stir well to combine thoroughly.
Serve with: hot spaghetti, linguine or bucatini.

367 WITH GREEN PEPPER

Add a seeded green pepper, chopped into small cubes, to the sauce before letting it stand. (Pictured centre.)
Serve with: hot pasta.

368 WITH MOZZARELLA

Add a handful of mozzarella cubes to the pasta and sauce as you toss them together. (Pictured bottom.)
Serve with: hot spaghetti.

369 Classic Bolognese sauce

This is the classic recipe for the rich meaty sauce from the city of Bologna. It uses only a little tomato purée and several kinds of finely chopped meat, which give the sauce a stew-like texture.

INGREDIENTS

100 g boneless pork loin
100 g boneless beef
100 g prosciutto
120 g butter
1 carrot, finely chopped
1 stalk celery, finely chopped
1 onion, finely chopped
70 g pancetta or bacon, finely chopped

1 generous tbsp (15 ml) tomato purée diluted with
120 ml hot water
Salt and black pepper
180 ml hot beef stock (see page 18) or water
Freshly grated Parmesan, to serve

MAKES sauce for 400 g pasta

Finely chop the meats together with a knife. In a large heavy-based pan, melt half the butter, then add the vegetables and pancetta or bacon and cook for 5 to 6 minutes, stirring over medium heat. Add the chopped meats and stir together to brown. Add the diluted tomato purée. Season with salt and pepper. Stir thoroughly, cover, and let simmer very gently for about 2 hours. Watch that it does not dry out; stir frequently and add a little hot water or stock as needed. After about 2 hours, when the meat is tender, add the remaining butter and stir. Remove from the heat. The sauce can be used now, but it improves with standing and reheating.

Serve with: hot pasta and freshly grated Parmesan cheese.

HANDY TIP

To save time, ask your butcher to mince the meats for you. Avoid buying ready-ground mince as the quality won't be as good as when you buy the whole cut of meat and have it ground to order.

Variations

370 WITH CREAM AND CHICKEN LIVER

Fry 240 ml sliced chicken livers in butter until cooked. Stir into the sauce at end of cooking time with 3 tablespoons (45 ml) double cream.
Serve with: tagliatelle, or use in a lasagne.

371 WITH EXTRA MINCED BEEF

Add 450 g minced beef to the pan with the other meats, and 400 g canned chopped tomatoes with the tomato purée.
Serve with: pappardelle.

372 WITH EXTRA MINCED PORK

Add 450 g minced pork to pan with the other meats, and add 400 g canned chopped tomatoes with tomato purée.
Serve with: spaghetti or fettuccine.

Don't just save it for pasta — try baked potato Bolognese too

373 WITH SAUSAGE AND MUSHROOM

Replace the pork, beef and prosciutto with 4 Italian sausages, skinned and crumbled, and a handful of dried porcini mushrooms, soaked in water for 30 minutes, then drained and chopped. Strain the mushroom soaking liquid and add to the pan with the stock.
Serve with: penne or rigatoni.

374 WITH PEAS

Add some fresh or frozen and thawed peas to the gently simmering sauce about halfway through the cooking process.
Serve with: penne or rigatoni.

375 WITH CHILLI

Add a ½ teaspoon (3 ml) dried chilli flakes to the saucepan with the tomato purée.
Serve with: spaghetti or fettuccine.

376 WITH RED WINE

Dilute the tomato purée with 140 ml red wine instead of water.
Serve with: spaghetti, or use in a lasagne.

377 WITH CHESTNUTS AND CREAM

Stir in 60 ml double cream 10 minutes before the end of the cooking time. Just before serving, stir in 55 g roughly chopped cooked chestnuts.
Serve with: fresh egg pasta such as fettuccine or tagliatelle.

378 WITH LENTILS

About 15 minutes before the end of the cooking time, stir in 100 g rinsed and drained canned green lentils.
Serve with: rice, soft polenta, baked potatoes or shepherd's pie.

379 Tomato Ketchup

This homemade ketchup is so good it almost puts the world's favourite condiment to shame. It's a little spicier, less sugary and a lot fresher than a sauce by any famous name!

INGREDIENTS

1 medium onion, chopped
1 small stick celery, trimmed and chopped
1 small carrot, chopped
1 kg ripe tomatoes, cored and roughly chopped
450 g canned peeled whole tomatoes, drained and roughly chopped (juices reserved)
60 ml tomato purée
2 garlic cloves, chopped
Salt
180 ml red wine vinegar
1 tsp (5 ml) black peppercorns
1 tsp (5 ml) coriander seeds
½ cinnamon stick
1 blade mace
4 allspice berries
6 cloves
2 bay leaves
6 tbsp (90 ml) soft light-brown sugar
½ tsp (3 ml) mustard powder
½ tsp (3 ml) paprika
1 tsp (5 ml) cornflour

MAKES 560 ml
Keeps in the fridge for 2 months in an airtight container or bottle

Place the onions, celery, carrot, tomatoes, tomato purée and garlic in a large saucepan with 160 ml of the reserved canned tomato juices, or water. Add a generous pinch of salt and bring to a boil. Simmer over medium heat for 50 minutes to 1 hour, stirring occasionally, and pressing down on the tomatoes to crush them, until you have a thick pulpy mush.

Meanwhile, place the vinegar in a saucepan with the peppercorns, whole spices and bay leaves and infuse over low heat for 10 minutes. Set aside.

Transfer the stewed tomatoes and vegetables to a blender, and process until you have a smooth, thick purée.

Pass the tomato and vegetable purée through a nylon sieve using a wooden spoon into a clean medium saucepan, rubbing the tomato mixture against the sides of the sieve to push through as much of the pulp as possible. Discard the remaining tomato skins, seeds and solids.

Strain the infused vinegar, discarding the spices, and add to the tomato mixture in the pan along with the tomato purée. Stir in the sugar, mustard powder and paprika and bring to a boil over medium heat, stirring occasionally. Reduce to a simmer and cook over low heat for 5 to 10 minutes – be careful the ketchup will spit.

Meanwhile combine the cornflour with a splash of cold water and stir until smooth. Add to the ketchup and continue to cook for a few more minutes, stirring constantly (this will help it spit less), until the ketchup thickens. Remove from the heat and add salt to taste.

Serve with: barbecued foods, eggs, chips, breaded or battered fish or seafood, breaded chicken nuggets or fingers.

HANDY TIP

To keep the ketchup for longer, pour the hot sauce into a jug and use a funnel to transfer it into sterilised bottles or jars. Clean the opening of the jars and bottles with a clean cloth, then seal immediately and cool completely before labelling and storing for up to 6 months. Once opened store in the fridge.

Variations

380 WITH SZECHUAN PEPPER AND ANISE

Omit the coriander seeds, cloves and allspice. Add 2 star anise and 1 tablespoon (15 ml) Szechuan peppercorns, which have been toasted until fragrant in a dry pan then crushed, to the vinegar to infuse.
Serve with: grilled or barbecued poultry, steak or burgers.

381 WITH DATES

Reduce the sugar to 2 tablespoons (30 ml). Soak 85 g pitted dates in just-boiled water until softened, 15 to 20 minutes. Drain, chop roughly, then blend to a smooth purée and stir into the sauce with the vinegar and sugar.
Serve with: hot dogs and burgers, with grilled or barbecued chicken, pork chops, beef or lamb steaks.

382 'SPIKED' BOURBON

Add 110 ml bourbon to the sieved tomato mixture before reducing on the hob.
Serve with: chicken, turkey or beef burgers, spicy fresh or smoked sausages or chips.

383 WITH GARLIC AND CAPERS

Increase the garlic to 4 cloves and stir 4 tablespoons (60 ml) finely chopped capers into the finished sauce.
Serve with: battered or breaded fish, prawns, scampi or calamari.

384 YELLOW TOMATO AND OREGANO

Replace the fresh red tomatoes and canned plum tomatoes with 85 g ripe yellow tomatoes, and add a small bunch of fresh oregano, stems and leaves, to the saucepan with the tomatoes and vegetables at the start of the recipe.
Serve with: barbecued or grilled fish, prawns, chicken or turkey.

385 WITH CHARRED TOMATOES AND BALSAMIC VINEGAR

Lightly char 1 kg red plum tomatoes under a very hot grill, turning occasionally, until blistered all over, and use in place of the fresh red tomatoes. Replace 85 ml of the red wine vinegar with balsamic vinegar. For an extra smoky flavour, add a drop of liquid smoke.
Serve with: steaks, pork chops, roasted vegetables, sausages, or bacon and egg sandwiches.

386 WITH BASIL

Add 1 bunch of basil, roughly chopped (leaves and stalks) to the saucepan with the tomatoes and vegetables at the start of the recipe.

Serve with: breaded or battered fish, calamari and chicken, or as a spread for chicken sandwiches and wraps.

387 WITH CHILLI

Add 2 teaspoons (10 ml) crushed dried chillies with the tomatoes and vegetables at the start of the recipe. For extra bite, add 1 to 2 teaspoons (5 to 10 ml) of hot sauce to the sieved tomato mixture before reducing on the hob.

Serve with: fried wontons, spring rolls, or spiced chicken wings, or as you would regular ketchup.

388 WITH CHILLI AND SWEET PEPPER

Add 2 red peppers, chopped, to the pan with the tomatoes and vegetables for the **Chilli Tomato Ketchup.**

Serve with: burgers, lamb meatballs, chips, sweet potato chips or sausages.

389 Tunisian-style Tomato Sauce

This sauce is based on a famous Tunisian dish where eggs are poached in a richly spiced tomato sauce. Sometimes the sauce is filled out with potatoes, at other times with aubergine, or it may be served simply with nothing else but soft, perfectly cooked eggs nestled inside and fresh chopped herbs sprinkled over the top.

INGREDIENTS

2 tbsp (30 ml) olive oil
1 medium onion, finely chopped
3 cloves garlic, minced
2 medium red peppers, seeded and diced
Salt and black pepper
2 tbsp (30 ml) harissa
1 tbsp (15 ml) tomato purée

1 tsp (5 ml) ground cumin
1 tsp (5 ml) paprika
½ tsp (3 ml) turmeric
300 ml strained tomatoes
200 ml canned crushed tomatoes

SERVES 4

Heat the oil in a large heavy-based saucepan over medium heat and add the onion. Cook for 5 to 6 minutes until softened. Add the garlic and cook, stirring, for a minute. Add the diced pepper with a generous pinch of salt and pepper and cook for 8 to 10 minutes until the peppers are tender. Add the harissa, tomato purée and ground spices and cook, stirring, for 2 minutes, then add the tomatoes. Reduce the heat, and simmer, stirring every now and then, for 15 minutes until the sauce is thick and significantly reduced. Taste and adjust seasoning. (Pictured opposite top.)

Serve with: rice, orzo, steak, grilled chicken, or fried or poached eggs.

HANDY TIP

Harissa, a fiery, spicy North African chilli condiment, is found in the ethnic section of most large supermarkets. To make your own, follow the recipe on page 100.

Variations

390 WITH OKRA AND CHICKPEA

Sauté 225 g sliced okra in a little olive oil in a very hot frying pan until browned and tender. Season with salt and set aside. Add to the sauce with 85 g drained and rinsed canned chickpeas in the final 10 minutes of cooking time.
Serve with: rice, orzo, chicken or red meats.

391 WITH SWEET POTATO

Add 1 medium sweet potato, diced, with the tomatoes. Make sure the sweet potato is cooked before removing the sauce from the heat. Stir 2 tablespoons (30 ml) chopped fresh parsley leaves into the finished sauce.
Serve with: rice, country-style bread, steak, or grilled chicken or portabello mushrooms.

392 WITH ARTICHOKE AND GREEN OLIVE

Stir 110 g chopped canned artichoke hearts and 3 tablespoons (45 ml) finely chopped pitted green olives into the sauce in the final 10 minutes of cooking.
Serve with: toasted bruschetta, soft polenta, grilled or roasted meats, or fish like haddock, cod and monkfish.

393 WITH YOGHURT AND MUSHROOM

Add 225 g sliced brown or white mushrooms, sautéed in a little butter until browned and tender to the finished sauce with 3 tablespoons (45 ml) thick plain yoghurt. Stir until smooth, simmer very gently for a minute then remove from the heat.
Serve with: toast, eggs or buttered egg noodles.

394 WITH BROAD BEANS

Add 150 g freshly shelled broad beans to the pan in the last 5 to 7 minutes of cooking time. (Pictured centre.)
Serve with: eggs, or beef, veal or pork medallions.

395 WITH PRAWNS

Add 16 peeled, cleaned raw medium prawns to the sauce in the final 3 to 4 minutes of cooking time. Remove the pan from the cooker as soon as the prawns are cooked. Stir in 2 tablespoons (30 ml) finely chopped fresh coriander leaves. (Pictured bottom.)
Serve with: pasta, gnocchi or rice.

396 Curry Ketchup

In Berlin this spicy tangy ketchup is a must-have accompaniment for one of the city's most beloved street foods, *curry wurst* – a chopped-up, grilled or boiled sausage slathered with a curry-infused ketchup and finished off with a sprinkle of cayenne.

INGREDIENTS

1 ½ tbsp (23 ml) vegetable or rapeseed oil
1 medium sweet onion, finely chopped
2 tbsp (30 ml) curry powder
½ tbsp (8 ml) paprika
½ tsp (3 ml) smoked paprika
¼ tsp (1 ml) garlic salt
¼ to ½ tsp (1 to 3 ml) cayenne pepper (depending on how spicy you like it)

½ tsp (3 ml) mustard powder
¼ tsp (1 ml) ground allspice
450 ml canned crushed tomatoes
110 g granulated sugar
70 ml cider vinegar
Salt

MAKES 400 ml
Keeps in the fridge for a month

Heat the oil over medium heat in a medium saucepan. Add the onion and cook, stirring, until softened and translucent, about 5 to 6 minutes. Add the curry powder and all the ground spices. Cook, stirring, for 1 minute. Add the tomatoes, sugar, vinegar and ¼ teaspoon (1 ml) salt. Simmer, stirring occasionally, until the sauce is really thick, about 30 minutes. Transfer to a blender or food processor and purée until smooth. Serve hot or warm.

Serve with: sausages, burgers, as a dip for chips and grilled or barbecued meats and poultry.

HANDY TIP

Feel free to customise this ketchup by changing up the spices or using different varieties of curry powder.

Variations

397 WITH TAMARIND

Reduce the cider vinegar to 55 ml and stir in 1 rounded tablespoon (15 ml) tamarind paste with the other ingredients.
Serve with: grilled, breaded or battered fish or seafood.

398 WITH BLACK MUSTARD

Cook 1 ½ tablespoons (23 ml) black mustard seeds in a little vegetable or rapeseed oil in a small frying pan until the seeds start to pop. Stir into the finished ketchup.
Serve with: grilled chicken, fish or seafood.

399 WITH CORIANDER AND MAYONNAISE

Stir 60 ml of the **Curry Ketchup** into 6 tablespoons (90 ml) mayonnaise along with 2 tablespoons (30 ml) finely chopped fresh coriander leaves.
Serve with: sandwiches, or burgers and chips.

400 Banana Ketchup

Don't be put off by the name of this sauce, it's amazingly good, and yes, it's really made with bananas with a hint of tomatoes. Sweet and spicy, it will bring an exotic touch to your next barbecue.

INGREDIENTS

1 ½ tbsp (23 ml) vegetable or rapeseed oil
1 medium onion
2 cloves garlic, chopped
½ red chilli, seeded and chopped
¼ tsp (1 ml) finely grated peeled ginger
3 medium very ripe, sweet bananas, well mashed
2 tbsp (30 ml) tomato purée
¼ tsp (1 ml) ground allspice
¼ tsp (1 ml) ground cinnamon
¼ tsp (1 ml) smoked paprika
¼ tsp (1 ml) ground turmeric
85 ml cider vinegar
3 tbsp (45 ml) dark honey
1 tsp (5 ml) Worcestershire sauce
1 tbsp (15 ml) soy sauce
Salt

MAKES about 480 ml
Keeps in the fridge in an airtight container or bottle for 2 weeks

Heat the oil over medium heat in a medium saucepan. Add the onion and cook, stirring, until softened and translucent, about 5 to 6 minutes. Add the garlic, chilli and ginger and cook for 30 seconds to 1 minute.

Add the remaining ingredients with 60 ml water and simmer for 15 minutes, stirring occasionally, until the mixture is thick and dark. Transfer to a blender and process to a smooth purée. This makes a thick, spoonable ketchup, if you prefer it to be pourable, add hot water, 1 tablespoon (15 ml) at a time. Season to taste with salt.

Serve with: chicken, turkey or beef burgers, steak or pork chops.

HANDY TIP

A quick and mess-free way to mash ripe bananas is to firmly massage the flesh through the skin, squishing it to a pulp without bursting the skin. Then, slit the peel open and spoon or squeeze out the pulp.

Variations

401 WITH CAJUN SPICES

Replace the allspice, cinnamon, cloves and smoked paprika with ½ teaspoon (3 ml) sweet paprika, ½ to 1 teaspoon (3 to 5 ml) ground cayenne, ½ teaspoon (3 ml) dried thyme leaves, ½ teaspoon (3 ml) dried oregano and ¼ teaspoon (1 ml) garlic powder.
Serve with: burgers, sausages or steak.

402 WITH FIG

Add 60 ml diced, stemmed, soft dried figs with the mashed bananas.
Serve with: grilled or barbecued beef or lamb steaks, or chicken, or pork loin or chops.

403 WITH RUM

Add 2 tablespoons (30 ml) of rum with the mashed banana.
Serve with: burgers or kebabs, grilled or barbecued pork or steaks, or grilled swordfish or tuna steaks.

SAVOURY FRUIT SAUCES

404 Cranberry & orange Sauce

No festive autumn or winter spread is complete without a bowl of cranberry sauce. But why rely on supermarket-bought versions when homemade is so easy? The simplest recipe only requires three ingredients, and it's so much more delicious than any can off a shelf.

INGREDIENTS

Finely grated zest and juice
  of 1 navel orange
80–120 g granulated sugar
225 g fresh or frozen
  cranberries

SERVES 4
Makes 255 ml

Place the orange zest, juice and sugar in a heavy-based medium saucepan over medium heat, and stir until the sugar has dissolved completely. Add the cranberries, bring to a boil, then reduce the heat and simmer, stirring, until the cranberries burst and the sauce is thick and jammy, about 8 minutes. (The longer you cook the sauce the more jam-like it will become.) Remove from the heat and serve warm or at room temperature. The sauce will thicken further upon cooling. Store in the fridge for up to one week in a jar or a covered container.

Serve with: roast turkey or chicken, or pork dishes when warm, and in sandwiches when cold or at room temperature.

HANDY TIP

Because of its thick, viscous consistency, cranberry sauce has a tendency to spit and splatter when cooking. To keep this to a minimum, keep the heat low and stir the sauce frequently to allow the steam to escape without exploding and causing a mess!

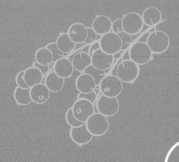

Variations

405 WITH CRYSTALLISED GINGER

Stir ¼ teaspoon (1 ml) ground ginger into the saucepan with the dissolved sugar and juice, and add 2 tablespoons (30 ml) minced crystallised ginger to the finished sauce.
Serve with: steaks, lamb or pork chops seasoned with an Asian-style rub or marinade.

406 WITH MAPLE SYRUP

Omit the sugar and add 120 ml maple syrup to the saucepan with the orange juice. Bring the liquid to a simmer before adding the cranberries.
Serve with: smoked or cured ham, roast, grilled or sautéed pork, or roast turkey or duck.

407 WITH CHILLI

Add ½ seeded, finely chopped red chilli, such as jalapeño, to the saucepan with the cranberries. For a really spicy kick, stir a dash of hot sauce into the finished sauce.
Serve with: lamb or chicken, or use as a stir-fry sauce.

408 WITH TEQUILA AND LIME

Replace half the orange juice and zest with the juice and zest of 1 lime, adding them to the saucepan with the sugar and orange juice. Cook until the sauce is thick, remove from the heat and stir in 3 tablespoons (45 ml) tequila.
Serve with: roast chicken, turkey or duck.

409 WITH POMEGRANATE

Replace the orange juice and zest with 160 ml pomegranate juice. Cook the sauce for 10 to 12 minutes until thickened, then stir in 3 to 4 tablespoons (45 to 60 ml) pomegranate seeds.
Serve with: lamb dishes.

410 WITH PORT

Use half the amount of orange juice and add 3 tablespoons (45 ml) port to the saucepan with the juice, zest and sugar.
Serve with: beef tenderloin or steaks, or game such as venison, pheasant or partridge.

411 WITH WALNUT

Make the **Cranberry and Port Sauce**, and add 28 g chopped walnuts with the cranberries.
Serve with: cold cuts, ham, red meat or game, or cheese.

412 WITH VODKA AND FIG

Make the **Cranberry and Port Sauce**, substituting 2 tablespoons (30 ml) vodka for the port, adding 55 g chopped dried figs with the cranberries.
Serve with: roast turkey, duck or goose.

413 WITH PECAN AND BOURBON

Make the **Port and Cranberry Sauce**, substituting 2 tablespoons (30 ml) bourbon for the port, and adding 28 g lightly toasted chopped pecans to the pan with the cranberries.
Serve with: burgers, or as an alternative to barbecue sauce for pork, lamb or poultry dishes.

414 Apple & Sage Sauce

Apples and pork go together as well as bread and butter. This pairing is said to date back centuries to the times when pigs roamed in orchards and grew plump on overly ripe apples. But don't reserve this sauce for pork roasts and chops, it's also great with chicken and even lamb. It is tangy and sweet but the sage imbues it with an aromatic, woodsy flavour.

INGREDIENTS

3 tbsp (45 g) unsalted butter, cut into small cubes

675 g apples, ideally Bramley, but Braeburn or Granny Smiths will also work well, peeled, cored and cut into small chunks

50 g granulated sugar

2 tbsp (30 ml) soft light-brown sugar

60 ml apple juice

3 tbsp (45 ml) lemon juice

2 whole cloves

1 tbsp (15 ml) finely shredded sage leaves

Salt

MAKES 560 ml sauce

Place all the ingredients except the sage and salt in a medium saucepan with 120 ml water and bring to a boil over medium-high heat stirring to melt the butter. Reduce the heat to medium-low and simmer for about 20 minutes until the apple breaks down to a mush, stirring frequently to help the apple chunks collapse.

Press any remaining large chunks of apple against the side of the pan to crush them, then remove the pan from the heat. Fish out and discard the cloves and stir in the sage. Season with salt to taste. (Pictured opposite top.)

Serve with: pork, chicken, turkey or lamb.

HANDY TIP

For a completely smooth sauce, process in the blender for 20 to 30 seconds before stirring in the sage.

Variations

415 WITH GINGER AND ALLSPICE

Add a 2-cm (1-inch) knob of ginger, peeled and finely minced, and ½ teaspoon (3 ml) allspice berries to the saucepan with the rest of the ingredients and omit the sage leaves at the end. Be sure to remove the allspice berries from the sauce before serving.
Serve with: pork or chicken dishes.

416 WITH PEAR AND CINNAMON

Replace half the apple with pear chunks. Replace the cloves with 1 cinnamon stick (remove before serving).
Serve with: roast pork, sautéed pork medallions, or chicken.

417 WITH ROSEMARY AND RAISIN

Add 45 g golden raisins to the saucepan with the apples, and replace the sage with 1 ½ teaspoons (8 ml) of finely chopped fresh rosemary leaves. (Don't purée this sauce; it's best left a little chunky.)
Serve with: pork, chicken, or calves' or chicken liver.

418 WITH APPLE BRANDY AND THYME

Add 1 tablespoon (15 ml) apple brandy in the final 10 minutes of cooking time. Replace the sage with 1 ½ teaspoons (8 ml) chopped fresh thyme leaves.
Serve with: sautéed duck, calves' or chicken livers, roast duck, chicken, goose, turkey or pork.

419 WITH CRANBERRY

Add 85 g fresh or frozen cranberries to the saucepan with the apples. This makes quite a tart sauce. For a sweeter sauce, add another 2 tablespoons (30 ml) of sugar to the pan. Omit the sage at the end, if you wish. (Pictured centre.)
Serve with: roast and pan-fried turkey, chicken or pork.

420 WITH APRICOT

Add 110 g chopped dried Turkish apricots to the rest of the ingredients in the saucepan. Omit the sage, if you wish. (Pictured bottom.)
Serve with: lamb, pork or chicken.

421 Classic Orange Sauce

This simple recipe is based on the classic French *canard a l'orange*, in which slow-roasted duck is served with a luscious orange sauce, but takes a fraction of the time to prepare. Perfect for entertaining, this sauce elevates simple duck or chicken breasts, or a whole roast bird, to something special.

INGREDIENTS

½ tbsp (8 ml) olive oil
½ tbsp (8 ml) butter
½ medium onion, sliced
1 large navel orange (or 2 small ones)
3 tbsp (45 ml) dry white wine
60 ml hot chicken stock (see page 16)

1 tbsp (15 ml) sherry vinegar
1 tbsp (15 ml) honey
Salt and black pepper
½ tsp (3 ml) cornflour

SERVES 2 to 3
Makes about 170 ml

Cook the onion in the oil and butter in a medium frying pan for 6 to 7 minutes until softened. Meanwhile zest and juice the orange. Combine in a measuring cup and set aside. You should have 160–180 ml of juice. Add the wine to the onions and simmer until the wine has almost disappeared. Add the zest and juice, stock, vinegar, honey and a generous pinch of salt and pepper, and simmer for 5 minutes.

Combine the cornflour with a splash of cold water in a small bowl and stir until smooth. Add to the pan and whisk into the sauce. Cook for a further minute until the sauce is slightly thickened. Adjust the salt to taste.

Serve with: roast duck, goose, chicken or game such as venison, or a vegetarian nut loaf.

HANDY TIP

To make a vegetarian sauce, simply replace the chicken stock with a well-flavoured vegetable stock (see page 16).

Variations

422 BLOOD ORANGE

Substitute 2 to 3 (depending on size) blood oranges for the navel oranges.
Serve with: roast duck, or confit duck legs, or sautéed calves' liver.

423 WITH MINT

Add 2 teaspoons (10 ml) finely sliced fresh mint leaves to the finished sauce.
Serve with: roasted or sautéed salmon, monkfish or prawns, chicken.

424 WITH GINGER

Add ¼ teaspoon (1 ml) peeled finely grated ginger to the saucepan with the orange juice and zest.
Serve with: roast or grilled chicken, pork or beef, game birds such as partridge, pheasant or quail, or use as a stir-fry sauce with lamb, chicken or beef.

orange sauce is traditionally served with duck — but try it with vegetarian dishes too

425 WITH KUMQUAT

Add 3 to 4 thinly sliced kumquats to the pan in the final 5 minutes of cooking time, before adding the cornflour.
Serve with: beef, pork tenderloin or roast rack of lamb, or use as a stir-fry sauce for mixed vegetables.

426 WITH COINTREAU

Replace the white wine with 2 tablespoons (30 ml) Cointreau.
Serve with: duck, goose, roast chicken or turkey.

427 CUMBERLAND SAUCE

Substitute ruby port for the white wine, omit the sherry vinegar and add 5 tablespoons (75 ml) red currant jelly and ¼ teaspoon (1 ml) finely grated peeled fresh ginger to the pan with the chicken stock and other ingredients. Whisk to dissolve, then simmer until thickened. Leave to cool.
Serve with: roast lamb, ham or venison.

428 WITH LEMONGRASS AND CHILLI

Add ½ tablespoon (8 ml) chopped lemongrass (from the tender lower bulb only), and a generous pinch dried chilli flakes with the orange zest and other ingredients. Strain the sauce before serving.
Serve with: beef, lamb, pork, prawns or even mixed vegetables as a stir-fry sauce.

429 WITH DIJON MUSTARD AND THYME

Stir ½ teaspoon (3 ml) Dijon mustard and 1 teaspoon (5 ml) finely chopped fresh thyme leaves into the finished sauce.
Serve with: duck, goose or pork.

430 WITH SZECHUAN PEPPERCORNS

Add ½ teaspoon (3 ml) crushed Szechuan peppercorns and a splash of soy sauce to the pan with the orange zest and other ingredients.
Serve with: Asian-style roasted pork and beef tenderloin, chicken steamed with soy or ginger, or as a stir-fry sauce.

431 Peach Chutney

This delicious and versatile chutney is a great way to use up a bushel of ripe summer peaches. Have it on hand to serve with cheeses and cold cuts, but it's also great with sandwiches and burgers. You can even serve it warm with barbecued pork or chicken.

INGREDIENTS

450 g firm, ripe peaches
1 tbsp (15 ml) olive oil
1 small red onion, thinly sliced
1 large clove garlic, minced
60 ml cider vinegar
2 tbsp (30 ml) white sugar

3 tbsp (45 ml) soft light-brown sugar
Salt

MAKES 400 g
This chutney will keep in an airtight container or jar in the fridge for 1 month.

Bring a saucepan of water to the boil over high heat. Fill a bowl with ice water. Score a small X on the bottom of each peach. Carefully drop the peaches into the boiling water. Bring back to the boil and, after 30 seconds, use a slotted spoon to transfer them to the ice water. Once the peaches are cool enough to handle, peel, halve, remove the pits, then cut into 2-cm (¾-inch) dice.

Cook the onion in the olive oil in a heavy-based saucepan over medium heat for 6 to 8 minutes until soft. Add the garlic, cider vinegar and sugar and stir. Simmer gently for 5 minutes. Add the peaches with a round ¼ teaspoon (2 ml) salt and 3 to 4 tablespoons (45 to 60 ml) water, then gently simmer, stirring every now and then, until the peaches are soft and the liquid syrupy, about 20 minutes. Add water, a tablespoon (15 ml) at a time, if the mixture looks too dry at any point.

Serve with: cold cuts, cheese, or sandwiches, or with roast, grilled or barbecued pork or chicken.

HANDY TIP

Try to use 'freestone' peaches as the flesh will separate easily from the pit.

Variations

432 WITH BLUEBERRIES

Add 55 g dried blueberries to the saucepan with the peaches and an extra 1 tablespoon (15 ml) water.
Serve with: duck, goose, turkey or chicken.

433 WITH SPICES

Add ½ tablespoon (8 ml) minced peeled ginger, 4 lightly cracked cardamom pods and a generous pinch dried chilli flakes to the saucepan with the peaches.
Serve with: cold cuts, ham, pork or chicken.

434 WITH CURRY

Prepare the **Peach Chutney with Spices**, adding 1 ½ teaspoons (8 ml) curry powder to the saucepan with the peaches.
Serve with: papadum, chicken, lamb or beef kebabs or koftas, or spicy Tandoori-style grilled meats.

435 Grilled Lemon Parsley Sauce

This complex, piquant sauce is one to reserve for adults.

INGREDIENTS

2 large lemons, pointed ends removed and halved across the middle
½ tbsp (8 ml) olive oil
2 small cloves garlic, minced
450 ml chicken stock (see pages 16)

½ tsp (3 ml) finely chopped thyme
Salt and pepper
1 tbsp (15 ml) cold unsalted butter
1 tbsp (15 ml) chopped parsley

SERVES 4 to 6
Makes about 300 ml

Place lemons cut flesh-side up in a roasting dish and drizzle with oil. Grill under high heat until browned and soft. When cool enough to handle, squeeze out flesh and juice, press through a fine sieve, and set aside, discarding the solids. Place the garlic, stock and thyme in a medium saucepan and bring to the boil. Simmer briskly to reduce by half. Stir in the reserved lemon juice and pulp and a pinch of salt and pepper. Simmer briskly for two more minutes. Remove from the heat, whisk in the butter and stir in the parsley. Season to taste and serve immediately.

Serve with: chicken or veal.

HANDY TIP

The butter must be really cold. If it is warm or soft, it will melt making for a greasy sauce!

Variations

436 WITH WHOLE-GRAIN MUSTARD

Whisk 2 teaspoons (10 ml) whole-grain mustard into the sauce before you add the butter at the end.
Serve with: pork or chicken.

437 WITH WHITE WINE AND TARRAGON

Add 85 ml dry white wine to the stock before reducing the liquid by half, and replace the parsley with 1 tablespoon (15 ml) chopped fresh tarragon.
Serve with: salmon, halibut, sea bass or prawns.

438 WITH CAPERS AND OREGANO

Replace the parsley with 1 tablespoon (15 ml) chopped rinsed capers and 2 teaspoons (10 ml) chopped fresh oregano.
Serve with: chicken, cod or monkfish.

439 Dark Cherry & Port Sauce

This fruit-filled sauce is just the thing to enliven steaks or poultry such as duck and goose.

INGREDIENTS

1 tbsp (15 ml) olive oil
1 small shallot, minced
1 sprig thyme
120 ml hot chicken stock (see page 16)
12 to 14 fresh or frozen (defrosted) large dark sweet cherries, halved and pitted

½ tbsp (8 ml) red currant jelly
½ tbsp (8 ml) honey
1 tbsp (15 ml) balsamic vinegar
2 tbsp (30 ml) port
Salt and black pepper
1 tbsp (15 ml) cold butter

SERVES 2 to 3
Makes about 180 ml

Heat the olive oil in a frying pan over medium heat. Add the shallot and thyme and cook, stirring, until the shallot is translucent, 4 to 5 minutes. Add the chicken stock, cherries, red currant jelly, honey, balsamic vinegar and port with a pinch of salt and freshly ground black pepper. Bring the sauce to a boil, stirring to combine everything well. Simmer for 5 to 7 minutes until reduced and syrupy. Remove from the heat, fish out and discard the thyme, then whisk in the butter. Adjust the salt and pepper to taste and serve immediately. (Pictured opposite top.)

Serve with: red meat such as beef or venison, or rich poultry such as duck or goose or game birds.

HANDY TIP

Butter-thickened sauces such as this one don't keep warm well as the butter will separate and melt. If you intend to serve this for a dinner party make the sauce right up to the final stage then store in the fridge in a covered container for up to 2 hours. Just before serving, gently reheat the sauce, then, when it's piping hot, remove from the heat, whisk in the butter and serve.

Variations

440 WITH MARSALA AND ROSEMARY

Replace the port with marsala wine and add ½ teaspoon (3 ml) finely chopped fresh rosemary.
Serve with: pork medallions, beef tenderloin or lamb chops.

441 WITH STAR ANISE

Add 1 star anise to the pan when sautéing the shallots. Remove the star anise before serving.
Serve with: beef, pork and lamb, or sautéed calves' or chicken livers.

442 WITH BRANDY

Add 1 fluid ounce (30 ml) brandy to the cooked shallots. Bring to a simmer then remove the pan from the heat and, using a long-handled lit match, carefully set the sauce aflame. Once the flame dies down, continue with the recipe, omitting the port.
Serve with: grilled or sautéed steak, roast beef tenderloin or venison medallions.

443 WITH ZINFANDEL

Replace the port with 85 ml of Zinfandel wine that has been boiled in a small saucepan and reduced to about 3 tablespoons (40 ml).
Serve with: duck, goose, beef or venison steaks.

444 WITH ORANGE

Add 1 teaspoon (5 ml) finely grated orange zest to the pan with the cherries and other ingredients. (Pictured centre.)
Serve with: duck, goose, partridge, pheasant or quail.

445 BLUEBERRY AND PORT

Replace the cherries with 85 g fresh blueberries. (Pictured bottom.)
Serve with: steak, smoked or cured ham, or roast or grilled pork.

446 Plum & Star Anise Sauce

Plums make a great ingredient for a sauce since they break down when cooking to a velvety sweet and piquant purée. This recipe is inspired by the popular Asian plum condiment, and infuses star anise, soy, chilli and ginger into a quick-cooking sauce.

INGREDIENTS

4 red plums, pitted and
   quartered
60 ml soft light-brown sugar
3 tbsp (45 ml) red wine vinegar
1 ½ tbsp (23 ml) soy sauce
½ tsp (3 ml) ground fennel

1 star anise
Pinch dried chilli flakes
¼ tsp (1 ml) finely grated
   peeled ginger

SERVES 4 to 6

Heat all the ingredients in a medium saucepan over medium heat. Bring to a boil, then reduce the heat and simmer, stirring occasionally, for about 15 minutes until the plums have broken down and the sauce is thick and syrupy. Remove the star anise before serving.

Serve with: red meat, pork, duck or chicken, or use as an alternative to supermarket-bought Asian plum sauce.

HANDY TIP

Since different varieties of plums vary in sweetness, you might need to add more sugar. Taste near the end of the cooking time, and stir in more sugar, if needed.

Variations

447 WITH CABERNET

Heat 110 ml Cabernet Sauvignon wine in a small saucepan and bring to the boil. Simmer briskly until the wine has reduced by at least two-thirds. Omit the star anise and add the red wine reduction to the plums in the saucepan.
Serve with: beef tenderloin or steaks, or venison.

448 WITH CINNAMON

Replace the star anise with 1 cinnamon stick. Be sure to remove the cinnamon before serving.
Serve with: pork, duck, goose, beef or venison steaks.

449 WITH FIVE-SPICE

Replace the ground fennel and star anise with 1 teaspoon (5 ml) five-spice powder.
Serve with: pork, steak and duck, or use as a stir-fry sauce.

450 WITH BALSAMIC VINEGAR

Replace the red wine vinegar with balsamic vinegar.
Serve with: beef, poultry, venison, partridge or pheasant.

451 WITH PORT AND ORANGE

Heat 6 tablespoons (90 ml) port and 3 tablespoons (45 ml) freshly squeezed orange juice in a small saucepan and bring to a boil. Reduce heat slightly and simmer briskly until the liquid has reduced by at least two-thirds. Add to the plums and other ingredients in the saucepan. (Pictured top.)
Serve with: game such as venison, or duck, goose, chicken or pork.

452 WITH CHERRY AND PINK PEPPERCORN

Add 2 tablespoons (30 ml) dried cherries, roughly chopped, and 1 ½ teaspoons (8 ml) crushed pink peppercorns to the saucepan with the plums. (Pictured top.)
Serve with: pork chops or tenderloin, steak, beef tenderloin or medallions, or meatloaf.

453 Pear & Raisin Relish

This full-flavoured fruity relish rivals any that you can buy and you can customise it many ways. Some variations are listed here, but feel free to experiment with your choice of spices, dried fruits and nuts.

INGREDIENTS

3 large firm ripe Bosc or Bartlett pears, peeled, cored and cut into small cubes
2 shallots, thinly sliced
1 tbsp (15 ml) salt
85 g golden raisins

4 tbsp (60 ml) granulated sugar
2 tbsp (30 g) light soft-brown sugar
6 tbsp (90 ml) white wine vinegar

MAKES about 675 g

Place the pears and shallots in a large bowl and sprinkle with the salt. Toss well, cover with cling film and refrigerate for 6 to 8 hours.

Drain the pears and shallots and rinse them thoroughly under cold, running water to wash off the excess salt. Place in a heavy-based saucepan with the raisins, sugars, vinegar and 60 ml water. Bring to the boil over medium heat, then simmer gently over low heat for 20 minutes, stirring occasionally, until the pears are tender and the liquid syrupy. Store in an airtight jar or container in the fridge for up to 1 month.

Serve with: pork dishes, or grilled or barbecued chicken or lamb.

HANDY TIP

Letting the cubed pears sit in salt for a number of hours draws out water from the fruit and helps the cubes keep their shape rather than disintegrating during the cooking process. This makes for a chunky rather than mushy relish. Do not to leave the pears for longer than 8 hours as they will absorb too much salt and the finished relish will be too salty.

Variations

454 WITH PERSIMMON

Replace the golden raisins with chopped dried persimmon slices.
Serve with: cheese, cold cuts or pork, chicken or turkey burgers.

455 WITH PECAN

Toast 55 g chopped pecans in a dry frying pan until fragrant and browned. Leave to cool. Reduce the raisins to 55 g and stir the toasted pecans into the finished relish.
Serve with: duck, roast turkey or turkey sandwiches.

456 WITH ASIAN SPICES

Add ½ tablespoon (8 ml) minced peeled, fresh ginger; 1 small jalapeño chilli, seeded and minced; and a drizzle of toasted sesame oil to the saucepan with the pears.
Serve with: barbecued or grilled pork or chicken, roast duck or goose, or use as a dipping sauce for spring rolls, satay and other Asian-style appetizers.

457 Mango cream sauce

A wonderful multipurpose sauce. For extra colour and flavour, garnish with mango salsa (see page 176).

INGREDIENTS

2 ripe mangoes, peeled and pitted

120 ml Mexican crèma or sour cream

Lemon juice, to taste

SERVES 6

Place all the ingredients in a food processor or blender and purée until smooth. Use right away or cover and refrigerate for up to 2 days.

Serve with: lobster-papaya quesadillas, or grilled chicken or fish fillets.

HANDY TIP

It's important to use ripe mangos, otherwise the sauce will be lumpy, fibrous and sour. Look for mangos that when squeezed gently give a little and aren't too firm and smell fragrant and fruity near their stems.

458 WITH PASSION FRUIT

Make the **Mango and Lime Cream Sauce**, stirring in the strained juice and pulp of 2 yellow or purple passion fruits. (Pictured left.)
Serve with: grilled fish.

Variations

459 WITH PAPAYA

Replace the mango with fresh papaya.
Serve with: chicken or seafood.

460 SPICY MANGO AND PAPAYA

Make the **Mango and Lime Cream Sauce** and replace half the mango with fresh, ripe papaya and season with a dash of hot sauce.
Serve with: grilled chicken.

461 SWEET MANGO

Replace the sour cream with double cream, and the lemon juice with lime. Add a little sugar to taste.
Serve with: fruit desserts.

462 WITH ORANGE

Replace the lemon juice with orange zest and juice.
Serve with: grilled or roasted chicken or duck.

463 WITH LIME

Replace the lemon juice with lime juice and zest. (Pictured right.)
Serve with: Caribbean-spiced dishes.

ASIAN SAUCES

464 Teriyaki sauce

Perhaps the best-known Japanese sauce, teriyaki sauce is traditionally brushed onto meat, chicken or fish, just as it comes off the grill, but it can also be served hot as a dipping sauce.

INGREDIENTS

120 ml mirin (sweetened rice wine)
2 tbsp (30 ml) soy sauce
1 tbsp (15 ml) tamari sauce
120 ml sake

MAKES 240 ml

Pour ingredients into a small saucepan and bring to a boil. Reduce heat and simmer gently for about 15 minutes, until the liquid has reduced a little.

Serve with: chicken or fish.

HANDY TIP

Tamari is a wheat-free Japanese soy sauce. While it is also made from fermented soybeans like soy, it is thicker, richer and darker than its Chinese counterpart, and of course, it's suitable for anyone with a wheat intolerance.

Variations

465 WITH GARLIC

Add 2 crushed garlic cloves after the sauce has boiled.
Serve with: fish and poultry.

467 WITH WASABI

Add 1 teaspoon (5 ml) wasabi paste with the rest of the ingredients.
Serve with: fish or chicken.

466 SWEET TERIYAKI

After the sauce has boiled, lower the heat and stir in 2 tablespoons (30 ml) rock or palm sugar until it dissolves.
Serve with: grilled chicken and seafood.

468 WITH MISO

Add 1 tablespoon (15 ml) red miso paste with the rest of the ingredients.
Serve with: chicken or vegetables.

Variations

469 WITH GINGER

Add 28 g fresh ginger, peeled and grated, after the sauce
has boiled.
Serve with: grilled vegetables and red meat.

473 DASHI SAUCE WITH GINGER AND DAIKON

Stir 28 g peeled and grated fresh ginger and 55 g daikon into
the **Dashi Sauce** just before serving.
Serve with: seafood or vegetables.

470 WITH GINGER AND PINEAPPLE

Make the **Teriyaki with Ginger Sauce**, and replace the
sake with the same amount of pineapple juice.
Serve with: chicken or salmon.

471 WITH CHILLI AND SPRING ONIONS

Add 1 red chilli, stalk and seeds removed and finely
chopped, and 2 spring onions, trimmed to the white bulbs
and finely chopped after the sauce has boiled.
Serve with: grilled lamb or prawns.

472 DASHI SAUCE

Add 160 ml dashi – a seaweed-flavoured stock prepared
from dried kelp (konbu) and dried fish flakes, or a brown
fish stock (katsuo-bushi) – available in Asian markets to
the other ingredients before heating.
Serve with: Japanese tempura.

474 Chinese Black Bean Sauce

Recreate your favourite takeout dishes with this simple sweet, salty and aromatic sauce. Fermented black beans are easy to find in an Asian supermarket, or you can order them online.

INGREDIENTS

1 ½ tbsp (23 ml) vegetable or rapeseed oil

2 large cloves garlic, minced

1 tsp (5 ml) finely minced peeled ginger

2 tbsp (30 ml) chopped Chinese fermented black beans

240 ml hot chicken or vegetable stock (see pages 16 and 17)

2 tbsp (30 ml) soy sauce, plus more as needed

1 tbsp (15 ml) Chinese rice wine or dry sherry

1 tsp (5 ml) granulated sugar

1 tbsp (15 ml) mirin (Japanese sweet rice wine)

1 tsp (5 ml) rice vinegar

½ tsp (3 ml) toasted sesame oil

2 ½ tsp (13 ml) cornflour

SERVES 4

Heat the oil in a wok or frying pan over medium heat. When very hot, add the garlic and ginger and stir-fry briskly for 30 seconds. Stir in the black beans and cook for a further minute, tossing. Add the chicken stock, soy sauce, Chinese rice wine, sugar, mirin, rice vinegar and sesame oil. Simmer for about 3 minutes. Combine the cornflour with a splash of cold water in a small bowl and stir until smooth. Whisk into the sauce and simmer for 2 to 3 minutes until the sauce is thickened and glossy.

Serve with: prawns, salmon or tuna; chicken, pork or beef; aubergine, courgette or red pepper; or Asian greens or tofu.

HANDY TIP

Mirin is a Japanese rice wine used almost exclusively for cooking. It is similar to sake but is sweeter in flavour and has lower alcohol content. You can substitute with sweet sherry or sake and a pinch of sugar.

Variations

475 WITH SPRING ONION AND SZECHUAN PEPPERCORN

Thinly slice 2 spring onions. Stir-fry the white and light-green parts with the garlic and ginger. Add the dark-green leaves with ¼ tsp (1 ml) crushed Szechuan peppercorns in the final minute of cooking the sauce.
Serve with: rice or noodles, steak, pork or tofu, lamb, cauliflower, Asian greens or Mediterranean vegetables.

476 WITH RED PEPPER AND CHILLI

Add 1 seeded and shredded red chilli with the garlic and ginger. Then add 1 small seeded thinly sliced red pepper and cook, tossing, for about 4 minutes until still a little crisp, before adding the black beans.
Serve with: rice or egg or rice noodles, stir-fried chicken, beef or pork, or mixed vegetables and tofu.

477 WITH SHIITAKE MUSHROOM

Soak 8 dried shiitake mushrooms in just-boiled water for 20 minutes or until soft. Drain, reserving 120 ml of the liquid. Discard the stems, thinly slice the caps and use in place of the red pepper in the **Chinese Black Bean, Red Pepper and Chilli Sauce**. Use 120 ml of stock and add to the pan with the reserved soaking liquid.
Serve with: rice, noodles, fish, prawns, Asian greens or tofu.

478 Red Thai Aubergine Curry

Curries are popular throughout Asia, the Thai version being very famous. Enriched with coconut milk, it is bittersweet from the Asian lime leaves and the Thai basil adds a hint of liquorice.

INGREDIENTS

1 tbsp (15 ml) vegetable oil
4 cloves garlic, crushed
2 shallots, peeled and sliced
2 dried chillies, left whole
3 tbsp (45 ml) Thai red curry paste
1 tbsp (15 ml) prawn paste
1 tbsp (15 ml) palm sugar
480 ml unsweetened coconut milk

250 ml chicken stock (see pages 16), or water
2 medium aubergines, cut into bite-sized pieces, or
12 small Asian aubergines, halved
6 fresh Asian lime leaves
Bunch of fresh Thai basil leaves
2 limes, quartered

SERVES 4 to 6

Heat oil in a wok or heavy saucepan. Stir in the garlic, shallots, and chillies until they begin to colour. Stir in the curry paste, prawn paste and palm sugar until mixture begins to darken. Add the coconut milk and stock, then toss in the aubergine pieces and lime leaves. Partially cover pan, and cook over a gentle heat for about 25 minutes, until the aubergines are tender. Stir in the Thai basil leaves and check seasoning. (Pictured opposite top.)

Serve with: jasmine rice and lime wedges.

HANDY TIP

The hallmark of an authentic Thai curry is a thin layer of oil floating atop the gravy. This is achieved by simmering the coconut milk until it separates and the oil rises to the surface. If your sauce doesn't do this, turn up the heat slightly so it simmers more briskly.

Variations

479 GREEN THAI

Replace the red curry paste with jarred green curry paste.
Serve with: steamed rice and garnish with coriander.

480 RED SWEET POTATO

Replace the aubergines with 2 sweet potatoes, peeled and cut into bited-sized chunks.
Serve with: jasmine rice and garnish with slices of fresh red chilli.

481 GREEN POTATO

Replace the red curry paste with jarred green curry paste, and the aubergines with 12 to 15 new potatoes, peeled and left whole.
Serve with: jasmine rice and garnish with coriander.

482   SAIGON AUBERGINE

Add 28 g fresh turmeric root, peeled and minced, to the garlic and shallots in the wok. Replace the Thai red curry paste with Indian curry paste and the Asian lime and Thai basil leaves with the leaves from a small bunch of fresh coriander, finely chopped.
Serve with: basmati rice and garnish with a tablespoonful of plain yoghurt.

483   GREEN SWEET POTATO

Replace red curry paste with jarred green curry paste and the aubergines with 2 sweet potatoes, peeled and cut into bite-sized chunks. (Pictured centre.)
Serve with: coconut rice.

484   RED POTATO

Replace the aubergines with 12 to 15 baby potatoes, peeled and kept whole. (Pictured bottom.)
Serve with: steamed rice and garnish with chopped chillies.

485 Spicy Kung Pao Sauce

When it comes to comfort food, Kung Pao chicken holds it own besides favourites such as meatloaf. Keep this recipe in mind for a mid-week feast.

INGREDIENTS

1 ½ tbsp (23 ml) soy sauce
1 tbsp (15 ml) hoisin sauce
1 tbsp (15 ml) Chinese rice wine
½ tsp (3 ml) sesame oil
2 tbsp (30 ml) vegetable or rapeseed oil
2 to 4 small dried chillies
2 large cloves garlic, thinly sliced
2 spring onions, thinly sliced, white and green parts kept separately
1 ½ tsp (8 ml) minced peeled fresh ginger
1 tbsp (15 ml) supermarket-bought chilli paste
½ medium red pepper, seeded and finely chopped
140 ml hot chicken or vegetable stock (see pages 16 and 17)
2 tsp (10 ml) cornflour
2 ½ tbsp (38 ml) roughly chopped roast, unsalted peanuts

SERVES 2 to 4

Combine the soy sauce, hoisin sauce, Chinese rice wine and sesame oil in a small bowl and set aside.

Heat the oil in a wok or frying pan over a medium-high heat. Stir-fry the chillies until fragrant and lightly blistered. Add the garlic, white parts of the green onion, and ginger and fry for a minute. Add the chilli paste and cook for a minute, stirring. Add the pepper and cook for 3 to 4 more minutes until tender. Add the sauces and bring to a boil. Stir in the stock and simmer for 2 minutes. Combine the cornflour with a little water in a small bowl and stir until smooth. Stir into the sauce and cook for 2 minutes longer until the sauce thickens. Add the peanuts and the green parts of the green onion. Remove the dried chillies before serving.

Serve with: rice or noodles, chicken, lamb, pork or beef, or stir-fried mixed vegetables and tofu.

HANDY TIP

Don't confuse Chinese rice wine for mirin – Chinese rice wine is far less sweet. Substitute with dry sherry.

Variations

486 WITH CASHEW NUTS

Replace the peanuts with chopped roast, unsalted cashew nuts.
Serve with: chicken, beef, pork, tofu or peppers, carrots, broccoli and Asian greens as a stir-fry sauce.

487 WITH SZECHUAN PEPPERCORNS

Add ½ teaspoon (3 ml) well-crushed Szechuan peppercorns to the wok with the mixture of sauces.
Serve with: rice or noodles, sliced steak, or pork or lamb chops, or as a stir-fry sauce with prawns, chicken, beef, pork or tofu.

488 WITH WATER CHESTNUTS

Omit the red pepper and add 100 g drained, canned sliced water chestnuts to the pan with the mixture of sauces.
Serve with: rice and noodles or as a stir-fry sauce with Asian greens, broccoli, peppers, tofu and meat, poultry or seafood.

489 Tomato, onion & Prawn Sambal

Fiery *sambals* in Southeast Asia are like ketchup in the West, but they are also served as a sauce when cooked with tomatoes.

INGREDIENTS

2 large cloves garlic, chopped

2 to 4 red chillies, such as Holland or jalapeño, seeded and chopped

2 cm (1 inch) piece ginger, peeled and chopped

½ medium shallot, chopped

1 tsp (5 ml) paprika

3 large or 4 medium ripe plum tomatoes, peeled, cored and chopped

2 tbsp (30 ml) vegetable oil

1 large onion, thinly sliced

8 fresh or dried curry leaves

1 tsp (5 ml) prawn paste, crumbled

450 g raw peeled prawns

Salt

1 tsp (5 ml) soft dark-brown sugar

½ to 1 tsp (3 to 5 ml) jarred tamarind concentrate (depending on the brand you use – some are more tart than others) or 1 tbsp (15 ml) lime juice

SERVES 4 to 6

Using a food processor or blender process the garlic, chillies, ginger, shallot and paprika to a paste with a splash of water. Set aside. Blend the tomatoes in a blender or food processor until puréed. Set aside.

Heat the oil in a wok or frying pan over medium heat. Add the onions and curry leaves and cook until the onion is tender and golden. Add the garlic and chilli and prawn pastes and cook for 3 minutes, stirring. Season the prawns with salt and add to the wok. Stir-fry over high heat until lightly cooked and turning opaque. Add the tomatoes with the brown sugar and tamarind paste. Cook, simmering for 6 to 8 minutes, until the sauce thickens. Adjust the salt to taste.

Serve with: rice or Indian- or Asian-style breads such as paratha, chapatti or naan.

HANDY TIP

Prawn paste is made from fermented ground prawns that are dried until it forms a pungent, salty cake.

Variations

490 WITH SQUID

Replace the prawns with rings of thinly sliced raw squid.
Serve with: rice or Asian- and Indian-style breads.

491 WITH EDAMAME

Use a medium onion and add 85 g frozen edamame to the sauce 3 to 4 minutes before the end of the cooking time. Simmer until the edamame is tender and the sauce thickened.
Serve with: basmati, wild or brown rice.

492 WITH SCALLOPS

Replace the prawns with queen scallops.
Serve with: rice or with Asian- and Indian-style breads.

493 Spicy Peanut Satay Sauce

This Indonesian dipping sauce is used for fried and grilled meats and steamed vegetables and is similar to the peanut sauces of Malaysia, Vietnam and Thailand.

INGREDIENTS

1 to 2 tbsp (15 to 30 ml) peanut or vegetable oil
1 shallot, peeled and finely chopped
2 cloves garlic, peeled and finely chopped
70 g unsalted peanuts, finely ground
1 tbsp (15 ml) Indonesian or Thai prawn paste
1 tbsp (15 ml) palm sugar
1 tbsp (15 ml) tamarind paste
1 tbsp (15 ml) Indonesian sweet soy sauce
1 tbsp (15 ml) chilli powder
300 ml water

SERVES 4

Heat oil in a heavy-based pan and cook the shallot and garlic until golden. Add the peanuts, prawn paste, and sugar, and fry for 3 to 4 minutes, until peanuts colour and release some of their oil. Stir in the tamarind paste, sweet soy sauce and chilli powder. Add water and bring the mixture to a boil. Reduce heat and simmer for 15 to 20 minutes, until mixture has reduced and thickened. Leave mixture to cool, then pour into a blender and process to a smooth sauce. It may be kept in the fridge, covered, for a week. (Pictured opposite top.)

Serve with: chicken or beef kebabs.

HANDY TIP

Indonesian sweet soy sauce is labelled as *Kecap Manis*. It is a thick, dark molasses-like soy sauce. If you don't have any, simply reduce regular soy sauce in a saucepan then stir in a couple of tablespoons of soft dark-brown sugar until completely dissolved.

Variations

494 THAI

Replace the tamarind paste, soy sauce and chilli powder with 1 to 2 tablespoons (15 to 30 ml) of Thai red curry paste.
Serve with: grilled prawns or chicken.

495 HOT AND SOUR ALMOND

Omit chilli powder and add 2 red chillies, seeded and chopped, with the shallot and garlic. Replace the peanuts with toasted almonds.
Serve with: grilled or pan-fried fish.

496 CREAMY SATAY

When the sauce is completely cool, stir in 60 ml good-quality mayonnaise.
Serve with: raw vegetables as a dip.

497 HOT AND SOUR WALNUT

Omit the chilli powder and add 2 red chillies, seeded and chopped, with the shallot and garlic. Replace the peanuts with walnuts.
Serve with: grilled fish or red meat.

498 VIETNAMESE

Replace the shallot, prawn paste and sugar with an extra clove of garlic and 2 red chillies, seeded and finely chopped. Stir the garlic and chillies in oil for 2 minutes before adding the peanuts. Replace the tamarind, soy sauce, chilli powder and water with 2 tablespoons (30 ml) each hoisin and fish sauce and 60 ml each coconut milk and chicken stock. Beat in a small bunch of finely chopped fresh coriander. (Pictured centre.)
Serve with: stir-fried vegetables.

499 HOT AND SOUR WITH MINT AND LIME

Add 2 red chillies, seeded and chopped, with the shallot and garlic. Replace the tamarind paste and chilli powder with the juice of 1 lime and 2 tablespoons (30 ml) finely chopped fresh mint leaves. (Pictured bottom.)
Serve with: grilled chicken and vegetables.

500 Nuoc cham Dipping Sauce

This Vietnamese sauce varies in degrees of sweet, sour and fiery flavours, depending on the cook and the region.

INGREDIENTS

4 cloves garlic
2 fresh red chillies, stem and
  seeds removed
3 to 4 tsp (15 to 20 ml) palm sugar
Juice of ½ lime

5 tbsp (75 ml) water
60 ml Vietnamese or Thai fish
  sauce

SERVES 4

Finely mince the garlic and chillies and transfer to a small bowl. Add the sugar, lime juice, water and fish sauce and stir to combine. Store in the fridge until ready to use, for a maximum of 2 weeks. (Pictured opposite top.)

Serve with: spring rolls, grilled meats or seafood.

HANDY TIP

Palm sugar is caramel-like sugar commonly used in Indian and Southeast Asian cuisine. It is made from the sap of the sugar palm tree – buy it in jars or discs from Asian supermarkets. As a substitute, use dark soft-brown sugar.

Variations

501 WITH GINGER

Add 28 g fresh ginger, peeled and chopped, to the garlic and chilli, and the juice of 1 whole lime.
Serve with: grilled or baked chicken.

502 SWEET AND SOUR LIME WITH MIRIN

Replace the lime, water, and fish sauce with 1 tablespoon (15 ml) rice vinegar, 2 tablespoons (30 ml) soy sauce, the juice of 2 limes and 120 ml mirin.
Serve with: vegetable spring rolls.

503 SWEET AND SOUR LIME WITH GINGER

Add 28 g ginger, peeled and finely minced, to the garlic and chilli. Omit the water and stir in juice of 2 limes with the fish sauce.
Serve with: chicken or salmon.

504 SPICY VINEGAR

Replace the water and fish sauce with 60 ml rice vinegar and 2 tablespoons (30 ml) soy sauce.
Serve with: grilled prawns.

505 WITH SOY SAUCE

Replace the water with 3 to 4 tablespoons (45 to 60 ml) soy sauce and reduce the fish sauce to 2 to 3 tablespoons (30 to 45 ml). (Pictured centre.)
Serve with: vegetable spring rolls or tempura.

506 CAMBODIAN WITH LEMONGRASS AND CORIANDER

Add 2 lemongrass stalks, tender bulbs only, trimmed and minced, and a small bunch of fresh coriander leaves, finely chopped, to the garlic and chilli, and use the juice of 2 whole limes. (Pictured bottom.)
Serve with: grilled beef or lamb.

507 Madras Curry Sauce

South Indian curries are often fiery hot, laden with aromatic spices and tempered with coconut milk. For a milder sauce, reduce the cayenne powder.

INGREDIENTS

FOR THE CURRY POWDER
½ to 1 tsp (3 to 5 ml) cayenne powder
2 tsp (10 ml) ground coriander
1 tsp (5 ml) ground cumin
½ tsp (3 ml) ground paprika
½ tsp (3 ml) ground fennel seeds
¼ tsp (1 ml) ground fenugreek
¼ tsp (1 ml) ground turmeric
3 large cloves garlic, chopped
2 cm (1 in) fresh ginger, peeled and chopped
Salt

FOR THE SAUCE
2 tbsp (30 ml) ghee (clarified butter, see page 14) or vegetable oil
1 cinnamon stick
1 to 2 dried chillies
1 star anise
8 fresh or dried curry leaves
1 tsp (5 ml) black mustard seeds
1 medium onion, chopped
2 ripe tomatoes, peeled, cored and chopped
140 ml chicken stock (see page 16)
140 ml coconut milk
Salt

SERVES 4

Combine the curry powder spices in a small bowl and set aside. Grind the garlic and ginger with a good pinch of salt to a paste in a pestle and mortar. Set aside.

Heat the ghee or oil in a heavy-based saucepan, add the cinnamon, chilli, star anise, curry leaves and mustard seeds. Cook for 1 minute, stirring, until the seeds start to pop. Add the onion and stir-fry until golden. Add the garlic and ginger paste and cook, stirring, for 1 minute. Add the spice powder and cook, stirring, for another minute. Add the tomatoes and cook, stirring, until they reduce to a thick pulp. Add the stock, coconut milk and ½ teaspoon (3 ml) salt and simmer for 5 to 7 minutes until thickened. Adjust salt to taste.

Serve with: rice, Indian breads, chicken, lamb or fish.

HANDY TIP

There are no good substitutes for curry leaves. If you can't find them, just leave them out.

Variations

508 WITH POTATOES

Add 1 medium to large red potato, peeled and cubed, to the sauce once the chicken stock and coconut milk comes to a boil. Simmer until the potato is cooked through and the sauce is thickened.
Serve with: rice or Indian breads, chicken or lamb.

509 WITH PEAS

Stir 110 g fresh green peas into the sauce 4 minutes before the end of the cooking time.
Serve with: rice or Indian breads, cooked chicken or lamb, or sautéed paneer (Indian cheese).

510 WITH RED LENTILS

Simmer 110 g red lentils in a pot of boiling salted water until al dente. Drain and add to the sauce once the chicken stock and coconut milk have come to a boil. Simmer for 5 to 10 minutes until the lentils are soft but not collapsed.
Serve with: rice, Indian breads, baked potatoes, prawns, lobster or scallops, or Asian greens and tofu.

511 Creamy Tikka Masala Sauce

This Anglo-Indian invention is creamy and spicy.

INGREDIENTS

1 tsp (5 ml) cumin seeds

1 tsp (5 ml) coriander seeds

½ tsp (3 ml) fennel seeds

½ tsp (3 ml) ground cayenne

¼ tsp (1 ml) turmeric

1 tsp (5 ml) paprika

¾ tsp (4 ml) ground garam masala

2 cm (1 inch) ginger, peeled and chopped

3 cloves garlic

1 tbsp (15 ml) tomato purée

1 tbsp (15 ml) finely ground almonds

1 tbsp (15 ml) desiccated coconut

3 tbsp (45 ml) ghee (clarified butter, see page 14) or vegetable oil

2 medium onions, thinly sliced

3 ripe plum tomatoes, peeled, cored, seeded and chopped

170 ml hot chicken or vegetable stock (see pages 16 and 17)

160 ml double cream

2 tbsp (30 ml) chopped fresh coriander leaves

SERVES 4 to 6

In a dry frying pan, toast the cumin, coriander and fennel seeds until fragrant and browned. Once cool, grind in a pestle and mortar until fine. Place with the cayenne, turmeric, paprika, garam masala, ginger, garlic, tomato purée, almonds and coconut in a blender and blend with a little water to form a paste. Set aside. Cook the onion in 2 tablespoons (30 ml) ghee or oil in a frying pan, stirring occasionally, until deep brown and caramelised. Transfer to the blender and process to a paste.

Heat the remaining ghee or oil in the frying pan, and add the reserved spice paste. Cook, stirring for a few minutes, then add the tomatoes with ½ teaspoon (3 ml) salt and cook until the tomatoes break down, 5 to 7 minutes. Add the blended onion and the stock. Bring to the boil, then simmer gently, covered, for 5 minutes. Stir in the cream and simmer, uncovered for 3 minutes. Remove from the heat, stir in the coriander and season to taste.

Serve with: plain or tandoori-style chicken or lamb, paneer (Indian cheese), sautéed vegetables and rice.

HANDY TIP

Garam masala is a spice blend frequently used in North Indian cuisine.

Variations

512 WITH SPINACH

Blanch 4 to 5 handfuls of spinach in boiling salted water until wilted. Drain, run under cold water to cool, then squeeze out as much water as possible. Roughly chop the spinach and add to the sauce with the cream.
Serve with: rice, naan or other Indian breads.

513 WITH CHICKPEAS

Stir 1 (425 g) can of drained and rinsed chickpeas into the pan a few minutes before adding the cream.
Serve with: rice, grilled or pan-fried plain or tandoori-style chicken or lamb cubes.

514 WITH MUSHROOM

Sauté 225 g sliced brown mushrooms, seasoned with salt and pepper, in a little ghee (clarified butter, see page 14) until tender and browned. Set aside. Stir into the sauce 1 minute before adding the cream.
Serve with: spicy roast chicken or lamb, tandoori-style lamb chops, or chicken, kebabs or sautéed paneer over rice or with naan or other Indian breads.

515 Filipino Adobo Sauce

This sauce is an adaptation of *adobo*, a kind of stew that's the unofficial national dish of the Philippines where it's served on every festive holiday.

INGREDIENTS

2 tbsp (30 ml) vegetable or
    rapeseed oil
1 medium onion, chopped
2 large cloves garlic, minced
340 ml hot chicken stock (see
    page 16)
1 bay leaf
2 tbsp (30 ml) soy sauce, plus
    more as needed

2 tbsp (30 ml) oyster sauce
5 tbsp (75 ml) apple cider
    vinegar
Dash Worcestershire sauce
1 tbsp (15 ml) soft brown sugar
1 ½ tsp (8 ml) cornflour

SERVES 4

Heat the oil in a wok or frying pan over medium heat. Stir-fry the onion until lightly golden, about 4 to 5 minutes. Add the garlic and cook for another minute. Stir in the chicken stock, bring to the boil, then simmer for 3 minutes. Add the bay leaf, soy sauce, oyster sauce, apple cider vinegar, Worcestershire sauce and sugar, then simmer gently for 10 to 12 minutes. Combine the cornflour with a splash of cold water in a small bowl and stir until smooth. Stir into the sauce and cook for 2 minutes until the sauce thickens. Taste and add more soy sauce if necessary. Discard the bay leaf before serving.

Serve with: roast or pot-roasted chicken, pork or beef.

HANDY TIP

For a vegetarian version, use vegetarian oyster sauce and vegetable stock.

Variations

516 WITH CHERRY TOMATOES

Add 1 tablespoon (15 ml) tomato purée with the garlic, and a handful of cherry tomatoes 5 minutes before the end of the cooking time. Simmer until the skins split.
Serve with: roast or grilled chicken or beef.

517 WITH ORANGE

Replace one third of the chicken stock with orange juice and stir the finely grated zest of 1 orange into the sauce 5 minutes before the end of the cooking time.
Serve with: chicken, pork or beef.

518 WITH COCONUT

Simmer 200 ml coconut milk in a saucepan until reduced by half. Add with the soy sauce and other ingredients. Omit the cornflour, if desired.
Serve with: noodles, or chicken, pork or beef.

519 Tamarind Sauce

This piquant sauce is ideal if you need just one condiment to go with a selection of Asian-inspired canapés.

INGREDIENTS

85 g block tamarind pulp
2 cloves garlic, minced
1.25 cm (½ inch) fresh ginger, peeled and finely minced or grated

3 tbsp (45 ml) soft brown sugar, plus more as needed
½ tbsp (8 ml) soy sauce
Salt

MAKES 250 ml
Serves 4 to 6 as a dipping sauce

Place the tamarind block in a small bowl and cover with 180 ml boiling water. Leave to soak for 30 minutes until very soft. Mash until collapsed, then pass through a sieve, rubbing with the back of a spoon to push as much as possible through. Discard the seeds and fibres. Set aside the strained pulp. Place the garlic, ginger, sugar and soy sauce in a saucepan with 80 to 120 ml water and bring to a boil. Add the tamarind pulp and simmer for 2 to 3 minutes, stirring. Season to taste with salt, and add more sugar, if needed. Cool before serving.

Serve with: Indian and Asian snacks such as samosas, spring rolls, fish cakes and kebabs.

HANDY TIP

Mouth-puckeringly tart tamarind is an essential ingredient in the Indian and Southeast Asian pantry. The soft, edible pulp is held inside the pods with several seeds. Most of the seeds are removed but, sometimes, a few errant seeds get left behind so be on the lookout for them.

Variations

520 WITH MINT

Stir 2 tablespoons (30 ml) finely shredded fresh mint leaves into the finished sauce.
Serve with: lamb kebabs, koftas, grilled prawns or salmon.

521 WITH MANGO AND CHILLI

Add ½ to 1 seeded and minced long red chilli with the strained tamarind pulp, and stir in the flesh of half of a medium ripe mango, finely diced to the finished sauce.
Serve with: Indian or Asian finger foods, burgers or barbecued chicken.

522 WITH YOGHURT AND CORIANDER

Whisk 3 tablespoons (45 ml) plain thick Greek yoghurt into the finished sauce, then add 2 tablespoons (30 ml) chopped fresh coriander.
Serve with: Indian or Asian finger foods, crudités.

SALSAS & VEGETABLE DIPS

523 Tzatziki

Greek tzatziki, traditionally served as an appetizer, can be left on the table as an accompaniment for other foods throughout the meal. The key to the best tzatziki is the thick creamy texture.

INGREDIENTS

1 tbsp (15 ml) olive oil
2 tsp (10 ml) lemon juice
480 ml thick Greek yoghurt
4 to 10 cloves garlic (or to taste), finely chopped
1 cucumber, peeled and finely diced or coarsely grated
Chopped fresh parsley, to garnish

MAKES 480 ml

Combine the olive oil and lemon juice in a mixing bowl by whisking gently together. Fold the yoghurt into the mixture slowly, making sure it is fully incorporated. Add the garlic, according to taste, and the cucumber. Stir until evenly distributed. Garnish with a little chopped parsley.

Serve with: crudités.

HANDY TIP

For a really thick dip, halve the peeled cucumber and scrape out and discard the watery seeds before dicing or grating the flesh.

Variations

524 WITH MINT

Add 3 tablespoons (45 ml) finely chopped fresh mint leaves to the mixture with the cucumber.
Serve with: lamb kebabs.

525 QUICK

Instead of the main recipe, wash and peel 2 cucumbers, then use a vegetable peeler to shave off thin strips. Place strips in a colander, sprinkle with salt, and let sit about 10 minutes to drain. Rinse well. Mix with finely minced fresh garlic, lots of fresh dill, and plain yoghurt.
Serve with: pitta bread.

Tzatziki complements spiced vegetable and meat dishes

526 WITH CHILLI

Add ¼ teaspoon (1 ml) finely chopped dried red chilli, or chilli flakes, to the mixture with the cucumber.
Serve with: grilled chicken.

530 WITH ROASTED GARLIC

Add gently roasted, peeled garlic cloves instead of fresh garlic for a softer, sweeter flavour. For roasting instructions, see pages 90 and 164.
Serve with: vegetable kebabs.

527 WITH TOMATO, CUCUMBER AND CUMIN

Toast 1 teaspoon (5 ml) cumin seeds in a dry frying pan, when cool roughly crush in a pestle and mortar. Use only half a cucumber, and add 2 seeded and diced plum tomatoes and the crushed cumin seeds to the yoghurt and cucumber.
Serve with: lamb kebabs.

531 MANGO AND COCONUT RAITA

Replace the cucumber in the **Classic Indian Cucumber Raita Dip** with the diced flesh of 1 large mango, and add 2 tablespoons (30 ml) desiccated coconut that's been lightly toasted in a dry frying pan and cooled, to the mango and yoghurt mixture.
Serve with: Indian curries.

528 WITH GINGER, CHILLI AND CORIANDER

Add 1.25 cm (½ inch) of finely grated or minced peeled ginger, 1 green or red jalapeño chilli (seeded and minced) and 3 tablespoons (45 ml) finely chopped fresh coriander to the cucumber and yoghurt mixture.
Serve with: baked fish.

532 CUCUMBER AND POMEGRANATE RAITA

Add 70 g pomegranate seeds, and ¼ teaspoon (1 ml) very finely minced or grated fresh ginger to the yoghurt in the **Classic Indian Cucumber Raita Dip**.
Serve with: warm flatbreads, crackers, spicy stews and curries or spice-rubbed grilled fish or chicken.

529 CLASSIC INDIAN CUCUMBER RAITA

Replace the garlic, lemon juice, olive oil and parsley with 2 tablespoons (30 ml) finely chopped fresh mint leaves and a generous pinch of ground cumin and stir into the cucumber and yoghurt mixture.
Serve with: spicy curries and stews, lamb burgers, crudités.

533 Wild Mushroom 'caviar' Dip

This rich, sherry-spiked dip, packed with the complex, earthy flavours of wild mushrooms, may not be quite as expensive as real caviar, but it's just as luxurious, and just as delicious.

INGREDIENTS

14 g dried mixed
  wild mushrooms
2 tbsp (30 ml) unsalted
  butter
½ tbsp (8 ml) olive oil
2 shallots, minced
2 cloves garlic, minced
450 g mixture of chanterelle,
  oyster, shiitake or morel
  mushrooms, stems
  trimmed or discarded if
  too tough, wiped clean
  and coarsely chopped
Salt and black pepper
3 tbsp (45 ml) sherry
1 ½ tsp (8 ml) chopped fresh
  thyme leaves, plus more
  to garnish
60 ml crème fraîche

MAKES 560 ml

Place the dried mushrooms in a bowl, pour over just enough boiling water to cover, then leave to soak for 20 minutes or until tender. Remove and squeeze dry. Strain the liquid to remove any grit and set aside. Chop the mushrooms finely and set aside.

Heat the butter and olive oil in a heavy-based frying pan over medium heat. Add the shallots and cook, stirring, until softened. Add the garlic and cook for a minute longer. Add all the mushrooms with ½ teaspoon (3 ml) salt and ¼ teaspoon (1 ml) pepper, and sauté until tender and browned. Add 160 ml of the reserved mushroom soaking liquid and cook until almost all of the liquid has evaporated, about 5 minutes. Add the sherry and cook for 1 to 2 minutes until the alcohol has bubbled away.

Remove from the heat and stir in the thyme. Leave to cool to room temperature then transfer to a food processor or blender with the crème fraîche. Process until everything is well combined and the mixture is still a little chunky or completely smooth, as you prefer. Adjust the seasoning, then serve at room temperature garnished with chopped fresh thyme leaves.

Serve with: crisp toast points and crackers, melba toasts or sliced grilled baguette topped with a dollop of crème fraîche for a canapé.

HANDY TIP

It's important to cool the mushrooms before processing with the crème fraîche, otherwise it will melt from the heat of the mushrooms and the dip will be very loose. If this happens, chill the dip until it sets up again.

Variations

534 WITH BACON

Cook 3 rashers of bacon in a frying pan over medium heat until crisp. Drain on kitchen paper, roughly chop and add to the food processor with the rest of the ingredients. Thin down dip with a little water or stock, if necessary.
Serve with: toasted sourdough or olive bread crostini, seeded crackers, or wedges of country-style bread.

537 WITH TRUFFLE

Stir 2 teaspoons (10 ml) truffle oil into the dip just before serving.
Serve with: beef burgers, or toast or crackers

535 WITH MASCARPONE

Replace the crème fraîche with mascarpone cheese.
Serve with: tortilla chips, slices of fresh baguette, ciabatta or foccacia bread, or crackers.

538 WITH CARAMELISED ONION

In a heavy-based frying pan, cook 1 medium onion, sliced, in 1 tablespoon (15 ml) olive oil and 1 tablespoon (15 ml) unsalted butter and a sprig of thyme until soft. Discard the thyme and leave to cool. Make the dip, using 1 shallot and adding the onions to the blender or food processor with the mushroom mixture and the crème fraîche. Thin down with a little water, if necessary.
Serve with: crispbreads, crackers or as a sandwich spread.

536 WITH ROASTED GARLIC

Replace the minced fresh garlic with roasted garlic. Place 6 to 8 large unpeeled garlic cloves in a baking dish and drizzle with olive oil. Pour 1 to 2 tablespoons (15 to 30 ml) of water over the top, cover with foil and bake in oven at 120°C (225°F) for 45 minutes until very soft. When cool, squeeze the cloves from their skins.
Serve with: blanched asparagus or broccoli florets, toast, crostini or thick-cut sandwiches.

539 WITH WALNUTS

Add 85 g chopped walnuts to the food processor with the mushrooms and crème fraîche. Season with a generous dash of hot sauce before serving.
Serve with: wholewheat crackers, bread, or as a sandwich spread.

540 WITH NEUFCHÂTEL

Replace the crème fraîche with 85 g softened Neufchâtel cheese.
Serve with: turkey or chicken sandwiches, burgers, or crostini and crackers.

541 WITH BRANDY

Replace the sherry with brandy.
Serve with: toast points, seeded crispbreads or breadsticks.

542 WITH RICOTTA AND ROSEMARY

Replace the thyme with 2 teaspoons (10 ml) finely chopped fresh rosemary leaves and the crème fraîche with 85 g full-fat ricotta cheese.
Serve with: crudités, sliced baguette or toast, or with hot penne or rigatoni pasta and loosened with 3 tablespoons (45 ml) of the pasta-cooking water.

543 Beetroot and Ginger Dip

This shocking pink dip will wake up the tastebuds.

INGREDIENTS

250 g cooked beetroot,
    roughly chopped
1 garlic clove, crushed
2 tsp (10 ml) ground coriander
½ tsp (3 ml) ground ginger

Salt and black pepper
180 ml plain Greek yoghurt
1 tsp (5 ml) chopped fresh
    mint leaves

SERVES 2

Place the beetroot, garlic, coriander and ginger in a food processor and season. Process to a smooth purée. Add the yoghurt. Season, then serve, sprinkled with mint.

Serve with: pitta bread.

HANDY TIP

To roast beetroot to use is this dip, peel small beetroot, cut in half, place on a baking sheet and toss with olive oil, salt and pepper. Roast in the oven at 180°C (360°F) for 35 to 40 minutes, turning once, until tender.

Variations

544 WITH ORANGE

Add the grated zest of half an orange with the yoghurt.
Serve with: crudités.

545 SPICY GINGER

Add 1 teaspoon (5 ml) harissa (see page 100) or 1 teaspoon (5 ml) paprika and a pinch of cayenne pepper.
Serve with: tortilla chips.

546 WITH GINGER AND CHIVES

Replace the mint with chopped chives.
Serve with: breadsticks.

547 Luscious Artichoke Dip

This smooth, mild and creamy dip is the perfect choice for those who want a reduced-fat dip.

INGREDIENTS

1 (400 g) can artichoke hearts, drained
1 garlic clove, crushed
1 tbsp (15 ml) extra-virgin olive oil
¼ tsp (1 ml) ground cumin
¼ tsp (1 ml) grated lemon zest
Salt and ground black pepper
1 tbsp (15 ml) chopped fresh parsley leaves

SERVES 4

Put the artichokes, garlic, oil, cumin and lemon zest in a food processor. Add salt and pepper, and blend to make a smooth purée. Check the seasoning and stir in the parsley. Scrape the dip into a bowl and serve. (Pictured opposite top.)

Serve with: plain tortilla chips or breadsticks.

Handy Tip

Thin out this dip with hot chicken or vegetable stock and serve it as a sauce with fish or chicken.

Variations

548 WITH CHIVES

Replace the parsley with chopped chives.
Serve with: raw vegetables.

549 WITH PAPRIKA

Add a good pinch of paprika to the food processor with the rest of the ingredients.
Serve with: seafood.

550 WITH FETA CHEESE

Add 85 g chopped feta to the food processor with the rest of the ingredients.
Serve with: cucumber, celery and carrot sticks, or seeded crackers.

551   EXTRA-CREAMY

Add 2 tablespoons (30 ml) crème fraîche with the parsley.
Serve with: raw vegetables.

552   WITH GREEN OLIVE AND THYME

Replace the parsley with 2 teaspoons (10 ml) fresh thyme
leaves and 110 g pitted green olives. (Pictured centre.)
Serve with: grilled chicken, swordfish or tuna kebabs,
vegetable crisps or breadsticks.

553   WITH PESTO

Replace the lemon zest and cumin with 1 to 2 tablespoons
(15 to 30 ml) of basil pesto. (Pictured bottom.)
Serve with: cheese crackers.

554 Courgette, Chilli & Caper Dip

This light and tangy dip makes another healthy choice if you want a smooth, creamy dip without a high calorie count.

INGREDIENTS

3 courgette, sliced
½ garlic clove, crushed
2 tsp (10 ml) capers, rinsed
Good pinch of dried chilli flakes

2 tbsp (30 ml) olive oil
Salt
Juice of ¼ lemon, to taste

SERVES 4 to 6

Steam the courgette for about 5 minutes, until tender. Place in a food processor with the garlic, capers, chilli and olive oil. Process to the desired consistency. Add salt and lemon juice to taste. (Pictured opposite top.)

Serve with: crackers or pitta breads, hot or cold.

HANDY TIP

You can steam the courgette in the microwave. Rinse the slices in running water then shake them but don't dry them completely. Place in a the bowl and cover with microwave-safe cling film, leaving one corner loose so the steam can escape. Cook on high for 3 to 5 minutes until tender.

Variations

555 WITH LEMON

Add ½ teaspoon (3 ml) grated lemon zest to the food processor with the lemon juice.
Serve with: seafood.

556 WITH TAHINI

Add 2 tablespoons (30 ml) tahini paste to the food processor with the rest of the ingredients. Garnish the finished dip with a couple of teaspoons (approximately 10 ml) of toasted sesame seeds.
Serve with: chicken or fish fingers, crispbreads, cheese sticks, crackers or carrot sticks.

557 WITH DILL

Add 1 tablespoon (15 ml) chopped fresh dill and 2 tablespoons (30 ml) crème fraîche with the lemon juice.
Serve with: grilled salmon.

558 WITH MINT

Add 1 teaspoon (5 ml) chopped fresh mint. Sprinkle with extra chopped fresh mint before serving.
Serve with: baked lamb steaks.

559 CREAMY

Omit the chilli flakes and add 3 tablespoons (45 ml) crème fraîche with the lemon juice. (Pictured centre.)
Serve with: tortilla chips.

560 WITH PARSLEY

Add 2 tablespoons (30 ml) chopped fresh parsley leaves. Sprinkle with more parsley when serving. (Pictured bottom.)
Serve with: crudités.

561 Aubergine Dip with Walnuts

The combination of walnuts and the sharpness of the red wine vinegar gives this Greek dip, called *melitzanosalata me karythia*, a nice tart taste.

INGREDIENTS

2 kg large aubergine(s)
3 cloves garlic
80 ml extra-virgin olive oil
3 tbsp (45 ml) red wine vinegar
1 tsp (5 ml) salt
½ tsp (3 ml) black pepper

½ bunch fresh flat-leaf parsley, finely chopped
7 tbsp (105 ml) coarsely chopped walnuts

MAKES 480 ml

Preheat oven to 190°C (375°F). Remove stems from the aubergines, rinse, and pat dry. Place the whole aubergines on a baking sheet and bake for just over an hour. Cool. As soon as they can be handled, remove skin (it will come off easily by hand) and place the pulp in a fine sieve to drain for about 15 minutes, or until it stops dripping.

Combine aubergine pulp with remaining ingredients in a food processor and process until blended. Alternatively, once the aubergine pulp has drained, chop finely, mash with a fork, and stir in all the other ingredients until well blended, adding the oil and vinegar alternately. Serve chilled or at room temperature. (Pictured opposite top.)

Serve with: pitta bread, raw vegetables or salty cheeses.

HANDY TIP

Sometimes, aubergines can burst while they are roasted due to a build-up of steam inside the vegetable. Avoid any unnecessary mess in your oven by piercing the skins a few times with a fork so the steam can escape.

Variations

562 WITH ALMONDS

Replace the walnuts with blanched almonds and halve the amount of vinegar.
Serve with: fish such as trout.

563 WITH PINE NUTS

Replace the walnuts with pine nuts and halve the amount of vinegar.
Serve with: grilled or baked chicken.

564 WITH LEMON JUICE

Omit the walnuts and replace the vinegar with 1 ½ tablespoons (23 ml) fresh lemon juice.
Serve with: baked white fish.

565 WITH CORIANDER

Halve the amount of vinegar and omit the walnuts.
Stir about 60 ml finely chopped fresh coriander leaves
into the finished dip.
Serve with: vegetable spring rolls.

566 WITH SOUR CREAM

Omit the walnuts, and add 60 ml sour cream to the food
processor with the aubergine, ensuring the aubergine is
cool. (Pictured centre.)
Serve with: beetroot chips, crisp potato skins, spiced and
roasted sweet potato wedges, crispbreads or breadsticks or
tortilla chips.

567 WITH CHILLI

Halve the amount of vinegar and stir 1 finely chopped
fresh red or green chilli into the finished dip. (Pictured
bottom.)
Serve with: tortilla chips.

568 Classic guacamole

Made with ripe, buttery avocados and tart lime juice, guacamole also has a bit of heat from chillies. Serve it right away, as it can discolour as it sits.

INGREDIENTS

2 large, ripe avocados

3 tbsp (45 ml) fresh lime juice

2 tbsp (30 ml) finely chopped fresh coriander

2 fresh jalapeño peppers, stemmed, seeded, and finely chopped

SERVES 4 to 6

Halve, pit, peel and slice the avocados into a bowl. With a fork, mash the avocados with the lime juice, coriander, and jalapeño until chunky but well blended. (Pictured opposite top.)

Serve with: tortilla chips or use as a garnish.

HANDY TIP

To make sure your avocados are ripe, choose ones that are darker in colour. Hold one in the palm of your hand and squeeze very gently with your fingers. If it yields to the pressure, it's ripe and ready to use.

Variations

569 GRILLED

Halve and pit the avocados, but do not peel. Grill the halves, cut side up, for 2 to 3 minutes or until you have good char marks on the flesh before using them. **Serve with:** pitta bread.

570 SMOKY TOMATO

Add 240 ml chopped fresh tomatoes and 1 teaspoon (5 ml) liquid smoke to the bowl with the lime juice. **Serve with:** barbecued food.

571 WITH LIME AND GARLIC

Add 1 teaspoon (5 ml) minced garlic and an additional 1 tablespoon (15 ml) fresh lime juice. **Serve with:** crudités.

572 EASY GUACAMOLE

Halve and pit the avocados. Scoop the flesh into a bowl, drizzle with the juice of 1 lime, mash with a fork, and add salt to taste.

Serve with: tortilla chips.

573 EXTRA-SPICY MANGO

Add a generous dash or two of hot sauce and the diced flesh of 1 small ripe mango to the mashed avocado. (Pictured centre.)

Serve with: fish or pork tacos, grilled, barbecued or pan-fried fish, chicken or pork.

574 WITH FRESH SWEETCORN

Using a sharp knife, remove the kernels from one ear of fresh, in season, sweet corn and add to the mashed avocado. (Pictured bottom.)

Serve with: nachos, fajitas, tacos or tortilla chips.

575 charred sweetcorn salsa

The secret to this tasty salsa is the hint of smokiness in the lightly blackened, blistered sweetcorn.

INGREDIENTS

3 ears sweetcorn
60 ml sour cream
Juice of 1 lime
1 tsp (5 ml) ground cumin
½ to 1 red jalapeño or Holland
  chilli, seeded and minced
½ small red onion, minced
3 tbsp (45 ml) chopped fresh
  coriander leaves

¼ tsp (1 ml) granulated sugar
Hot sauce
Salt and black pepper

MAKES 560 ml

Balance each of the ears of corn over a gas burner on the cooker grate directly over a medium-high flame. Turn with tongs until they are charred and blistered in spots, 2 to 3 minutes. The corn will pop a little as it chars, so be sure to stand back. Transfer to a plate and leave to cool for a few minutes. Shave off the kernels with a sharp knife and set aside. Discard the cobs.

When completely cool, combine the charred sweetcorn kernels with the sour cream, lime juice, cumin, chillies, red onion, coriander and sugar in a medium bowl and toss gently. Season with hot sauce and salt and pepper to taste. (Pictured opposite top.)

Serve with: nachos or tortilla chips.

HANDY TIP

The easiest way to remove the kernels from a cob is to hold the top with one hand with the tip pressed firmly into the base of a shallow bowl. Use long, downwards strokes to cut the kernels away.

variations

576 WITH QUESO FRESCO

Use 2 ears of sweetcorn instead of 3, and add 140 g crumbled queso fresco cheese.
Serve with: tacos or fajitas, spiced corn crisps or sprinkle over chilli con carne.

577 WITH PEACH

Use 2 ears of sweetcorn instead of 3, and add the diced flesh of 1 large peeled ripe peach. Stir in 1 tablespoon (15 ml) tequila (optional) and let the salsa sit for 30 minutes at room temperature before serving.
Serve with: tortilla chips or nachos, spicy Mexican dishes, or cooked king prawns.

578 WITH AVOCADO

Use 2 ears of sweetcorn instead of 3, and add the diced flesh of 1 small avocado (about 140 g).
Serve with: nachos and tortilla chips.

579 WITH JICAMA

Use 2 ears of sweetcorn instead of 3, and 140 g jicama, peeled and finely chopped or grated. Combine the lime juice with 2 tablespoons (15 ml) orange juice and 1 tablespoon (15 ml) honey before adding to the bowl with the sweetcorn.

Serve with: crackers, nachos, corn crisps or tortilla chips, or fish or chicken tacos.

580 WITH PAPAYA

Replace 1 ear of sweetcorn with 140 g diced, fresh papaya. (Pictured centre.)

Serve with: grilled, pan fried or barbecued fish, chicken or pork, nachos or tortilla chips.

581 WITH CHORIZO

Thinly slice 2 small fresh chorizo sausages and fry or grill until cooked through. When cool, chop into a similar-sized dice as the corn kernels. Use 2 ears of sweetcorn instead of 3, and add the chorizo to the salsa ingredients in the bowl. (Pictured bottom.)

Serve with: grilled or barbecued chicken, steak or pork chops, or in fajitas or burritos.

582 Pineapple Salsa

Golden fresh pineapple makes a delicious salsa.

INGREDIENTS

480 ml chopped fresh pineapple
120 ml chopped fresh coriander
  leaves
1 fresh jalapeño pepper,
  stemmed and seeded

½ tsp (3 ml) crushed red
  pepper flakes
Salt

MAKES 600 ml

Place the pineapple, coriander, jalapeño pepper and red pepper flakes in a blender or food processor. Process until somewhat smooth. Add salt to taste. It will keep, covered, in the fridge for up to 3 days.

Serve with: grilled chicken tacos, fish, shellfish or pork.

HANDY TIP

To bring out the flavours, let the finished salsa sit at room temperature for about 30 minutes before serving.

Variations

583 PANTRY SHELF

Use drained, canned pineapple, in place of fresh.
Serve with: fish tostadas.

584 MANGO

Replace the pineapple with mango. Add lime juice to taste.
Serve with: spicy samosas.

585 WITH STRAWBERRY

Replace 240 ml pineapple with strawberries.
Serve with: smoked or cured ham steaks.

586 Pepita Salsa

Made with *pepitas*, toasted pumpkin seeds, this salsa has a toasty flavour that goes well with grilled foods.

INGREDIENTS

130 g toasted pumpkin seeds (pepitas)

2 cloves garlic

Zest and juice of 1 lime

240 ml chopped fresh coriander

60 ml olive oil

360 ml canned diced tomatoes with green chillies

MAKES about 480 ml

Place all ingredients in a blender or food processor and purée until almost smooth. Keep at room temperature until ready to serve.

Serve with: grilled or barbecued chicken.

HANDY TIP

To toast fresh pumpkin seeds, spread clean, dry seeds in a single layer on a baking tray. Drizzle with 2 tablespoons (30 ml) olive oil, and sprinkle with salt and pepper then toss well. Bake in the oven at 180°C (350°F) for 6 to 8 minutes, until light brown and crisp.

Variations

587 DOCTORED-UP

Instead of the main recipe, blend 50 g toasted pumpkin seeds with 240 ml supermarket-bought pipian (a pumpkin seed mole). Add olive oil, lime juice, canned tomatoes with green chillies and chopped fresh coriander to taste.

Serve with: hamburgers.

588 SPANISH ALMOND

Use toasted sliced almonds in place of pumpkin seeds. Toast 100 g sliced almonds on a baking sheet in a 180°C (350°F) oven until lightly browned; let cool.

Serve with: baked fish or chicken.

589 DOUBLE PUMPKIN SEED

Use 180 ml canned pumpkin in place of 180 ml of the canned tomatoes with green chillies.

Serve with: pork steaks.

590 salsa cruda

Made from raw ingredients, this salsa is perfect with tortilla chips and a margarita or a Mexican beer.

INGREDIENTS

2 cloves garlic, minced
60 ml finely chopped onion
120 ml grated peeled fresh jicama
120 ml finely chopped cucumber
60 ml chopped fresh coriander leaves
450 g firm, ripe red tomatoes, stemmed and chopped

Juice of 2 limes
1 fresh jalapeño pepper, stemmed, seeded, and finely chopped
Salt and pepper

MAKES 480 ml

Combine all ingredients in a bowl. Season to taste and let sit at room temperature until ready to serve. (Pictured opposite top.)

Serve with: tortilla chips.

HANDY TIP

Raw onion can sometimes be harsh and acerbic to eat. To take the bite out of it, and also bring out the more subtle flavours of the onion, soak the whole peeled bulb in a bowl of cold water for 20 minutes, before drying and chopping.

variations

591 FROZEN

Freeze the salsa in a metal bowl, stirring every 30 minutes, until slushy, about 4 hours.
Serve with: chilled, cooked prawns or oysters.

592 GOLDEN

Replace the red tomatoes with yellow tomatoes, and the jalapeño with a yellow pepper. Add ½ teaspoon (3 ml) ground chipotle.
Serve with: baked chicken.

593 TOMATO AND ROASTED TOMATILLO

Roast 225 g fresh tomatillos, de-husked, in an oven at 220°C (425°F) until browned. Once cool, finely chop and add to the rest of the ingredients, adding extra lime juice to taste.
Serve with: nachos, tortilla chips, or fish, chicken or pork.

594 MIXED TOMATOES

Use an assortment of different varieties of fresh tomatoes in place of the red tomatoes.
Serve with: beef burgers.

595 CHERRY TOMATOES

Replace the regular red tomatoes with halved cherry tomatoes. (Pictured centre.)
Serve with: salmon steaks.

596 TOMATO AND AVOCADO

Add the diced flesh of 1 large avocado to the rest of the ingredients. (Pictured bottom.)
Serve with: nachos, toasted tortilla shards, or grilled or barbecued fish, prawns or chicken.

MEAT & SEAFOOD DIPS

597 creamy Salmon Rillettes

The trick to this pretty, rich, pink fish dip is to use a light hand when combining the ingredients. Only gently break up the salmon, without mashing it, so the texture is rough and rustic.

INGREDIENTS

1 small onion, peeled and quartered
1 small carrot, roughly chopped
1 stick celery, roughly chopped
1 bay leaf
½ tsp (3 ml) whole black peppercorns
240 ml dry white wine
Salt
450 g centre-cut, skinless salmon fillet cut into 4 pieces
110 g smoked salmon cut into very fine strips
3 tbsp (45 ml) mayonnaise
3 tbsp (45 ml) crème fraîche
1 tbsp (15 ml) lemon juice, plus more as needed
Black pepper

SERVES 4 to 6

Place the onion, carrot, celery, bay leaf, whole peppercorns and white wine in a saucepan with 560 ml water. Bring to the boil, reduce the heat and simmer gently for 30 minutes.

Season the salmon fillet generously with salt, and add to the saucepan. Poach over very low heat until the fish is barely cooked in the centre, about 6 to 8 minutes. Remove the pan from the heat and leave to stand for 5 minutes before transferring the fish to a plate using a slotted spoon. When the salmon is cool enough to handle, flake it with your fingers, removing and discarding any bones. Transfer the salmon to a medium bowl and leave to cool completely. Discard the poaching liquid.

Add the smoked salmon to the bowl with the flaked fish together with the mayonnaise, crème fraîche, lemon juice and a generous pinch of pepper. Use a fork to gently mix everything together, breaking up the salmon a little. Adjust the salt, pepper and lemon juice to taste.

Serve with: toasted, thinly sliced sourdough bread, rice cakes, seeded crackers, lavash shards or warm blinis.

HANDY TIP

Make this easy-to make dip even easier by using supermarket-bought cooked salmon.

Variations

598 WITH CHIVES

Add 2 ½ tablespoons (38 ml) chopped fresh chives to the flaked salmon and other ingredients in the main recipe.
Serve with: endive and chicory leaves, cherry tomatoes, fennel wedges, raw julienned jicama or fresh bread.

599 WITH FENNEL AND PERNOD

Sauté 1 small shallot, minced, and ½ bulb fennel, finely diced in 2 tablespoons (30 ml) butter until softened and very tender. Leave to cool. Add to the flaked salmon and the rest of the ingredients in the main recipe with 1 tablespoon (15 ml) Pernod (or ouzo or Sambuca).
Serve with: crudités, crackers, whole-grain or white toast.

600 WITH MIXED HERBS

Add ½ tablespoon (8 ml) each of finely chopped fresh chervil leaves, parsley leaves, chives and dill to the flaked salmon.
Serve with: vegetable crisps, cucumber, red pepper and carrot sticks, crackers, crispbreads or pretzels.

601 TARRAGON AND WHOLE-GRAIN MUSTARD

Add 1 tablespoon (15 ml) whole-grain mustard and 1 ½ tablespoons (23 ml) finely chopped tarragon to the bowl with the salmon.
Serve with: rye toast, ciabatta crostini and warm blinis, or use as a sandwich spread.

602 WITH LEMON AND GHERKINS

Add 1 finely diced medium-to-large gherkin and the finely grated zest of 1 lemon to the flaked salmon.
Serve with: pitta bread, a selection of fresh breads and seeded crackers, or use as sandwich spread.

603 WITH HORSERADISH AND CHERVIL

Add 1 ½ tablespoons (23 ml) prepared horseradish and 2 tablespoons (30 ml) finely chopped fresh chervil with the flaked salmon.
Serve with: vegetable crisps, julienned cucumber, red pepper and carrots, radishes, fennel, or fresh and toasted breads.

604 WITH CUCUMBER

Finely dice half a seeded English cucumber and combine with the flaked salmon, together with 2 tablespoons (30 ml) chopped fresh dill.

Serve with: warm blinis, sourdough toast, grilled crostini and fresh baguette.

605 THAI SPICED

Sauté 1 minced large shallot in a little vegetable oil until tender, add 1 tablespoon (15 ml) Thai red curry paste and cook for a further minute. Let the mixture cool to room temperature, then add to the bowl with the flaked salmon together with 2 tablespoons (30 ml) finely chopped fresh coriander leaves.

Serve with: naan and pitta bread, Asian prawns, rice crackers or crudités.

606 SMOKY SALMON AND PRAWNS

Use only 225 g salmon and poach it with 225 g peeled and cleaned raw prawns. Chop the cooked prawns finely and combine with flaked salmon together with ½ teaspoon (3 ml) smoked paprika.

Serve with: seeded crackers, thinly sliced fresh and toasted baguette, crudités.

607 Prawn & Almond Dip

A grown up dip for die-hard seafood fans, this is salty, peppery, tangy and crunchy; what's not to love?

INGREDIENTS

55 g unsalted butter
1 large clove garlic, finely sliced
1 medium shallot, finely minced
350 g raw medium prawns, peeled and cleaned
Salt
1 tsp (5 ml) finely grated lemon zest
3 tbsp (45 ml) lemon juice

½ tsp (3 ml) freshly ground black pepper
2 tbsp (30 ml) chopped or crushed smoked almonds, plus more to garnish
2 tbsp (30 ml) mayonnaise
2 tbsp (30 ml) chopped fresh dill

SERVES 4

Heat the butter in a frying pan over medium-low heat. Add the garlic and shallot and cook until translucent, but not coloured. Increase the heat to medium-high, add the prawns and ½ teaspoon (3 ml) salt. Cook, stirring, for 4 to 5 minutes, until the prawns are opaque and just cooked through. Remove from the heat and leave to cool for about 15 minutes, or until room temperature. Transfer the prawn mixture to a food processor and add the lemon zest, lemon juice and the pepper. Process very briefly so the prawns are well-chopped but not minced to a fine paste. Turn out into a bowl, add the smoked almonds, mayonnaise and dill and stir until thoroughly combined. Adjust the salt to taste. Garnish with extra chopped smoked almonds. (Pictured opposite top.)

Serve with: seeded crackers, crispbreads, rye crackers and toasted sliced onion or poppy seed bread.

HANDY TIP

The smoked almonds add a delicious crunch to this dip, but if you are making this for a nut-free party, it's just as tasty without them.

Variations

608 WITH CRAYFISH

Replace the prawns with 675 g cooked, roughly chopped crayfish. Add to the pan with the cooked shallot and garlic mixture and heat through for 1 to 2 minutes until piping hot. Transfer to the food processor and continue with the recipe as directed.
Serve with: chicory, endive or Romaine lettuce leaves, cheese crackers, pretzel chips and fresh baguette.

609 WITH MUSTARD

Omit the lemon zest and freshly ground black pepper, replace the dill with chopped fresh tarragon and add a rounded 1 teaspoon (5 ml) Dijon mustard with the mayonnaise and almonds.
Serve with: spiced or herbed cheese crackers, seeded crispbread, toast points, rye and multigrain bread.

610 WITH BASIL AND TOASTED PINE NUT

Omit the lemon zest, replace the smoked almonds with chopped toasted pine nuts, and the dill with finely shredded fresh basil leaves.
Serve with: seeded crispbread, rye crackers, crostini or sliced ciabatta and focaccia bread.

611 MEXICAN SPICED AND TOASTED PUMPKIN SEED

Add 1 teaspoon (5 ml) Mexican spice blend and a dash of Hot sauce (if desired) to the pan with the prawns. Omit the lemon zest and ground black pepper, and replace the dill with chopped fresh coriander and the smoked almonds with chopped toasted pumpkin seeds.
Serve with: soft flour and corn tortillas, nachos, corn and tortilla crisps.

612 LIME-CHILLI AND DRY-ROASTED EDAMAME

Replace the lemon zest and juice with lime zest and juice, add 1 tablespoon (15 ml) sweet chilli sauce with the mayonnaise and replace the smoked almonds with lightly crushed dry-roasted edamame. Omit the dill. (Pictured centre.)
Serve with: Asian-style rice and prawn crackers, cheese crackers and seeded crispbreads.

613 WITH SESAME AND WASABI PEAS

Add a drizzle of toasted sesame oil to the chopped prawn mixture with the mayonnaise, replace the smoked almonds with lightly crushed wasabi peas and omit the freshly cracked pepper and dill. (Pictured bottom.)
Serve with: Asian-style rice and prawn crackers, spiced cheese crackers, seeded crispbreads, chicory, endive and romaine leaves.

614 Hot Crab Dip

Tasty crabmeat combined with cream cheese and hot horseradish makes a dip that's bound to please.

INGREDIENTS

225 g cream cheese, softened
1 tbsp (15 ml) milk
170-200 g flaked, cooked crabmeat
3 tbsp (45 ml) finely chopped onion
½–1 tsp (3–5 ml) prepared horseradish
½ tsp (3 ml) fine kosher or sea salt

½ tsp (3 ml) black pepper
6 drops hot sauce
1 tsp (5 ml) Worcestershire sauce

SERVES 8

Preheat the oven to 190°C (375°F). Combine all ingredients in a bowl until well blended. Spoon the dip into a baking dish. Bake for 15 minutes or until bubbling. Serve hot.

Serve with: crackers, dark rye bread or toasted baguette.

HANDY TIP

Cooked, ready-picked crabmeat is a convenient, mess-free option. While you can use pasteurized canned crabmeat if fresh isn't available, always opt for the latter when crabs are in season as it tastes inordinately better with a sweet and briny flavour redolent of the sea.

Variations

616 CAJUN SPICED

Add ¼ teaspoon (1 ml) cayenne powder, ½ teaspoon (3 ml) dried thyme, ½ teaspoon (3 ml) dried oregano, ½ teaspoon (3 ml) garlic powder and ¼ teaspoon (1 ml) smoked paprika to the crabmeat.
Serve with: nachos, crispy tortilla shards, corn crisps or toast.

617 WITH RED PEPPER AND HERB

Replace the onion with 60 ml finely chopped red pepper, and add 1 tablespoon (15 ml) each chopped fresh parsley leaves chives to the crab mixture.
Serve with: toasted pitta or flatbread, baguette or toasted whole-grain bread.

618 WITH BACON

Cook 2 to 3 rashers of bacon until crisp, then drain on kitchen paper and crumble into small pieces when cool enough to handle. Add to the rest of the ingredients.
Serve with: crackers, crispy potato skins or toasted sourdough bread.

615 WITH MUSTARD AND GREEN ONION

Replace the onion with 2 finely sliced green onions and the horseradish with 1 teaspoon (5 ml) Dijon mustard.
Serve with: toasted baguette, crackers and bread.

619 WITH CHORIZO AND CORIANDER

Finely dice 55 g cured and smoked chorizo sausage and add it to the crabmeat with 2 tablespoons (30 ml) chopped fresh coriander leaves.
Serve with: garlic crostini or pumpernickel toast.

620 PRAWNS

Replace the crab with small canned prawns, drained.
Serve with: crackers or sliced, toasted baguette.

621 CRAB RANGOON DIP

Replace the onions with 2 finely chopped green onions, the horseradish with 1 minced garlic clove, the Hot sauce with ½ teaspoon (3 ml) soy sauce and the black pepper with ground white pepper, and reduce the Worcestershire sauce to ½ teaspoon (3 ml).
Serve with: fried wontons.

622 CURRIED PRAWNS

Replace the crab with small canned prawns, drained, the onion with chopped green onions, and the horseradish and Worcestershire sauce with 1 teaspoon (5 ml) curry powder.
Serve with: papadums, crackers or flatbreads.

623 CRAB-STUFFED MUSHROOMS

Spoon the dip into 450 g cleaned mushroom caps. Arrange the stuffed mushrooms on a cookie sheet and bake in the oven at 190°C (375°F) for 15 minutes, or until bubbling.
Serve with: salad.

624 Smoked Mackerel Pâté

Serve this quick appetizer with salad for a formal dish.

INGREDIENTS

200 g smoked mackerel fillets, skinned
120 ml plain Greek yoghurt
Black pepper
Juice of ¼ to ½ a lemon
Chopped fresh parsley to garnish

SERVES 2

Put the fish and yoghurt in a food processor, season with black pepper, and process to a paste. Transfer to a bowl and stir in lemon juice to taste. Garnish with parsley.

Serve with: wholewheat toast.

HANDY TIP

For a fancier alternative, use hot-smoked salmon.

625 WITH PAPRIKA

Add 2 chopped garlic cloves and 1 teaspoon (5 ml) smoked paprika with the rest of the ingredients.
Serve with: toasted multi-grain and rye bread.

626 WITH TARRAGON

Add the finely grated zest of 1 lemon and 2 teaspoons (10 ml) chopped fresh tarragon. Garnish with tarragon.
Serve with: sourdough bread, seeded crispbreads.

627 WITH HERBS

Add 1 teaspoon (5 ml) toasted, crushed fennel seeds, and ½ tablespoon (8 ml) each chopped fresh chives, chervil and dill to the mixture.
Serve with: crudités, toast or crackers.

628 Bagna cauda

In its native Piedmont, Italy, the name of this dish translates to 'hot bath'. It is traditionally served fondue-style with crudités.

INGREDIENTS

180 ml olive oil
55 g unsalted butter

10 anchovy fillets
5 large garlic cloves
Salt and black pepper

SERVES 4 to 6

Heat the oil and butter in a small saucepan over medium heat. When the butter has melted add the anchovies and the garlic, reduce the heat to low and cook gently for 10 minutes until the garlic is tender and golden, stirring occasionally. Pour the mixture into a food processor or blender and blend until you have a smooth purée. Season with salt and pepper. Transfer to a fondue pot, or a small, flame proof, preheated ceramic bowl to keep warm.

Serve with: crudités.

HANDY TIP

Don't be alarmed if the dip separates when you serve it; it's supposed to. Simply give it a stir, or leave it as is.

Variations

629 TRUFFLED BAGNA CAUDA

Just before serving, drizzle some truffle oil into the dip.
Serve with: raw or lightly grilled portabello mushrooms, blanched asparagus and broccolini and vegetable crudités.

630 WITH HERBS

Stir ½ tablespoon (8 ml) each finely chopped fresh parsley, chervil and tarragon, and ½ teaspoon (3 ml) freshly grated lemon zest into the dip just before serving.
Serve with: baby potatoes, grilled fennel wedges, small chicory, endive and Romaine lettuce leaves, and crudités.

631 MEDITERRANEAN STYLE

Stir 2 tablespoons (30 ml) finely minced pitted black olives and 2 tablespoons (30 ml) finely shredded fresh basil leaves into the finished dip.
Serve with: crudités.

632 Beef Rendang Dip

This is based on a curry from Indonesia and Malaysia.

INGREDIENTS

SPICE PASTE
½ medium shallot, chopped
1 tbsp (15 ml) chopped ginger
1 stalk lemongrass, 5 cm
  (2 inches) from the lower white
  bulb, chopped
2 large cloves garlic, chopped
½ tsp (3 ml) ground turmeric
1 tsp (5 ml) paprika
3 dried red chillies, soaked in hot
  water for 15 minutes until soft,
  then chopped

DIP
1 tbsp (15 ml) vegetable oil
½ medium onion, chopped
1 cinnamon stick

1 star anise
3 cardamom pods, crushed
300 g ground beef
240 ml thick coconut milk
  (see Handy Tip)
Rounded 1 tsp (5 ml)
  tamarind concentrate
1 ½ tsp (8 ml) soft dark-brown
  sugar
½ tbsp (8 ml) soy sauce
2 dried or fresh Asian lime
  leaves
Salt
Freshly squeezed lime juice
2 tbsp (30 ml) chopped fresh
  coriander leaves

SERVES 4 to 6

Put the paste ingredients in a food processor and blend until smooth; add water to bring it together. Set aside.

Heat the oil in a saucepan, add the onion, cinnamon, star anise and cardamom and cook until the onion softens. Stir in the paste and cook, stirring occasionally, until thick and fragrant. Add the beef and cook, stirring, until browned. Add the coconut milk, tamarind, sugar, soy sauce, lime leaves and ½ teaspoon (3 ml) salt. Bring to the boil, then simmer for 25 minutes or until thick and there's a layer of oil on the surface. Remove from the heat, add lime juice and adjust the salt to taste. Discard the whole spices and lime leaves, and stir in the coriander.

Serve with: Asian rice crackers, warm pitta or crudités.

HANDY TIP

For thick coconut milk, leave a can for an hour or two so that the thick, creamy component rises to the top. Spoon out enough of the thick creamy layer as you need.

Variations

633 WITH LAMB

Replace the ground beef with ground lamb.
Serve with: chicory and endive leaves, rice cakes or crackers, bread or warm pitta.

634 WITH SWEET POTATO

Add 1 small or half a medium-sized peeled and diced sweet potato to the pan with the meat mixture 15 minutes before the end of the cooking time. Cook until tender.
Serve with: spiced crackers, crispbreads or pitta, crudités.

635 WITH PEAS

Add 110 g frozen peas to the pan 5 to 10 minutes before the end of the cooking time.
Serve with: Asian rice crackers, warm flatbreads such as pita and naan, or crudités.

636 chilli con carne Dip

This dip needs little introduction. It tastes just like the original, only you can eat it with your fingers!

INGREDIENTS

2 tbsp (30 ml) olive oil
1 medium yellow onion, finely chopped
2 cloves garlic, minced
1 tsp (5 ml) paprika
1 tsp (5 ml) ground cumin
¼ tsp (1 ml) cayenne
340 g minced beef
1 (425 g) can chopped tomatoes
2 tbsp (30 ml) tomato purée
½ tsp (3 ml) dried oregano
Pinch sugar
Salt
½ (425 g) can kidney beans, drained and rinsed
2 tbsp (30 ml) finely chopped fresh coriander leaves
Sour cream, to serve

SERVES 6

Heat the oil in a pan over medium heat. Add the onion and cook, stirring, until softened. Stir in the garlic, paprika, cumin and cayenne and cook for 2 to 3 minutes. Increase the heat, add the beef and cook, stirring, until browned.

Add the chopped tomatoes, tomato purée, oregano, sugar and ½ teaspoon (3 ml) salt and bring to the boil. Reduce the heat, cover the pan and simmer for 20 minutes, stirring occasionally. Add the kidney beans and cook for 5 to 10 minutes, until the dip is thick and rich (add a little water if it becomes too dry.) Adjust the salt to taste, remove from the heat, then stir in the coriander. Leave to stand for at least 15 minutes to allow the flavours to fuse before serving with sour cream.

Serve with: nachos, corn crisps, toasted tortilla shards, or soft tacos.

HANDY TIP

When browning the beef, be sure to cook it over high heat to achieve an even golden-brown sear on the crumbled ground meat; this will ensure plenty of rich flavour in the finished chilli.

Variations

637 WITH CHICK PEAS

Replace the kidneys beans with canned, drained and rinsed chick peas.
Serve with: nachos, corn crisps, soft corn and flour tortillas, or warm flatbreads.

638 WITH SOUR CREAM

Stir 2 to 3 tablespoons (30 to 45 ml) sour cream into the dip until combined.
Serve with: tortilla and corn crisps, or small chicory, endive and Romaine lettuce leaves.

639 EXTRA-SPICY

Increase the cayenne to ¾ teaspoon (4 ml), and for a real kick, stir in a couple of dashes of hot sauce into the finished dip.
Serve with: corn and tortilla crisps and spicy nachos, soft flour or corn tortillas or warm flatbreads.

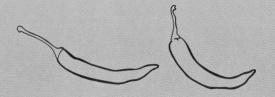

640 THREE-BEAN CHILLI

Combine red and white kidney beans and pinto beans to make a total of 250 g and use in place of the kidney beans.
Serve with: soft corn or flour tortillas, seasoned nachos, corn or tortilla crisps, or crispy potato skins.

641 WITH RED WINE

Add 70 ml red wine to the pan with cooked beef and simmer for 5 minutes until the wine is reduced by at least half, before adding the chopped tomatoes and the other ingredients.
Serve with: fresh sliced sourdough bread, ciabatta and crusty white bread, or with corn and tortilla crisps.

642 WITH CHOCOLATE

Stir 2 squares, very dark chocolate (preferably 85% cacao) to the saucepan with the chopped tomatoes.
Serve with: spicy nachos, corn crisps, soft tortillas or fresh sourdough bread.

643 SMOKY BEEF AND BACON

Replace ½ teaspoon (3 ml) regular paprika with ½ teaspoon (3 ml) smoked paprika, and mix 2 to 3 rashers of smoked bacon, cooked until crisp and crumbled, into the dip about 2 minutes before you remove it from the heat.
Serve with: beef burgers, hot dogs, nachos or spicy tortilla crisps.

644 WITH A HOT CHEESE TOPPING

Transfer the finished dip to an ovenproof casserole dish and top evenly with 85 g grated Cheddar cheese. Place under a hot grill until bubbly and golden.
Serve with: fresh bread, soft corn or flour tortillas, seasoned nachos, corn and tortilla crisps or crispy potato skins.

645 WITH A CRUNCHY CHEESE TOPPING

Combine a large handful of roughly crushed potato crisps with 55 g grated Parmesan cheese and 2 tablespoons (30 ml) melted and cooled butter. Transfer the finished dip to an ovenproof casserole dish, sprinkle over the cheese and crisps topping and cook under a hot grill for a few minutes until golden brown.
Serve with: fresh bread, soft corn or flour tortillas, seasoned nachos, or corn and tortilla crisps.

646 Spinach & Sausage Dip

There are few dishes containing spinach that are considered a rare treat. This dip is one of them.

INGREDIENTS

1 ½ tbsp (23 ml) olive oil

1 small yellow onion, finely chopped

½ red pepper, finely diced

1 clove garlic, minced

225 g spicy or sweet Italian-style sausages, removed from their casings and crumbled

1 (425 g) can chopped tomatoes, drained

1 tsp (5 ml) chopped fresh oregano

120 ml dry white wine

170 g frozen spinach, defrosted, squeezed dry and chopped

Generous 85 g cream cheese

2 tbsp (30 ml) sour cream

Salt and pepper

SERVES 4

Heat the oil in a large frying pan over medium heat. Add the onion and cook for about 3 to 4 minutes until softened. Add the red pepper and the garlic and cook until the pepper is very tender. Push the vegetables to one side of the pan and add the sausage meat. Cook, stirring and breaking up the sausage with a wooden spoon until browned, crumbly and cooked through. Combine the sausage with the onion and pepper mixture and add the tomatoes, oregano and wine. Cook until the tomatoes break down and the mixture is thick with the wine almost completely evaporated.

Add the cream cheese and crème fraîche and stir until melted. Add the chopped spinach and cook for 2 to 3 minutes until the spinach is piping hot. Season with salt and pepper to taste, then remove the pan from the heat. Serve hot. (Pictured opposite top.)

Serve with: crispy potato skins, corn and tortilla crisps, bagel chips and fresh or toasted baguette and ciabatta.

Variations

647 WITH ARTICHOKE

Replace the spinach with 170 g defrosted and chopped frozen artichoke hearts.
Serve with: fresh or toasted crusty white bread, ciabatta or focaccia bread, tortilla or corn crisps.

648 WITH PINTO BEANS

Add half the quantity of pinto beans from a 425 g can (drained and rinsed) to the pan with the chopped spinach.
Serve with: soft corn and flour tortillas, nachos and corn and tortilla crisps.

649 WITH FRESH CHORIZO

Replace the Italian sausage with fresh chorizo sausage.
Serve with: soft corn and flour tortillas, nachos, and corn and tortilla crisps.

650 WITH MERGUEZ SAUSAGE

Replace the Italian sausage with fresh merguez lamb sausage.
Serve with: warm pitta and other Mediterranean flatbreads.

651 WITH MUSHROOM

Replace the spinach with 200 g chopped brown mushrooms which have been sautéed with a little butter, salt and plenty of black pepper. (Pictured centre.)
Serve with: crackers, warm baguette, ciabatta or multi-grain bread.

652 WITH LENTILS

Add half the quantity of green lentils from a 425 g can (drained and rinsed) to the pan with the chopped spinach. (Pictured bottom.)
Serve with: crusty white, whole-grain and ciabatta bread, warm Mediterranean flatbreads or crispy potato skins.

653 Chicken Liver Pâté

Smooth, rich chicken liver pâté is irresistible and perfect for parties as it can be made in advance.

INGREDIENTS

120 g butter
2 garlic cloves, crushed
400 g chicken livers, trimmed and chopped
2 tbsp (30 ml) brandy
½ tsp (3 ml) fresh thyme leaves
Salt and ground black pepper

SERVES 4 to 6

Melt one-quarter of the butter in a small nonstick pan and cook the garlic gently for 1 minute. Add the chicken livers and cook for about 5 minutes, until browned, then place them in a food processor, with all the pan juices. Add the remaining butter, brandy and thyme, and process until smooth. Season to taste with salt and pepper and transfer to a bowl. Cover and chill for at least 2 hours or until firm.

Serve with: toasted baguette or sourdough bread.

HANDY TIP

When preparing the chicken livers, be sure to remove and discard any tough, sinewy parts or greenish bits as they can make the finished pâté taste bitter. If you have some extra time, and want to ensure that your pâté is creamy and sweet with no hint of bitterness, soak the livers in 480 ml each of milk and water with 2 teaspoons (10 ml) of salt for 1 hour. Drain and rinse the livers well before using.

Variations

654 WITH DUCK LIVERS

Replace the chicken livers with duck livers.
Serve with: toasted brioche and caramelized onion chutney.

655 WITH SHERRY

Replace the brandy with sherry.
Serve with: wholewheat toast.

656 WITH CHIVES

Stir 1 tablespoon (15 ml) chopped fresh chives into the pâté before chilling.
Serve with: rye crispbreads.

Enjoy a classic chicken liver pâté with crackers instead of breads

657 WITH OREGANO

Replace the thyme with oregano.
Serve with: toasted ciabatta.

660 WITH CAPERS

Add 1 tablespoon (15 ml) rinsed capers and 1 teaspoon (5 ml) anchovy paste to the food processor with the rest of the ingredients.
Serve with: toasted pumpernickel and sourdough bread, and whole grain crackers.

658 WITH MARSALA

Replace the brandy with 2 ½ tablespoons (38 ml) marsala.
Serve with: toast points, garlic-rubbed toasted baguette slices, or wedges of country-style bread.

661 WITH BOURBON AND ROSEMARY

Replace the brandy with bourbon, and the thyme with 2 teaspoons (10 ml) chopped fresh rosemary leaves.
Serve with: seeded crackers and crispbreads, fresh and toasted sliced baguette and warm pitta bread.

659 WITH BALSAMIC ONION

Sauté 1 thinly sliced, small yellow onion in butter and a generous pinch of soft dark-brown sugar until softened and golden, about 20 minutes. Add a splash of balsamic vinegar and cook for 2 to 3 minutes longer. Add to the food processor with the chicken livers.
Serve with: toasted sourdough bread, crispbreads and crackers.

662 WITH APPLE AND SAGE

Cook 1 diced, peeled and cored Granny Smith apple with the chicken livers, until the apple is tender and the livers browned. Process with the rest of the ingredients and 1 tablespoon (15 ml) roughly chopped fresh sage leaves.
Serve with: garlic-rubbed crostini, toasted sourdough fingers and whole-grain crackers.

663 Buffalo Chicken Dip

A tribute to Buffalo wings; this version combines all the flavours of the original dish in a decadent dip.

INGREDIENTS

225 g cream cheese
110 ml whole milk
½ rotisserie chicken, skin discarded and meat finely shredded (should yield about 250 g meat)
85 g finely minced celery

2 green onions, finely sliced
2 to 4 tbsp (30 to 60 ml) hot sauce
70 g crumbled blue cheese

SERVES 6 to 8

Preheat the oven to 210°C (400°F).

Place the cream cheese and milk in a medium saucepan and cook over medium-low heat, stirring, until the mixture is smooth and piping hot. Remove from the heat, and add the chicken, celery, green onion and hot sauce and stir to combine everything thoroughly.

Transfer the mixture to a round baking dish and sprinkle the blue cheese over the top. Bake until hot, bubbly and golden brown, about 20 minutes. Leave to rest for 5 to 7 minutes before serving. (Pictured opposite top.)

Serve with: carrot, celery and cucumber sticks as well as with soft corn and flour tortillas and sliced fresh or toasted crusty white bread.

HANDY TIP

Different brands of hot sauce can vary significantly in strength, so it's best to add the condiment 1 or 2 tablespoons (15 to 30 ml) at a time, tasting as you go, to ensure you hit just the right amount of heat.

Variations

664 BARBECUE

Use 1 tablespoon (15 ml) of hot sauce, and add 3 tablespoons (45 ml) of your favourite barbecue sauce to the dip before baking.
Serve with: crispy potato skins, crudités, corn and tortilla crisps, cheese crackers and sliced fresh bread.

665 WITH SMOKED SAUSAGE

Add 140 g diced smoked sausage to the chicken and cream cheese mixture.
Serve with: fresh crusty bread, crackers, corn and tortilla crisps, or crudités.

666 TEX MEX

Reduce the hot sauce to ½ tablespoon (8 ml); add 2 teaspoons (10 ml) Mexican spice blend and ½ small red pepper, finely minced, to the cream cheese and chicken mixture; and replace the blue cheese with grated Monterey Jack or Pepper Jack cheese.
Serve with: soft flour and corn tortillas, spicy nachos, corn and tortilla crisps and crudités.

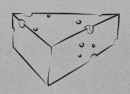

667   FIERY CHIPOTLE AND BACON CHICKEN DIP

Omit the hot sauce in the main recipe and add 3 slices cooked, crispy bacon, crumbled, and 1 to 2 finely minced canned chipotle chillies in adobo sauce, plus ½ tablespoon (8 ml) of the adobo sauce to the chicken and cream-cheese mixture.

Serve with: crispy potato skins, corn and tortilla crisps.

668   WITH CURRY

Sauté 1 medium onion with 8 dried curry leaves (optional) in 2 tablespoons (30 ml) vegetable oil or ghee (clarified butter, see page 14). When the onion is soft, add 1 rounded tablespoon (15 ml) curry powder and cook for a minute. Add to the chicken and cream-cheese mixture. (Pictured centre.)

Serve with: crudités, papadums and warm flatbreads such as naan and pitta.

669   WITH CHEDDAR CHEESE

Replace the blue cheese with grated Cheddar cheese. (Pictured bottom.)

Serve with: crispy potato skins, crudités, or corn and tortilla crisps.

CREAMY CHEESE, BEAN & LENTIL DIPS

670 Hummus

Hummus is one of the best-known and most popular Middle Eastern dips. Served with fresh or toasted pitta bread, hummus makes a great snack or appetizer.

INGREDIENTS

400 g canned chickpeas or garbanzo beans
60 ml water or vegetable stock (see page 17)
3 to 5 tbsp (45 to 75 ml) lemon juice (depending on taste)
1 ½ tbsp (23 ml) tahini
2 cloves garlic, crushed
½ tsp (3 ml) salt
1 to 2 tbsp (15 to 30 ml) olive oil
Chopped fresh parsley, to garnish

SERVES 4 to 6

Drain the chickpeas, reserving liquid from the can. Combine the chickpeas, water or stock, lemon juice, tahini, garlic and salt in a blender or food processor. Add 60 ml of the reserved liquid from the chickpeas. Blend for 3 to 5 minutes on low speed until the mixture is smooth.

Transfer to a serving bowl, create a shallow well in the centre using the back of a spoon, and pour olive oil into it. Serve immediately garnished with chopped parsley. If preferred, cover and refrigerate until required and add the oil and parsley garnish just before serving.

Serve with: warm or toasted pitta bread, marinated artichokes.

HANDY TIP

To make this entirely from scratch, start with dried chickpeas. First rinse and place 125 g dried chickpeas in a bowl. Soak the chickpeas overnight in 8 cm (3 inches) of cold water and ½ tbsp (8 ml) baking soda. The next day, rinse and drain, then place the chickpeas in a saucepan with another 8 cm (3 inches) of cold water. Bring to a boil, then reduce the heat and simmer very gently – adding more water to keep the beans submerged, if necessary, for 2 to 2 ½ hours, or until the chickpeas are tender. Drain and use.

variations

WITH CUMIN

Prepare the hummus, omitting the tahini. When it is smooth and creamy, add 1 teaspoon (5 ml) ground cumin.
Serve with: raw vegetables.

WITH KALAMATA OLIVES

Stir a handful of chopped, pitted Kalamata olives and a large pinch of dried oregano into the finished hummus. Omit the parsley garnish.
Serve with: barbecued meats.

WITH ARTICHOKE

Place the chickpeas and tahini in the food processor with one 1 (400 g) can artichoke hearts (drained). Slowly blend in lemon juice, garlic and olive oil. If it is too thick, gradually add water or vegetable stock. Season with salt and pepper.
Serve with: tortilla crisps.

WITH TOASTED PINE NUTS

Toast 3 tablespoons (45 ml) pine nuts in a dry frying pan until golden and fragrant and stir into the finished dip.
Serve with: toasted pitta, carrot and celery sticks, sugar snap peas and cherry tomatoes.

WITH ROASTED GARLIC

Mix the chickpeas, water or stock, lemon juice and salt in blender or food processor. Omit the tahini and raw garlic but add 6 cloves of roasted garlic (for instructions see pages 90 and 164), olive oil and ½ teaspoon (3 ml) dried oregano. Add extra olive oil, ½ teaspoon (3 ml) at a time, if the hummus is too thick.
Serve with: raw vegetables.

WITH ROASTED BROCCOLI

Toss the trimmed florets of half a head of broccoli in olive oil, salt and pepper and roast in a 200°C (400°F) oven for 40 minutes until golden brown. Leave to cool, then roughly chop. Add to the food processor or blender with the chickpeas.
Serve with: lavash, pitta and other flatbreads and raw and blanched vegetable crudités.

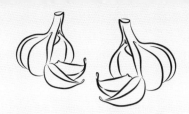

WITH MIXED HERBS

Add 1 tablespoon (15 ml) each roughly chopped fresh parsley, coriander and basil leaves to the food processor or blender with the chickpeas.

Serve with: toast points, sesame crackers, whole-grain crackers, and raw and blanched vegetable crudités.

SPICY RED PEPPER

Roughly chop 2 jarred whole roasted peppers and add to the food processor or blender with a generous pinch dried chilli flakes and ¼ teaspoon (1 ml) paprika with the chickpeas.

Serve with: crudités, warm flatbreads, rye crackers and other crisp biscuits, as well as cooked cocktail sausages.

WITH HORSERADISH

Add 1 ½ tablespoons (23 ml) prepared horseradish to the food processor with the chickpeas.

Serve with: crudités, crispbreads, rice cakes, poached or grilled, tail-on prawns, in a steak or roast beef sandwich.

680 Edamame & Tofu 'Hummus' Dip

This quirky take on traditional hummus has a rich, sweet almost pea-like flavour.

INGREDIENTS

255 g frozen edamame
170 g silken tofu, drained
1 large clove garlic, chopped
½ tsp (3 ml) ground cumin
¼ tsp (1 ml) ground coriander
¼ tsp (1 ml) onion powder
Pinch chilli flakes
3 tbsp (45 ml) extra-virgin olive oil
2 tbsp (30 ml) lime juice, plus more as needed
Salt and black pepper

SERVES 6 to 8

Bring a saucepan of water to a boil. Add the edamame, bring back to a boil and cook for 4 to 6 minutes until tender. Drain, and run under cold running water for 20 seconds or until cold. Place the edamame in a food processor with the tofu, garlic, cumin, coriander, onion powder, chilli, olive oil, lime juice, ½ teaspoon (3 ml) salt and ¼ teaspoon (1 ml) pepper. Process until blended. Adjust salt, pepper and lime juice to taste.

Serve with: whole-grain toast, sesame crispbreads, rice crackers or crudités.

HANDY TIP

Silken tofu brings a creamy texture to dips without adding calorie-laden ingredients such as sour cream.

variations

682 WITH SESAME

Add 1 teaspoon (5 ml) sesame oil with the rest of the ingredients to the food processor. Serve garnished with toasted sesame seeds.
Serve with: Asian-style rice crackers, crusty white bread, Melba toast and crudités.

683 WITH SPICED PEPITAS

Preheat oven to 190°C (375°F). Toss 65 g raw pumpkin seeds with 1 teaspoon (5 ml) olive oil, and ¼ teaspoon (1 ml) each salt, paprika and ground coriander. Spread in a single layer on a baking sheet and bake for 5 minutes or until golden brown. Cool, then scatter over the dip.
Serve with: tortilla crisps and warm pitta bread.

684 WITH TOASTED PECANS

Scatter 55 g pecans on a baking sheet and bake in the oven at 190°C (375°F) for 5 to 8 minutes until toasted. Cool, then finely chop and stir into the finished dip.
Serve with: fresh or toasted slices of rye, walnut or olive breads, sesame crispbreads and crudités.

681 WITH THYME

Add 2 teaspoons (10 ml) fresh thyme leaves to the food processor with the rest of the ingredients.
Serve with: flatbreads, vegetable crisps and rice cakes.

685 WITH LEMON AND TARRAGON

Replace the lime juice with lemon juice. Add the grated zest of a large lemon and 1 tablespoon (15 ml) chopped tarragon leaves with the rest of the ingredients.
Serve with: grilled asparagus wrapped in prosciutto, endive and romaine leaves, rice cakes and crispbreads.

WITH CHEESE

Add 3 tablespoons (45 ml) finely grated Parmesan cheese with the rest of the ingredients.
Serve with: corn and tortilla crisps, vegetable crisps, breadsticks, fresh and toasted sliced baguette, and crudités.

WITH SMOKED PAPRIKA

Replace the regular paprika with ½ tsp (3 ml) smoked paprika.
Serve with: sesame crispbreads, black pepper crackers, rice cakes and crudités.

WITH TAHINI AND PARSLEY

Add 1 tablespoon (15 ml) tahini and 2 tablespoons (30 ml) chopped fresh parsley leaves with the other ingredients to the food processor.
Serve with: warmed or grilled pitta bread or other flatbreads, crispbreads, bread sticks and crudités.

WITH FIVE-SPICE

Replace the cumin and coriander with 1 rounded teaspoon (5 ml) five-spice powder.
Serve with: Asian-style rice and prawn crackers, steamed Chinese pancakes, crudités and supermarket-bought fried Chinese bread sticks (*youtiao*).

690 Cannellini & Pesto Dip

Whet the appetite by serving this creamy bean dip.

INGREDIENTS

368 g canned cannellini beans, drained and rinsed
1 garlic clove, crushed
¼ tsp (1 ml) dried chilli flakes

3 ½ tbsp (53 ml) basil pesto
2 tbsp (30 ml) olive oil
1 tsp (5 ml) lemon juice, to taste

SERVES 4

Process the beans, garlic, chilli, pesto and oil in a food processor to a smooth purée. Add lemon juice to taste.
Serve with: crudités.

HANDY TIP

Cannellini beans are very popular in Italian cooking. If you can't find them, substitute with navy beans.

KIDNEY BEAN AND RED PESTO

Replace the cannellini beans with kidney beans and the green pesto with red pesto.
Serve with: tortilla crisps.

WITH COURGETTE

Slice 1 courgette and steam for 5 minutes, until tender. Add to the food processor with the beans.
Serve with: pitta bread.

WITH RED PEPPER

Add 2 bottled roasted red peppers with the beans.
Serve with: breadsticks.

694 Mexican Three-Layer Dip

It's questionable whether Mexicans eat this dish but it's a must-have at any party.

INGREDIENTS

½ yellow medium onion, finely chopped
1 ½ tbsp (23 ml) olive oil
1 large garlic clove, minced
½ to 1 jalapeño chilli, seeded and minced
½ tsp (3 ml) ground cumin
½ tsp (3 ml) ground coriander
¼ tsp (1 ml) cayenne
½ tsp (3 ml) paprika

425 g canned pinto beans, rinsed and drained
110 ml chicken stock (see page 16)
Salt
2 tbsp (30 ml) lime juice
255 g supermarket-bought guacamole
85 g shredded Cheddar cheese

SERVES 4

Cook the onion in the oil in a frying pan until softened. Add the garlic and spices and cook, stirring, for 2 minutes. Stir in the beans, stock and ¼ teaspoon (1 ml) salt and simmer for 5 to 7 minutes, stirring. Using a potato masher, squash the beans into a thick paste. Stir in the lime juice, adjust the salt to taste, remove from the heat, and leave to cool. When at room temperature, spread into the base of a small serving bowl, cover with the guacamole, then sprinkle the Cheddar over the top, and serve.

Variations

695 FOUR-LAYER

Add a layer of sour cream, about 230 g, before sprinkling over the cheese.
Serve with: cheese crackers, tortilla and corn crisps, spiced nachos, vegetable crisps and crudités.

696 FIVE-LAYER

Sauté the kernels from 2 ears of sweetcorn in butter until tender. Stir in 2 tablespoons (30 ml) chopped fresh coriander leaves and season with hot sauce and salt. Leave to cool completely, then add the corn to the dip in an even layer over the guacamole and beneath the sour cream.
Serve with: warm corn and flour tortillas, corn crisps, nachos, crispbreads and crudités.

697 FIVE-LAYER SPICED BLACK BEAN

Prepare the **Four-Layer Dip**, making a second layer of beans using 425 g canned black beans instead of the pinto beans. Place the black beans in the bottom of the bowl, top with guacamole, pinto beans, supermarket-bought tomato salsa then sour cream. Garnish with grated cheese.
Serve with: warm corn and flour tortillas, corn chips, spiced nachos, tortilla chips, vegetable chips and crudités.

698 French Green Lentil Dip

This unassuming lentil dip packs a powerful punch of flavour, and is remarkably healthy

INGREDIENTS

2 tbsp (30 ml) olive oil
½ small onion, finely chopped
2 large cloves garlic, minced
½ small carrot, peeled and finely chopped
½ small rib celery, finely chopped
2 sprigs thyme
1 bay leaf
80 ml dry white wine
170 g French green lentils, well-rinsed

Salt and black pepper
450 ml hot chicken or vegetable stock, (see pages 16 and 17), plus more as needed
1 tsp (5 ml) Dijon mustard
2 tsp (10 ml) red wine vinegar, plus more as needed
110 ml extra-virgin olive oil

SERVES 4

Heat the 2 tablespoons (30 ml) of olive oil in a saucepan. When hot, add the onion, garlic, carrot, celery, thyme and bay leaf. Cook, stirring occasionally, until the vegetables are soft. Add the wine and simmer until the wine has almost completely evaporated. Add the lentils, stock, ½ teaspoon (3 ml) salt and a generous pinch pepper. Simmer gently, covered, adding more stock if needed, until the lentils are tender. Remove from the heat and discard the thyme and bay leaf. Stir in the mustard and vinegar.

Transfer to a food processor and add the extra-virgin olive oil. Blend to a smooth purée, adding up to 60 ml hot water if the mixture is too thick. Adjust the seasoning and the vinegar to taste.

Serve with: fresh or toasted baguette, garlic-rubbed crostini, walnut and olive bread, or crudités.

HANDY TIP

French green lentils are the most delicately flavoured of all their brethren. But for the crème de la crème, opt for Puy lentils, which are known as the caviar of lentils.

Variations

WITH HERBS

Add ½ tablespoon (8 ml) each chopped fresh tarragon, parsley and chervil to the food processor with the lentils.
Serve with: crudités, crackers, crispbreads and baguette.

WITH BACON

Cook 30 g (1½ ounces) diced smoked bacon in a frying pan until crisp and all the fat has rendered. Pour away and discard all but 1 tablespoon (15 ml) of the fat. Prepare the lentils in the bacon fat, using just 1 tablespoon (15 ml) olive oil. Blend the cooked bacon with the lentil mixture in the food processor.
Serve with: fresh multigrain bread, toasted walnut bread and crudités.

WITH BACON AND CREAM

Prepare the **French Green Lentil and Bacon Dip**, making sure the lentil and bacon mixture is completely cool before transferring to the food processor and blending to a purée with 2 to 3 tablespoons (30 to 45 ml) crème fraîche.
Serve with: crudités, vegetable crisps, crackers and crispbreads.

702 Indian Lentil Dip

If you've ever enjoyed *dal* at an Indian meal, you know exactly what this lentil dip is about; hearty, full of earthy, spicy flavour and undeniably addictive.

INGREDIENTS

1 ½ tbsp (23 ml) vegetable or rapeseed oil
1 small onion, finely chopped
2 cloves garlic, minced
2 cm (¾-inch) piece ginger, minced or grated
Pinch turmeric
¼ tsp (1 ml) ground cumin
1 tsp (5 ml) curry powder

140 g moong dal (hulled and split mung bean lentils), washed and drained
2 small plum tomatoes (or 1 large), peeled, seeded and chopped
2 tbsp (30 ml) chopped fresh coriander leaves
Salt

SERVES 6

Heat the oil in a medium saucepan over medium heat. When hot add the onion and cook, stirring, for 3 to 4 minutes until the onion is softened and golden. Add the garlic and ginger and cook for a minute longer. Stir in the spices, and after 2 minutes, add the moong dal. Pour in 675 ml water, add the chopped tomato and ½ teaspoon (3 ml) salt, then bring the mixture to a boil. Reduce the heat and simmer the lentils for 40 to 50 minutes, stirring every now and then, and pressing down with the back of a spoon or a potato masher to break down lentils to a thick purée. Season to taste with salt, stir in the coriander leaves and serve warm.

Serve with: naan, pitta and chapatti breads, papadums or crudités.

HANDY TIP

This is a thick dip with some texture. For a smooth purée, transfer the cooked, mashed lentils (before adding the coriander leaves), to the food processor and process until creamy and smooth. Stir in the coriander before serving.

Variations

703 WITH CARROT

Add 1 small, peeled and diced carrot to the lentils 10 minutes before the end of the cooking time. Simmer until the carrot is tender and the lentils have broken down completely.
Serve with: flatbreads, Romaine and endive leaves, chicken and fish fingers or vegetable fritters.

704 WITH AUBERGINE

Add 1 small, diced, baby aubergine to the lentils 10 to 15 minutes before the end of the cooking time. Cook until the lentils have broken down completely and the aubergine is tender.
Serve with: flatbreads, spiced crackers or crispbreads.

705 WITH CRÈME FRAÎCHE

Serve with crème fraîche spooned over the top.
Serve with: vegetable crisps, crudités, papadums and flatbreads.

Serve a simple lentil dip with spiced crackers and crisp lettuce leaves

WITH SPINACH

Defrost 140 g frozen spinach, squeeze dry and finely chop. Add to the lentils 5 minutes before the end of the cooking time. Simmer until the spinach is piping hot.
Serve with: crudités, vegetable crisps, corn and tortilla crisps and flatbreads such as pitta and naan.

WITH LEEK

Add 1 small leek, halved lengthwise and thinly sliced into crescents, to the pan with the onion. Cook until the leek is tender and the onion softened and golden before adding the garlic and ginger.
Serve with: warm naan, pitta or chappati flatbreads, crudités and vegetable crisps.

WITH FRIED ONIONS

Stir 2 tablespoons (30 ml) supermarket-bought fried onions into the finished dip and serve with a little extra fried onions sprinkled over the top.
Serve with: sliced fresh crusty white bread, warm flatbreads, spiced and herbed crackers and crudités.

WITH MINCED LAMB

Sauté 110 g minced lamb in a little vegetable oil, seasoned with salt and pepper and ¼ teaspoon (1 ml) each ground cumin, ground coriander and garlic powder until well-browned. Stir into the finished lentil dip before serving.
Serve with: corn and tortilla crisps, warm flatbreads, or crusty white and multigrain breads.

WITH SWEET POTATO

Add half a medium diced, sweet potato to the lentils 10 to 15 minutes before the end of the cooking time. Cook until the lentils have broken down and the potato is tender.
Serve with: tortilla and corn crisps, papadums, warm flatbreads and crudités.

EXTRA SPICY

Add ¼ to ½ teaspoon (1 to 3 ml) cayenne powder to the pan with the rest of the ground spices before adding the moong dal.
Serve with: crudités, warm flatbreads and breadsticks, chicken and fish fingers and vegetable fritters.

712 Tomato, Black Pepper & Feta Dip

A bold dose of coarsely crushed black pepper elevates this dip to something special.

INGREDIENTS

½ to ¾ tsp (3 to 4 ml) black peppercorns
110 g crumbled feta cheese
3 tbsp (45 ml) extra-virgin olive oil
225 g Greek yoghurt

85 g minced drained sun-dried tomatoes, packed in oil
1 clove garlic, minced
2 tbsp (30 ml) chopped fresh parsley leaves
Salt

SERVES 4

Crush the peppercorns until coarsely ground using a pestle and mortar. Set aside. Combine the feta, olive oil and yoghurt in a bowl and mix well, mashing the cheese with a fork until a thick paste forms. Stir in the tomatoes, garlic, parsley, crushed peppercorns and a scant ½ teaspoon (3 ml) salt. (Pictured opposite top.)

Serve with: pretzel and bagel chips, crostini, crudités.

HANDY TIP

Try to use sun-dried tomatoes packed in oil, rather than those that are dry-packed since the former are more tender and juicy. If you have some of the dry-packed variety you need to use up, soak them in hot water for 15 minutes first.

Variations

714 WITH GREEN ONIONS

Add 2 finely chopped green onions to the bowl with the tomatoes and the other ingredients.
Serve with: blanched asparagus wrapped in prosciutto, baby potatoes, broccolini and tomatoes, or crispbreads.

715 WITH PESTO

Add 2 tablespoons (30 ml) jarred pesto with the tomatoes. (Pictured centre.)
Serve with: crackers, rice cakes or crispbreads, olive and walnut breads, or cooked, cooled pasta for a pasta salad.

716 WITH PROSCIUTTO

Add 45 g finely chopped prosciutto with the tomatoes and the other ingredients. (Pictured bottom.)
Serve with: crudités, toasted olive and plain focaccia.

717 WITH SMOKED ALMONDS

Prepare the **Tomato, Black Pepper and Feta Dip**, adding 2 tablespoons (30 ml) chopped smoked almonds with the tomatoes.
Serve with: crackers, bread sticks and crudités.

713 WITH GOAT'S CHEESE

Replace the feta cheese with soft goat's cheese.
Serve with: crackers, breadsticks, focaccia and ciabatta bread or crudités.

718 WITH WALNUTS

Make the **Tomato, Smoked Almond and Feta Dip**, replacing the smoked almonds with chopped walnuts.
Serve with: seeded crackers or bread.

719 Queso al Horno

This Mexican baked cheese appetizer is served hot.

INGREDIENTS

1 large onion, chopped
1 ½ tbsp (23 ml) vegetable oil
2 fresh, large tomatoes, peeled, seeded, and coarsely chopped
4 to 6 fresh jalapeño peppers, stemmed, seeded, and diced
¼ tsp (1 ml) ground dried chipotle chilli

Salt
900 g grated Monterey Jack cheese
1 small, whole jalapeño pepper, to garnish

SERVES 10 to 12

Sauté the onion in the oil until soft. Add tomatoes and jalapeños and cook until soft. Season with chipotle and salt. Preheat oven to 180°C (350°F). Place cheese in a 25-cm (10-inch) round dish 3.5 cm (1 ½ inches) deep. Spread tomato mixture onto the centre to a 15-cm (6-inch) diameter. Bake for 25 to 30 minutes. Garnish with the jalapeño.

Serve with: tortilla crisps.

HANDY TIP

Substitute Muenster or Gouda for the Monterey Jack.

WITH CHICKEN

Garnish with 125 g chopped cooked chicken.
Serve with: pitta bread.

WITH SHREDDED PORK

Garnish with 125 g shredded pork.
Serve with: crusty bread.

WITH CHORIZO

Garnish with 125 g cooked, crumbled chorizo.
Serve with: celery sticks.

723 Baked Cheesy Artichoke & Spinach Dip

Hefty amounts of iron-rich spinach and artichoke hearts make this cheesy dip seem almost virtuous.

INGREDIENTS

1 large shallot, minced

1 ½ tbsp (23 ml) olive oil

1 large garlic clove, minced

½ green jalapeño chilli, seeded and minced

½ tsp (3 ml) fresh thyme leaves

Salt and black pepper

200 g jarred artichoke hearts, drained and thinly sliced

255 g frozen spinach, defrosted, squeezed dry and finely chopped

2 tbsp (30 ml) lemon juice

3 tbsp (45 ml) good-quality mayonnaise

110 g cream cheese, softened

140 g sour cream

155 g grated pecorino cheese

SERVES 6

Preheat the oven to 220°C (425°F).

Cook the shallot in the oil in a medium frying pan over medium heat, until softened and golden. Add the garlic, chilli and thyme and cook for 1 minute. Season with a pinch of salt and pepper, and remove from the heat. Transfer to a bowl and combine with the artichokes, spinach, lemon juice, mayonnaise, cream cheese, sour cream and all but 42 g of the pecorino cheese. Season with ½ teaspoon (3 ml) salt and ½ teaspoon (3 ml) black pepper. Transfer to a round baking dish and sprinkle the remaining pecorino over the top. Bake for 25 to 30 minutes. Leave to rest for at least 5 minutes before serving.

Serve with: baguette, country and multigrain bread, corn crisps, endive and fennel.

HANDY TIP

Squeeze out as much of the excess water from the spinach as possible, otherwise the dip will be too wet.

Variations

724 WITH CHIPOTLE

Replace the jalapeño chilli with 1 chipotle chilli (from a can of chipotle in adobo sauce), finely minced, and add to the bowl with the artichokes and the rest of the ingredients. Add a little of the adobo sauce as well, if desired.
Serve with: corn and flour tortillas, nachos.

725 WITH GRUYÈRE

Replace the pecorino cheese with grated Gruyère.
Serve with: crispbreads, ciabatta, crostini, or crudités.

726 WITH FOUR CHEESES

Replace the pecorino cheese with a mixture of grated Asiago, pepper jack and mozzarella cheese.
Serve with: black pepper crackers, whole-grain crackers, crostini and crudités.

727 Roasted Fennel & Mascarpone Dip

Sweet, mellow and buttery, roasted fennel is one of the most underrated culinary feats, in my opinion. Here, it is combined with unctuous mascarpone cheese and piquant sherry vinegar.

INGREDIENTS

1 large bulb fennel [(about 675 g to 785 g), trimmed of stalks, quartered and cut into 5 mm (¼-inch) slices, fronds reserved]

2 tbsp (30 ml) olive oil

Salt and black pepper

6 tbsp (90 ml) mascarpone cheese

1 ½ tbsp (23 ml) sherry vinegar

SERVES 4 to 6

Toss the fennel slices with the olive oil in a large bowl, and season generously with salt and pepper. Transfer to a roasting pan and bake until soft and golden brown, 50 minutes to an hour. Leave to cool to room temperature. Meanwhile, chop the reserved fennel fronds to make up 3 to 4 tablespoons (45 to 60 ml).

Place the cooled, roasted fennel in a food processor with the mascarpone, sherry vinegar, ½ teaspoon (3 ml) salt and ¼ teaspoon (3 ml) pepper and blend until smooth. Adjust seasoning and stir in the chopped fennel fronds.

Serve with: rye bread, toasted baguette, ciabatta or Irish soda bread, crudités or grilled prawns.

HANDY TIP

Be sure not to discard the fennel stems and leftover fronds; add them to a pot of stock together with the usual vegetables such as carrots, onions and celery (see page 17).

Variations

WITH BACON

Cook 2 rashers of bacon until browned and crisp. Drain on kitchen paper, and crumble well. Stir into the fennel purée before transferring to the baking dish.
Serve with: bread, crackers and flatbreads.

WITH WALNUTS

Add 2 to 3 tablespoons (30 to 45 ml) coarsely chopped walnuts to the food processor with the roasted fennel.
Serve with: crudités, breadsticks, fresh and toasted whole-grain bread, cocktail sausages and grilled prawns.

WITH BLUE CHEESE AND CHIVES

Add 25 g crumbled blue cheese to the main recipe, and stir 1 tablespoon (15 ml) finely chopped fresh chives into the fennel purée.
Serve with: celery and carrot sticks, spicy Buffalo-style chicken wings.

731 Caramelised onion & goat's cheese Dip

Slow-cooked onions are blended with creamy goat's cheese and enlivened with lemon and oregano.

INGREDIENTS

2 tbsp (30 ml) butter
1 tbsp (15 ml) olive oil
2 large onions
Salt and black pepper
1 tsp (5 ml) granulated sugar
110 g sour cream

140 g soft goat's cheese
2 tsp (10 ml) roughly chopped fresh oregano
1 tbsp (15 ml) lemon juice

SERVES 4 to 6

Melt the butter and olive oil in a frying pan. Add the onions and ¼ teaspoon (1 ml) each salt and pepper and cook, stirring, until soft. Stir in the sugar and cook over a medium-low heat, stirring, until golden brown and soft, 30 to 40 minutes. Leave to cool to room temperature. Transfer to a food processor and add the sour cream, goat's cheese, oregano, lemon juice and ½ teaspoon (3 ml) salt, and blend until smooth. Season to taste.

Serve with: lightly grilled vegetables, breadsticks and olive or sun-dried tomato crostini.

HANDY TIP

Caramelising onions is a labour of love: keep the heat low, and stir every now and then so they don't stick to the pan.

Variations

733 WITH BALSAMIC VINEGAR

Add 2 tablespoons (30 ml) balsamic vinegar to the pan with the sugar and omit the lemon juice.
Serve with: crudités, crispbreads and fresh or toasted whole-grain, rye or sourdough bread.

734 WITH CHIVES

Replace the oregano with 2 to 3 tablespoons (30 to 45 ml) chopped fresh chives.
Serve with: sliced baguette, ciabatta or focaccia bread, breadsticks and crispbreads.

735 WITH ROSEMARY

Replace the oregano with chopped fresh rosemary leaves.
Serve with: crudités, crusty bread and crackers.

732 WITH THYME

Replace the oregano with fresh thyme.
Serve with: herb-flavoured breads, crackers or crudités.

736 WITH MASCARPONE

Replace the goat's cheese with mascarpone.
Serve with: seeded crackers, sesame crispbread and multi-grain bread or baguette.

WITH RICOTTA

Replace the goat's cheese with ricotta cheese.
Serve with: olive or sun-dried tomato crostini, sliced fresh or toasted sourdough or ciabatta bread, crudités.

WITH HORSERADISH

Add 1 ½ tablespoons (23 ml) prepared horseradish to the food processor with the rest of the ingredients.
Serve with: celery and cucumber sticks, endive and small romaine leaves, seeded crispbreads and crackers.

WITH WHOLE-GRAIN MUSTARD

Add 1 to 2 tablespoons (15 to 30 ml) whole-grain mustard to the food processor with the rest of the ingredients.
Serve with: sweet potato chips, roasted baby potatoes and butternut squash, crudités, multigrain or rye bread.

WITH NEUFCHÂTEL

Replace the goat's cheese with Neufchâtel cheese.
Serve with: crudités, baguette, crostini and grissini.

741 Olive Dip

This Italian-inspired dip is ideal for an elegant party.

INGREDIENTS

45 g pine nuts
200 g whole-milk ricotta
100 g pitted green olives, finely chopped
2 tbsp (30 ml) olive oil
Pinch dried chilli flakes

Finely grated zest of 1 lemon
1 ½ tbsp (23 ml) lemon juice
3 tbsp (45 ml) chopped parsley
Salt and pepper

SERVES 4

Toast the pine nuts in a frying pan, chop or crush, then combine with the other ingredients. Season to taste.

Serve with: crackers, crostini, baguette or crudités.

HANDY TIP

To crush the pine nuts, place in a freezer bag and pound with a rolling pin.

WITH STUFFED OLIVES

Replace the pitted green olives with pimento-stuffed olives.
Serve with: olive and sun-dried tomato crostini, bread.

WITH BASIL

Replace the parsley with a handful of shredded basil.
Serve with: crispbreads, crudités, chicken fingers.

WITH PISTACHIOS

Replace the pine nuts with roasted shelled pistachio nuts.
Serve with: crackers, crudités, chicken and fish fingers.

OIL & VINEGAR DRESSINGS

745 Classic Vinaigrette

If you ask for a salad in France, you will be given a bowl of mixed-green salad leaves – no cucumber, no tomatoes, and no croutons or cheese – tossed in a vinaigrette.

INGREDIENTS

180 ml extra-virgin olive oil
60 ml good-quality
   white wine vinegar
Salt and black pepper

SERVES 5 to 6

Place all the ingredients in the blender and process for 30 seconds, until a creamy emulsion forms. Taste, adjust the seasoning with salt and pepper, and add more vinegar 1 to 2 teaspoons (5 to 10 ml) at a time, to taste.

Serve with: a green salad.

HANDY TIPS

This is best made fresh, but it will keep for a few days covered in the fridge. To use, bring to room temperature, and whisk briefly. If you do not have a blender, you can whisk the ingredients in a bowl, or shake in a jar. You could also use any light neutral-flavoured oil, such as rapeseed.

Variations

746 HONEY-MUSTARD

Add 1 rounded teaspoon (5 ml) Dijon mustard and 2 teaspoons (10 ml) clear honey.
Serve with: potato or green salads, cold smoked fish.

748 CITRUS

Replace the white wine vinegar with lemon juice.
Serve with: seafood or waxy potato salads.

747 SPICY

Replace the olive oil with chilli oil, and add ½ a finely-chopped fresh chilli at the end.
Serve with: Thai-style beef salad.

749 WALNUT-MUSTARD

Replace half the olive oil with walnut oil, and add 1 rounded teaspoon (5 ml) Dijon mustard.
Serve with: salad niçoise.

750 WITH SMOKED PAPRIKA

Add 1 teaspoon (5 ml) smoked paprika.
Serve with: cold roasted peppers or hot cooked pasta.

753 CITRUS BASIL

Add 1 teaspoon (5 ml) lemon juice and 60 ml freshly chopped basil leaves to the blender with the other ingredients. After blending, add 1 chopped shallot and blend again until it is completely incorporated.
Serve with: a tomato or a green salad.

751 SPICY SESAME

Add 1 teaspoon (5 ml) toasted sesame seeds to the **Spicy Vinaigrette**.
Serve with: bresaola, cold noodle or prawn salad.

754 LEMON POPPY SEED

Add 1 teaspoon (5 ml) fresh lemon juice and 1 to 2 tablespoons (15 to 30 ml) poppy seeds to the blender with the main ingredients.
Serve with: grilled meat and a green salad.

752 WITH FRENCH MUSTARD AND DILL

Add 1 rounded teaspoon (5 ml) Dijon mustard and 1 teaspoon (5 ml) of freshly chopped dill.
Serve with: braised leeks and salmon salad.

755 Red onion, Mint & Cucumber Vinaigrette

This punchy dressing has all the flavours of summer.

INGREDIENTS

¼ red onion, finely diced

¼ cucumber, seeded and finely diced

2 tsp (10 ml) red wine vinegar

2 tbsp (30 ml) olive oil

Pinch of sugar

Salt and ground black pepper

2 tsp (10 ml) chopped fresh mint

SERVES 2

Put the onion and cucumber in a small bowl and cover with the vinegar and oil. Sprinkle with the sugar and season with salt and pepper, then stir to combine. Fold in the mint and season to taste.

Serve with: oysters.

HANDY TIP

For a mess-free method of seeding a cucumber, slice it in half, lengthwise, then working with a half at a time, hold the cucumber over the trash can and use a teaspoon to scrape all the way down the centre, scooping out the seeds directly into the trash.

Variations

756 WITH SHALLOT AND TARRAGON

Replace the red onion with ½ finely chopped shallot and the mint with tarragon.
Serve with: grilled chicken.

757 WITH TOMATO

Replace the cucumber with 1 finely chopped, seeded tomato.
Serve with: roast or pan-fried fish fillets.

758 WITH GREEN ONION AND CHILLI

Replace the red onion with 2 finely chopped green onions, and add a good pinch of dried chilli flakes.
Serve with: barbecued meats.

759 Raspberry Vinaigrette

Vibrantly coloured, and bursting with bright berry flavours, this honeyed piquant dressing is sure to win over the most ardent salad-haters!

INGREDIENTS

45 g (about 12) fresh raspberries
1 tbsp (15 ml) lime juice
2 tbsp (30 ml) raspberry vinegar
1 tbsp (15 ml) honey
85 ml extra-virgin olive oil
Salt and black pepper

MAKES 170 ml

Place the raspberries, lime juice, vinegar, honey and olive oil in a blender with ¼ teaspoon (1 ml) salt and a generous pinch of pepper and blend until smooth. Adjust salt and pepper to taste.

Serve with: green or mixed salads, cold-poached or baked salmon, and grilled or poached prawns.

HANDY TIP

Depending on how sweet or tart the raspberries you use are, you might need to tweak the amount of lime juice or vinegar and honey. This dressing will keep in the fridge, stored in an airtight container, for 3 days. Whisk dressing or shake jar or container well before using.

Variations

760 WITH RED WINE VINEGAR AND PINK PEPPERCORNS

Replace the raspberry vinegar with red wine vinegar, and add a rounded ¼ teaspoon (1 ml) crushed pink peppercorns in place of regular black pepper.
Serve with: mixed mesclun leaves, wilted greens, blanched or steamed green beans, grilled prawn salad.

761 WITH TARRAGON

Add 1 to 1 ½ tablespoons (15 to 23 ml) chopped tarragon leaves to the ingredients in the blender.
Serve with: baby spinach, rocket and watercress or a roasted duck and chicken breast salad.

762 WITH CAYENNE AND MAPLE SYRUP

Replace the honey with 1 tablespoon (15 ml) maple syrup and add a generous pinch of cayenne to the blender with the rest of the ingredients.
Serve with: mixed greens, baby spinach and rocket, or raw shredded kale salads.

Fruit vinegars will add zing to a simple salad dressing

763 STRAWBERRY LEMON

Replace the raspberries with chopped, ripe strawberries, and the lime juice with lemon juice, and add 1 teaspoon (5 ml) finely grated lemon zest to the blender with the rest of the ingredients.
Serve with: steamed green beans, mixed-green salad, goat's cheese and rocket salad.

764 STRAWBERRY PECAN

Make the **Strawberry Lemon Vinaigrette**, adding 1 ½ tablespoons (23 ml) chopped, toasted and cooled pecans to the finished dressing.
Serve with: chopped chicken and avocado salad, mixed-green salad, chopped turkey, avocado and tomato salad.

765 WITH WALNUT

Replace 1 tablespoon (15 ml) of olive oil with 1 tablespoon (15 ml) walnut oil, and add 1 ½ tablespoons (23 ml) chopped, toasted walnuts to the finished dressing.
Serve with: sliced avocado, mixed greens, baby spinach and watercress or rocket salads.

766 SPICED

Add ¼ to ½ teaspoon (1 to 3 ml) allspice to the blender with the rest of the ingredients.
Serve with: mango, spinach and watercress or green salad.

767 WITH ORANGE

Add 1 teaspoon (5 ml) finely grated orange zest and 3 tablespoons (45 ml) orange juice that has been simmered and reduced to 1 tablespoon (15 ml), then cooled, to the blender.
Serve with: endive and orange, spinach and berry salad or mixed-green and chopped feta salads.

768 WITH ONION AND POPPY SEED

Add 1 teaspoon (5 ml) finely grated onion to the blender with the rest of the ingredients. Whisk ½ teaspoon (3 ml) poppy seeds into the finished dressing.
Serve with: crudités, or spinach and chopped peach salad.

769 Warm Bacon Vinaigrette

This is the ideal dressing for a cold-weather salad – warm and rich with tangy red wine vinegar. Top off your dressed greens with crisp, crumbled bacon.

INGREDIENTS

4 rashers of unsmoked bacon, diced
1 small shallot, minced
2 ½ tbsp (38 ml) red wine vinegar
1 tsp (5 ml) honey
1 tsp (5 ml) Dijon mustard
60 ml extra-virgin olive oil
Salt and black pepper

MAKES 100 ml

Cook the bacon in a small frying pan over medium heat, stirring occasionally, until crisp and browned. With a slotted spoon, transfer the bacon to a plate lined with kitchen paper. Pour off all but 2 tablespoons (30 ml) of the hot bacon fat in the frying pan. Add the shallot and cook, stirring occasionally, until softened, about 3 minutes. Remove from the heat and whisk in the vinegar, honey and mustard. Scrape the bottom of the frying pan with a spoon to dislodge any stuck-on browned bits. Transfer the mixture to a bowl, then gradually whisk in the olive oil until the dressing is emulsified and thickened. Season with salt and pepper. (Pictured opposite top.)

Serve with: steamed green vegetables, baby spinach, red mustard leaves, and radicchio, potato salad or roasted sweet potatoes.

HANDY TIP

Dice your bacon straight out of the fridge – chilled bacon is nice and firm making it easier to chop.

Variations

770 WITH MAPLE BACON

Replace the honey with 1 ½ tablespoons (23 ml) maple syrup, and increase the Dijon mustard to 1 teaspoon (5 ml).
Serve with: tomato and avocado; apple, mixed-leaf and walnut; or green salads.

771 WITH FRESH HERB

Stir 1 tablespoon (15 ml) chopped fresh chives and 1 tablespoon (15 ml) chopped fresh parsley into the finished dressing.
Serve with: mesclun greens; spinach, orange and watercress; or endive salads.

772 WITH CHORIZO AND SHERRY

Make the **Warm Chorizo Vinaigrette**, replacing the red wine vinegar with sherry vinegar.
Serve with: a tomato or endive and orange salad, or wilted greens.

773   SMOKY BACON

Use smoked bacon and add ¼ teaspoon (1 ml) smoked paprika with the honey and mustard. For an extra smoky flavour, add a drop of natural liquid smoke.
Serve with: a spinach and steak or chicken salad, a Cobb salad, or mashed root vegetables.

774   WITH CHILLI

Add ½ to 1 minced seeded red jalapeño chilli with the shallot. (Pictured centre.)
Serve with: roasted butternut squash or sweet potato chunks, steamed or blanched greens, or a mixed salad.

775   WITH CHORIZO

Replace the bacon with 110 g diced chorizo sausage prepared in the same way as in the main recipe. (Pictured bottom.)
Serve with: a spinach and mixed mesclun green salad, cooked green beans, or blanched or roasted asparagus.

776 champagne, Walnut & grape Vinaigrette

If you're looking for a unique dinner-party-worthy vinaigrette, look no further. This fruity, complex dressing is a cinch to put together but tastes like you laboured for hours. Use champagne vinegar if you can – it really does add a special flavour.

INGREDIENTS

FOR THE GRAPES
½ tbsp (8 ml) olive oil
85 g red seedless grapes
2 tbsp (30 ml) honey
Salt

FOR THE DRESSING
1 ½ tbsp (23 ml) champagne
  vinegar
1 small clove garlic, crushed
2 tbsp (30 ml) extra-virgin
  olive oil
60 ml walnut oil
Salt and black pepper

MAKES 170 ml

Preheat oven to 220°C (425°F). Combine the grapes with the honey, sherry vinegar and a pinch of salt in a small roasting pan. Roast for 10 to 12 minutes, stirring once, until soft and juicy but not collapsed. Remove from the pan using a slotted spoon and set aside. Pour the juices from the pan in a small bowl and add the vinegar and garlic. Whisk to combine, then slowly drizzle in the oils, whisking all the time, until emulsified. Season with salt and pepper. Stir in the roasted grapes and serve warm or at room temperature.

Serve with: fresh herbs and mesclun salad leaves such as lamb lettuce, mizuna, radicchio and rocket.

HANDY TIP

Choose a red grape variety such as Red Flame that has a sweet flavour with a firm, crunchy texture so that, when roasted, the fruit maintains its shape.

Variations

777 BALSAMIC

Replace the champagne vinegar with aged balsamic vinegar.
Serve with: a simple green salad; mixed mesclun greens, crumbled blue cheese and crouton salad; and a grilled steak and spinach salad.

778 WITH HAZELNUT AND SHERRY VINEGAR

Substitute hazelnut oil for the walnut oil, and sherry vinegar for the champagne vinegar.
Serve with: steamed or blanched snow peas, green beans or mixed mesclun greens.

779 WITH TARRAGON

Use white grapes instead of red, omit the walnut oil and using 60 ml olive oil. Add 1 tablespoon (15 ml) chopped fresh tarragon leaves to the finished dressing.
Serve with: a spinach and watercress; mesclun greens; rocket; or lamb lettuce and chopped pecan salads.

780 Classic Italian Dressing

If there's one salad dressing to fit any and every occasion, this is it. Remarkably flexible, it suits just about every salad composition to perfection.

INGREDIENTS

2 ½ tbsp (38 ml) red wine vinegar
¼ tsp (1 ml) dried oregano
Generous pinch dried thyme
1 tbsp (15 ml) chopped fresh
   parsley leaves
Pinch white sugar

1 clove garlic, crushed
Salt and black pepper
85 ml extra-virgin olive oil

MAKES 100 ml

Place the vinegar, oregano, thyme, parsley, sugar and garlic in a small bowl with a ¼ teaspoon (1 ml) salt and a generous pinch of pepper, and briefly whisk to combine. Drizzle in the olive oil, whisking, until the dressing is emulsified. Adjust salt and pepper to taste. It will keep in the fridge, in an airtight container, for 2 days. Whisk dressing or shake container well before using.

Serve with: a mesclun greens, mixed or tomato and red onion salad, or with fusilli or penne pasta for a salad.

HANDY TIP

For a really delicious dressing, invest in a gourmet or artisanal red wine vinegar. The best vinegars are tart but balanced with complex, mellow aftertones.

Variations

781 BALSAMIC

Replace the red wine vinegar with aged balsamic vinegar.
Serve with: pasta, a mixed mesclun greens, radish and cucumber or a Cobb salad.

782 WITH APPLE

Replace the red wine vinegar with apple cider vinegar, and add 1 tablespoon (15 ml) grated, unpeeled Granny Smith apple with the vinegar and other ingredients.
Serve with: chopped Romaine leaves, baby spinach and lamb lettuce or endive, or cooked pasta.

783 WITH ORANGE AND RED ONION

Add 1 tablespoon (15 ml) orange juice that has been simmered, reduced by two-thirds and cooled, to the bowl with the vinegar and other ingredients. Stir ¼ small sweet red onion, very thinly sliced, to the finished dressing.
Serve with: green, pasta, orzo or bulgur wheat salads.

784 WITH PESTO

Add 2 teaspoons (10 ml) supermarket-bought Italian pesto and a squeeze of lemon juice with the vinegar and other ingredients.
Serve with: a green, pasta, Cobb, or chicken and feta cheese salad, or steamed or blanched greens.

785 WITH OLIVES

Add 1 ½ tablespoons (23 ml) minced pitted green olives to the finished dressing.
Serve with: roasted baby potatoes, mashed potatoes, cooked pasta and mixed greens.

786 WITH GORGONZOLA

Add 25 g finely crumbled gorgonzola cheese with the vinegar and the other ingredients.
Serve with: mixed mesclun greens, baby spinach, rocket, butter lettuce and watercress.

787 WITH FRESH HERB

Replace the dried thyme and oregano with 1 teaspoon (5 ml) chopped fresh thyme leaves, 1 teaspoon (5 ml) chopped fresh oregano.
Serve with: mixed-greens salads, as a marinade for chicken, lamb chops and steak.

788 WITH SHERRY

Replace the red wine vinegar with sherry vinegar and add a generous pinch of smoked Spanish paprika with the vinegar and other ingredients.
Serve with: chopped chicken, carrot and celery for a crunchy chicken salad, a tomato and avocado salad, with cooked pasta or orzo and a green salad.

789 WITH TOMATOES

Add 1 small plum tomato, peeled, seeded and finely diced, and replace the parsley with 1 tablespoon (15 ml) finely shredded basil leaves.
Serve with: steamed, roasted or blanched green beans, snow peas and asparagus or mesclun greens.

790 Tomato & Herb Vinaigrette

This is a full-flavoured vinaigrette that adds zing to simply cooked fish.

INGREDIENTS

480 ml coarsely chopped fresh
    or canned plum tomatoes,
    drained
120 ml fresh Italian parsley
60 ml fresh coriander leaves
60 ml fresh mint leaves
2 tbsp (30 ml) fresh oregano
60 ml chopped
    yellow onion
3 peeled garlic cloves
½ tsp (3 ml) cayenne pepper

1 tsp (5 ml) salt
1 tsp (5 ml) freshly ground
    black pepper
80 ml olive oil
80 ml sherry vinegar
60 ml water

MAKES 480 ml

Place all ingredients in a food processor and process until smooth. The vinaigrette is best served the same day but will keep, covered, in the fridge for up to 5 days.

Serve with: any cooked fish or shellfish, or asparagus salad.

HANDY TIP

If you are using fresh tomatoes and prefer a smoother sauce, peel the tomatoes before using. Score the bottoms with a cross and place in a bowl. Cover with just-boiled water, and leave for 1 to 2 minutes, until the skin around the scored cross pulls away. Drain and rinse them under cold running water, then peel away the skin.

Variations

791 WITH LEMON-DILL

Omit the tomatoes and decrease the salt and pepper to ½ teaspoon (3 ml) each. Replace the coriander, mint and oregano with dill and the vinegar with lemon juice.
Serve with: fish or chicken.

792 CHIMICHURRI DRESSING

Omit the tomatoes and decrease the salt and pepper to ½ teaspoon each.
Serve with: grilled meat, particularly beef steaks.

793 SAUCE VIERGE

Replace the vinegar with 60 ml lemon juice, omit the coriander and mint, replace the oregano with basil and add 2 canned anchovy fillets. Process until chopped but not blended. Chill for 2 to 4 hours before use.
Serve with: shellfish and white fish.

794 Miso-Ginger Dressing

Salty, gingery and with a hint of sweetness, this Japanese-inspired dressing is both refreshing and irresistibly addictive. Don't be tempted to use olive oil – it will overwhelm the other ingredients.

INGREDIENTS

60 ml peanut or rapeseed oil

60 ml rice vinegar

1 ½ tbsp (23 ml) mirin (Japanese rice wine)

1 tsp (5 ml) sugar

1 tbsp (15 ml) soy sauce

1 to 1 ½ tbsp (15 to 13 ml) chopped, peeled ginger

1 small garlic clove, chopped

2 tbsp (30 ml) red miso

1 tsp (5 ml) toasted sesame oil

MAKES 140 ml

Combine all the ingredients, beginning with just 1 tablespoon (15 ml) chopped ginger, in a blender, and blend until mixture is smooth. Taste and blend in extra chopped ginger, if desired. The dressing will keep in the fridge, stored in an airtight container, for 2 days.

Serve with: rocket, red mustard leaves, watercress, mixed-greens salads with julienned jicama and carrot, shredded sugar snap peas, thinly sliced red pepper, bean sprouts and blanched edamame; chicken salads; shredded raw kale, cabbage or brussels sprouts.

Handy Tip

Miso is a thick, pungent paste made from fermented soybeans cut with varying amounts of barley, rice and other grains. It comes in three main varieties; white, yellow and red. White miso is made with a large percentage of rice and the end result is a sweet, nutty and nuanced soy flavour. Red miso has the strongest flavour since it is fermented for longer and has a higher percentage of soybeans than the other varieties. If you prefer a more subtle taste, opt for white or yellow miso, which is mild and earthy.

Variations

795 SPICY

Add ½ red jalapeño or Holland chilli, seeded and chopped, to the blender with the rest of the ingredients.
Serve with: a mixed vegetable slaw, roasted aubergine, red peppers or new potatoes, or grated carrot.

796 WITH CHIVE

Add 1 tablespoon (15 ml) finely chopped fresh chives to the finished main recipe.
Serve with: a mixed-vegetable slaw, egg or soba noodles, or a mixed-greens salad.

797 WITH TOASTED SESAME SEEDS

Lightly toast 2 teaspoons (10 ml) sesame seeds in a small frying pan until golden. Set aside. Stir into the finished dressing.
Serve with: grilled or sautéed tofu, egg noodles or mixed greens.

798 WITH WASABI

Add 1 teaspoon (5 ml) wasabi paste to the blender with
the rest of the ingredients.
Serve with: grilled or sautéed chicken and steak, tofu, a
mixed-greens salad or crudités.

799 WITH LIME

Replace 2 tablespoons (30 ml) of the rice vinegar with 2
tablespoons (30 ml) lime juice, and add the finely grated
zest of 1 lime to the blender. Taste the finished dressing,
and add more lime juice, if necessary. (Pictured top.)
Serve with: grilled or sautéed fish and chicken, a Cobb
salad and mixed greens.

800 WITH CARROT

Add 1 peeled and chopped small carrot to the blender with
the rest of the ingredients. Thin the dressing with a little
water, if necessary. (Pictured bottom.)
Serve with: wilted greens, blanched green beans,
cucumber, radish, jicama and iceberg lettuce salad.

801 Rice Vinegar & Sesame Oil Dressing

Rice vinegar (known as rice wine vinegar) is a mild, slightly sweet vinegar made from fermented glutinous rice that is first converted to alcohol and then to vinegar.

INGREDIENTS

120 ml white rice vinegar

28 g fresh ginger, peeled and grated

2 tbsp (30 ml) soy sauce

2 tbsp (30 ml) granulated sugar

2 tsp (10 ml) sesame oil

2 cloves garlic, peeled and crushed

2 green onion bulbs, trimmed and finely chopped

1 tsp (5 ml) chilli powder

MAKES 240 ml

In a bowl, whisk together the rice vinegar, ginger and soy sauce. Beat in sugar until it has dissolved. Stir in the sesame oil, garlic, green onions and chilli powder, and put aside for 1 to 2 hours to allow the flavours to mingle before serving. This dressing keeps well, in a covered container, in the fridge. (Pictured opposite top.)

Serve with: salad and grilled foods.

HANDY TIP

If you can't find rice vinegar, substitute it with apple cider or white wine vinegar with a small pinch of sugar added and diluted with a little water since rice vinegar is less acidic than its western counterparts.

Variations

802 WITH WHITE RADISH

Replace the green onions with 56 g fresh white radish, peeled and grated.
Serve with: poultry as a marinade, or as a dip.

803 WITH LIME

Replace the garlic and green onion with the zest and juice of 1 lime.
Serve with: seafood as a dressing or dip.

804 WITH WASABI

Beat 1 to 2 tablespoons (15 to 30 ml) Japanese hot mustard paste – wasabi – (available in Asian stores) or, alternatively, 1 to 2 tablespoons (15 to 30 ml) powdered mustard combined with 1 tablespoon (15 ml) of water into the dressing.
Serve with: red meat as a marinade before barbecuing, or as a dressing or dip.

805 WITH HONEY

Replace the sugar with 2 tablespoons (30 ml) honey.
Serve with: raw vegetables.

806 WITH CHILLI

Replace the chilli powder with 1 to 2 chillies, seeded and
finely chopped. (Pictured centre.)
Serve with: vegetable spring rolls.

807 WITH ROASTED SESAME SEEDS

Roast 2 tablespoons (30 ml) sesame seeds in a frying
pan until they emit a nutty aroma. Stir most of the seeds
into the dressing, then scatter the rest on top. (Pictured
bottom.)
Serve with: raw vegetables as a dip or dressing.

CREAMY DRESSINGS

808 Classic Caesar Dressing

Don't think great Caesar salad can only be had at restaurants; the dressing is surprisingly simple to make with easily available ingredients.

INGREDIENTS

2 cloves garlic, smashed
Sea salt
5 canned anchovy fillets, packed in oil, drained and finely chopped
1 tsp (5 ml) Worcestershire sauce
Dash hot sauce (optional)
Rounded ½ tsp (3 ml) Dijon mustard
2 tbsp (30 ml) lemon juice, plus more as needed
2 large very fresh egg yolks, lightly beaten
3 tbsp (45 ml) extra-virgin olive oil
5 tbsp (75 ml) rapeseed or vegetable oil
Black pepper

MAKES 155 ml

Place the smashed garlic cloves in a pestle and mortar with a pinch of sea salt and grind to a smooth purée. Add the anchovies and continue to grind until a semi-smooth paste forms. Transfer the mixture to a medium bowl.

Alternatively, grind the cloves with a pinch of sea salt against a chopping board with the flat side of a knife until puréed, then transfer to a bowl with the anchovies. Use a fork or the back of a spoon to mash the anchovies and combine with the garlic paste.

Whisk the Worcestershire, hot sauce (if using), mustard and lemon juice into the mixture in the bowl. Whisk in the egg yolks, then slowly drizzle in the oils, whisking constantly until the dressing is thick, creamy and shiny. Season with pepper, salt, and more lemon juice, if needed, to taste. Use immediately, or store in an airtight container or jar in the fridge for up to 6 hours.

Serve with: whole or chopped Romaine lettuce leaves, plenty of freshly grated or flaked Parmesan cheese and crunchy croutons sautéed in butter. Top with cooked sliced chicken, salmon or prawns, if desired.

HANDY TIPS

If you are worried about using raw fresh egg, especially if you have young, pregnant or elderly diners, opt for pasteurised eggs which are available in many large supermarkets. Alternatively, use this method from food writer Harold McGee to render regular eggs bacteria-free. Combine 2 large egg yolks with 1 ½ teaspoons (23 ml) water and 1 teaspoon (5 ml) fresh lemon juice in a small glass bowl and cover tightly with cling film. Cook on high for 45 seconds, until the mixture bubbles. Stir the mixture then cover and cook again until it bubbles again, about 20 seconds. Let the yolks bubble for 5 seconds, then stir, and leave to cool to room temperature before using.

Variations

 ## WITH LIME

Replace the lemon juice with lime juice, and add the finely grated zest of 1 lime with the lime juice.
Serve with: chopped Romaine leaves, grated Asiago cheese and sourdough croutons.

 ## BALSAMIC

Replace the lemon juice with 2 tablespoons (30 ml) aged balsamic vinegar. Add a squeeze of lemon juice to the finished dressing, if desired.
Serve with: steak or roast beef sandwiches, burgers, or Romaine lettuce with grated Parmesan cheese and ciabatta croutons.

 ## VEGETARIAN KALAMATA OLIVE

Replace the anchovies with 2 to 3 tablespoons (30 to 45 ml) roughly chopped pitted Kalamata olives.
Serve with: chopped or whole Romaine lettuce, crumbled Feta cheese and rye bread croutons.

 ## WITH GHERKINS AND CAPERS AND PARSLEY

Add ½ tablespoon (8 ml) each minced rinsed and drained gherkins and capers and 1 tablespoon (15 ml) chopped fresh parsley to the finished dressing.
Serve with: fish wraps and burgers; crudités; Romaine lettuce, grated Parmesan cheese and French bread croutons.

 ## WITH SHALLOT AND CHIVES

Add 1 tablespoon (15 ml) finely minced shallot with the Worcestershire sauce and other ingredients, and stir 1 tablespoon (15 ml) finely chopped fresh chives into the finished dressing.
Serve with: Romaine lettuce or spinach, grated Parmesan cheese, toasted pine nuts or croutons, and sliced grilled chicken or steak.

 ## EASY CHEESY

Place all the ingredients in the man recipes with 3 tablespoons (45 ml) grated Parmesan cheese in a blender and process until smooth.
Serve with: a mixed green salad or spinach and watercress salad, tomato and red onion salad, grilled asparagus and croutons, or crudités.

CREOLE SPICED

Replace the Dijon mustard with a hot and spicy Creole-style mustard, and add ½ teaspoon (3 ml) smoked paprika, a generous pinch cayenne powder, ¼ teaspoon (1 ml) dried thyme, and ¼ teaspoon (1 ml) dried oregano to the anchovy paste.

Serve with: wraps, sandwiches, chicken or steak fajitas, green salads.

ROASTED GARLIC

Replace the raw garlic with roasted garlic. Place 6 to 8 large unpeeled garlic cloves in a small baking dish, drizzle with olive oil, then pour a couple of tablespoons (about 30 ml) of water over. Cover with foil and bake in the oven at 120°C (250°F) for 45 minutes to an hour, or until very soft. When cool enough to handle, squeeze the cloves from their skins, mash well and use to make the dressing.

Serve with: Romaine lettuce with grated Parmesan or Asiago cheese and multigrain croutons; mixed salads.

SKIP'S EGGLESS

Mash 2 cloves garlic with a pinch of salt to form a paste. Work in the juice of 1 small lemon then add 4 minced anchovies with a pinch of pepper and mash until smooth but with some texture. Stir in 1 teaspoon (5 ml) Dijon mustard, 3 tablespoons (45 ml) grated Parmesan and 1 teaspoon (5 ml) Worcestershire sauce, then gradually whisk in 6 to 7 tablespoons (90 to 105 ml) olive oil until thick and glossy.

Serve with: Romaine lettuce with Parmesan cheese and French bread croutons; a mixed green salad, or crudités.

818 Tarragon Buttermilk Dressing

With its bittersweet, anise flavour, tarragon perfectly complements buttery, sour buttermilk in this elegant dressing. For a special occasion use champagne vinegar, which bears the same crisp and complex flavours as the sparkling wine.

INGREDIENTS

1 clove garlic, well-crushed
1 ½ tbsp (23 ml) champagne
 or white wine vinegar
3 tbsp (45 ml) good-quality
 mayonnaise
½ tsp (3 ml) granulated
 sugar

1 ½ tbsp (23 ml) minced shallot
85 ml buttermilk
1 ½ tbsp (23 ml) finely chopped
 fresh tarragon leaves
Sea salt and black pepper

SERVES 2 to 4

Place the garlic in a small bowl with the vinegar, mayonnaise, sugar and shallots and whisk briefly to combine. Whisk in the buttermilk and season with ¼ teaspoon (1 ml) salt and a generous pinch pepper. Adjust seasoning to taste. The dressing will keep in the fridge, in an airtight container, for 3 to 4 days.

HANDY TIP

The recipe calls specifically for sea salt because the flakes are coarser and more abrasive than table salt. This creates extra friction in the pestle and mortar or between the knife and chopping board, helping to break down the garlic into a paste.

Variations

819 WITH POPPY SEED

Stir 1 teaspoon (5 ml) poppy seeds into the finished dressing.
Serve with: a mixed-greens, grated carrot and chopped tomato, or Cobb salad.

820 MIXED HERB

Use only ½ tablespoon (8 ml) tarragon and add ½ tablespoon (8 ml) each chopped fresh chervil and chopped fresh dill.
Serve with: a mixed green salad, or use as a marinade for chicken breast before grilling or baking.

821 WITH FENNEL SEEDS

Toast ½ teaspoon (3 ml) fennel seeds in a dry frying pan over medium heat until fragrant and slightly darker. Set aside to cool, then roughly crush in a pestle and mortar. Add to the finished dressing.
Serve with: a mixed-greens or chopped chicken, sweet corn and chopped Romaine salad, as a marinade for chicken before grilling or roasting.

WITH ORANGE

Add 1 ½ teaspoons (8 ml) finely grated orange zest with the vinegar, mayonnaise and shallots. If desired, stir 2 tablespoons (30 ml) finely chopped orange segments into the finished dressing.
Serve with: a spinach, sliced fennel and prawn salad, or Bibb lettuce and shredded cabbage.

WITH SWEET ONION AND CHIVE DRESSING

Cook ½ medium onion, finely chopped, in a little olive with a pinch of sugar, over medium-low heat for 15 to 20 minutes, stirring, until dark golden and caramelised. Leave to cool. Replace the shallot with the caramelised onion, and the tarragon with chopped fresh chives.
Serve with: mixed mesclun greens, sliced tomatoes, or baked, grilled or roast chicken.

HONEY MUSTARD AND CHERVIL

Replace the tarragon with chervil, and add 1 ½ teaspoons (8 ml) mild honey mustard to the bowl with the vinegar, mayonnaise and shallots.
Serve with: grilled or roasted asparagus, broccoli and other vegetables, a mixed green salad.

WITH ASIAGO CHEESE AND SHERRY VINEGAR

Omit the tarragon, replace the champagne or white wine vinegar with sherry vinegar, and add 1 ½ to 2 tablespoons (23 to 30 ml) finely grated Asiago cheese with the vinegar.
Serve with: an iceberg lettuce, tomato and bacon; mixed green; or tomato salad.

WITH CUMIN AND CORIANDER

Toast ½ teaspoon (3 ml) cumin seeds in a dry frying pan over medium heat until fragrant and slightly darkened. Set aside to cool, then roughly crush in a pestle and mortar. Replace the tarragon with fresh coriander leaves and add the crushed cumin seeds to the finished dressing.
Serve with: a tomato, cucumber, celery and radish salad; crudités; as a marinade for chicken.

BALSAMIC BASIL

Replace the champagne or white wine vinegar with aged balsamic vinegar and the tarragon with thinly sliced fresh basil leaves.
Serve with: a tomato; Bibb lettuce and tomato; rocket and thinly sliced red onion; or sweet corn, iceberg lettuce and fennel salad.

828 Creamy Maple-Mustard Dressing

Elevate a bowl of mixed greens, or boiled new potatoes to dizzying heights of deliciousness with this tasty sweet and tangy dressing.

INGREDIENTS

2 ½ tbsp (38 ml) maple syrup

2 tbsp (30 ml) whole-grain mustard

3 tbsp (45 ml) apple cider vinegar

1 tbsp (15 ml) lemon juice

3 tbsp (45 ml) crème frâiche

110 ml olive oil

Salt and black pepper

MAKES 225 ml

Add all the ingredients to a blender with ½ teaspoon (3 ml) salt and ¼ teaspoon (1 ml) pepper and blend until creamy, smooth and thoroughly combined. The dressing will keep in the fridge, stored in an airtight container or jar, for 1 week.

Serve with: raw or blanched shredded green cabbage, brussels spouts, kale or grilled broccoli and cauliflower florets, a mixed green salad and boiled new potatoes.

HANDY TIP

If you can't find crème frâiche, substitute with sour cream. The main difference between these two tangy dairy products is that sour cream has a lower fat content since it is made with single cream to which a bacterial culture is added. Crème frâiche, on the other hand, is similarly cultured but made with cream with a higher fat content resulting in a thicker, richer end product.

Variations

WITH WALNUT AND TARRAGON

Replace the olive oil with walnut oil and add 1 tablespoon (15 ml) finely chopped fresh tarragon leaves to the finished dressing.
Serve with: watercress, baby spinach or rocket, served alone or with salmon or chicken.

WITH ORANGE

Add 1 teaspoon (5 ml) finely grated orange zest with the maple syrup and vinegar, and stir 2 to 3 tablespoons (30 to 45 ml) chopped fresh orange segments into the finished dressing.
Serve with: a sliced beef salad with watercress, or a mixed-greens salad.

WITH SHALLOT AND CHIVE

Add 1 rounded tablespoon (15 ml) finely minced shallot with the maple syrup, and 1 tablespoon (15 ml) finely chopped fresh chives to the finished dressing.
Serve with: crushed or roasted new potatoes, a mixed green salad with chicken or salmon.

832 Russian Salad Dressing

Despite the name of this dressing, it was actually invented in the American state of New Hampshire! Its name is probably due to the fact that the original early 20th-century recipe contained caviar – an ingredient commonly associated with Russia.

INGREDIENTS

110 ml good-quality mayonnaise

3 tbsp (45 ml) tomato ketchup

1 tsp (5 ml) Worcestershire sauce

Dash Hot sauce

2 tbsp (30 ml) sweet relish or finely chopped sweet piccalilli

1 ½ tbsp (23 ml) chopped fresh dill

Salt and black pepper

MAKES 170 ml

Combine all the ingredients in a bowl with ¼ teaspoon (1 ml) salt and ¼ teaspoon (1 ml) black pepper, and whisk thoroughly. Adjust seasoning to taste. The dressing will keep in the fridge, stored in an airtight container, for 1 week.

Serve with: iceberg wedges, shredded cabbage, a mesclun mixture such as lamb's lettuce, rocket, endive, mizuna and radicchio or as a substitute for mayonnaise in sandwiches, wraps and burgers.

HANDY TIP

Since this dressing contains a good dose of mayonnaise, it's important to use a really good-quality, whole-egg mayonnaise. If using supermarket-bought, opt for the fresh, refrigerated kind or, for an especially delicious tasting dressing, opt for making the mayonnaise using the recipe on page 31 (for this dressing you'll need a little less than half the quantity the recipe makes).

Variations

SPICY

Replace 1 tablespoon (15 ml) tomato ketchup with 1 tablespoon (15 ml) sweet chilli sauce. For an extra kick add a dash or two of hot sauce.
Serve with: shredded jicama, carrots, cabbage and bean sprouts for an Asian-style coleslaw, as a dip for crudités, with potato or sweet potato chips.

WITH MIXED HERBS

Reduce the fresh dill to ½ tablespoon (8 ml) and add ½ tablespoon (8 ml) each chopped fresh chervil, parsley and chives.
Serve with: iceberg lettuce wedges, burgers, sandwiches and wraps.

SKINNY

Use just 55 g low-fat mayonnaise and add 55 g low-fat Greek yoghurt to the rest of the ingredients.
Serve with: a mixed green salad, cold cooked prawns and lobster, or crudités.

836 Red Pepper & Basil Dressing

A vibrant dressing full of spritely Mediterranean flavour – just the thing for summer salads, or to brighten up a dreary cold-weather plate of greens.

INGREDIENTS

110 g drained jarred roasted red peppers, chopped

2 cloves garlic, chopped

8 to 10 large fresh basil leaves, torn

2 ½ tbsp (38 ml) red wine vinegar

2 tbsp (30 ml) good-quality mayonnaise

2 tbsp (30 ml) freshly grated Parmesan cheese

Salt and black pepper

70 ml extra-virgin olive oil

MAKES 285 ml

Combine the first four ingredients in a blender or food processor and process until smooth. Add the mayonnaise, Parmesan cheese, ¼ teaspoon (1 ml) salt and ¼ teaspoon (1 ml) pepper and process until thoroughly mixed. Slowly drizzle in the olive oil, with the motor running, and blend the dressing until thick and creamy. Adjust seasoning to taste. The dressing will keep in the fridge, stored in an airtight container, for 1 week.

Serve with: steamed greens, raw shredded cabbage, kale and brussels sprouts.

HANDY TIP

To roast your own red pepper, preheat the grill to high, then remove and discard the core of 1 medium to large red pepper. Cut the pepper into 4 large pieces and place them skin side up on a baking sheet lined with foil. Cook under the hot grill until blistered and blackened on the surface. Remove and place the pepper in a plastic bag, seal the bag and leave to steam for 10 to 15 minutes. Peel off and discard the loosened skin with your fingers. The roasted peppers are now ready to use.

Variations

WITH CHIPOTLE

Add ½ to 1 canned chipotle chilli in adobo sauce to the blender, with ½ teaspoon (3 ml) of the adobo sauce for extra heat.
Serve with: steamed greens, shredded raw brussels sprouts, mixed salad greens, or use as dip.

WITH CAPERS AND PARSLEY

Add ½ to 1 tablespoon (15 to 23 ml) drained and rinsed capers, and 2 tablespoons (30 ml) fresh parsley leaves in place of the basil.
Serve with: roasted Mediterranean vegetables, mixed salad greens.

WITH PAPRIKA AND SUN-DRIED TOMATOES

Add 2 tablespoons roughly chopped and drained, jarred sun-dried tomatoes, packed in oil, and ½ teaspoon (3 ml) paprika to the blender with the other ingredients.
Serve with: grilled chicken or fish, halved boiled or roasted new potatoes.

840 Peanut & Sesame Dressing

Laced with creamy peanut butter and fragrant toasted sesame seeds, this satisfyingly rich, chilli-spiked dressing is just the thing for nut lovers.

INGREDIENTS

2 tbsp (30 ml) sesame seeds

2 tbsp (30 ml) smooth peanut butter

1 tbsp (15 ml) soft dark-brown sugar

2 tbsp (30 ml) lime juice

2 tbsp (30 ml) soy sauce

½ tsp (3 ml) toasted sesame oil

1 tbsp (15 ml) vegetable or rapeseed oil

2 spring onions, thinly sliced, white and green parts kept separate

1 large clove garlic, minced

¼ tsp (1 ml) finely grated fresh peeled ginger

2 tsp (10 ml) supermarket-bought chilli paste

110 ml coconut milk

MAKES 170 ml

In a frying pan, lightly toast the sesame seeds until golden and fragrant. Set aside. Combine the peanut butter, brown sugar, lime juice, soy sauce and sesame oil in another small bowl and stir until smooth.

Heat the vegetable oil in the frying pan, add the white parts of the spring onions, and stir-fry for 1 to 2 minutes or until softened. Add the garlic, ginger and chilli paste and cook, stirring, for a further minute. Stir in the peanut butter mixture, cook for 30 seconds, then pour in coconut milk and bring to a boil. Simmer for 3 minutes until reduced and thickened. Remove from the heat and stir in the reserved green parts of the spring onions and about half to two-thirds of the toasted sesame seeds. Serve warm, using the remaining sesame seeds as a garnish.

Serve with: sautéed or grilled tofu, steamed Asian greens, a chicken or steak mixed salad, potato salad.

HANDY TIP

Different brands of chilli paste vary in heat, so use the amount suggested in the recipe as a guide.

Variations

WITH CASHEW

Replace the sesame seeds with 2 to 3 tablespoons (30 to 45 ml) chopped roasted unsalted cashew nuts, and sprinkle the dressed salad with extra chopped cashews.
Serve with: tofu, grilled chicken, or a mixed salad.

WITH CORIANDER

Omit the spring onions, using 1 small shallot in place of the white green onion parts, and adding 3 tablespoons (45 ml) chopped fresh coriander leaves to the finished dressing.
Serve with: shredded raw cabbage or kale, a chicken or beef salad.

SPICY GREEN CURRY

Replace the chilli paste with 1 tablespoon (15 ml) Thai green curry paste.
Serve with: egg or rice noodles, chicken, steak or lamb chops, a mixed green salad.

844 Blue Cheese Dressing

Easy to whip up, this luscious, undeniably naughty dressing is possibly the most indulgent condiment to grace a leaf of lettuce. But if you're going for indulge, go big and don't forget the generous garnish of crumbled crispy bacon!

INGREDIENTS

110 g blue cheese, crumbled
110 ml sour cream
2 tbsp (30 ml) good-quality mayonnaise
60 ml whole milk
2 tbsp (30 ml) cider vinegar

1 tbsp (15 ml) lemon juice
½ tsp (3 ml) celery salt, plus more as needed
Black pepper
2 tbsp (30 ml) finely chopped fresh chives

MAKES 285 ml

In a medium bowl, mash the blue cheese with a fork, then, using a whisk, work in the sour cream, mayonnaise, milk, vinegar and lemon juice until the dressing is smooth. Stir in the celery salt, ¼ teaspoon (1 ml) pepper and the chopped chives. Adjust seasoning to taste. Store in an airtight container or jar in the fridge for up to 2 days.

Serve with: iceberg lettuce topped with crispy bacon bits, a mixed green salad, sliced tomatoes, crudités, Buffalo wings, sandwiches and wraps.

HANDY TIP

You can use any variety of blue cheese for this recipe, however Roquefort or Gorgonzola are particularly good and both will bring a robust, well-rounded flavour to the dressing. If you prefer a more subtle flavour, opt for Fourme d'Ambert, a creamy French blue with a nutty, fruity flavour and earthy scent.

Variations

845 CHIPOTLE AND CORIANDER

Add 1 to 2 teaspoons (5 to 10 ml) minced canned chipotle chilli in adobo sauce to the dressing, replace the chives with chopped fresh coriander leaves.
Serve with: crudités, chicken fingers, tacos or fajitas, chicken or steak, a mixed green salad, Buffalo wings.

846 WITH BUTTERMILK

Replace the mayonnaise and milk with 85 ml buttermilk.
Serve with: a mixed green or Cobb salad, or burgers.

847 WITH WALNUTS

Toast 70 g walnut halves in a dry frying pan over medium heat for 2 to 3 minutes. Remove from the heat. Chop when cool then set aside. Stir half the chopped walnuts into the finished dressing and sprinkle the remaining walnut pieces over the top.
Serve with: shredded jicama, carrots, radishes and kohlrabi; a mixed-greens salad.

848 WITH PECANS

Make the **Walnut and Blue Cheese Dressing**, replacing the walnuts with pecan halves.
Serve with: crudités, Buffalo wings, Cobb and spinach or mixed-greens salads.

WITH BACON

Cook 2 rashers of bacon until crisp, then drain on kitchen paper. When cool, crumble into fine pieces and stir into the finished dressing. (Pictured left.)
Serve with: iceberg wedges, a spinach and watercress salad, crudités, fresh bread, Buffalo wings, roasted sweet potato chunks and new potatoes.

SWEET CHILLI

Add 2 tablespoons (30 ml) sweet chilli sauce with the sour cream. (Pictured right.)
Serve with: egg noodles, roasted new potatoes and sweet potato chunks, a steak and spinach salad.

851 Best-ever Ranch Dressing

When you taste this homemade version, you'll soon realise just how addictive this dressing is.

INGREDIENTS

1 clove garlic, well crushed
55 ml good-quality mayonnaise
55 ml buttermilk
55 ml sour cream
1 tbsp (15 ml) white wine vinegar
½ tsp (3 ml) Worcestershire sauce
Dash hot sauce

1 ½ tbsp (23 ml) chopped fresh parsley leaves
1 ½ tbsp (23 ml) chopped fresh chives
Salt and black pepper

MAKES 170 ml

Place the garlic in a small bowl and stir in the mayonnaise, buttermilk and sour cream and mix until smooth. Whisk in the white wine vinegar, Worcestershire sauce and hot sauce, then add the fresh herbs with ¼ teaspoon (1 ml) salt and a generous pinch of black pepper. The dressing will keep in the fridge, stored in an airtight container, for up to 1 week.

Serve with: crudités, a chicken salad, mashed potatoes, a mixed salad or salad greens.

HANDY TIP

If you can't find buttermilk, it's easy to make a substitute. Add 1 tablespoon (15 ml) lemon juice or white vinegar to 110 ml of milk and leave at room temperature for 10 minutes. Alternatively, use plain yoghurt thinned with a little water.

Variations

853 TEX-MEX

Add ¼ teaspoon (1 ml) ground cumin, ¼ teaspoon (1 ml) onion powder, ½ teaspoon (3 ml) Mexican spice blend and ½ finely minced seeded large red jalapeño chilli to the bowl before adding the vinegar.
Serve with: mixed green salad, crudités, a chicken salad, scrambled eggs.

854 CURRIED

Sauté 1 medium shallot, minced, in a little olive oil until softened. Add 2 teaspoons (10 ml) curry powder and a pinch of salt and cook for 2 minutes, stirring. Make the dressing, replacing the parsley with coriander. Stir the cold curry mixture into the finished dressing.
Serve with: a green salad with chicken and coriander, or a warm beef and spinach or watercress salad.

855 ROASTED RED PEPPER

Add 2 tablespoons minced, drained, jarred roasted red peppers to the dressing with the herbs.
Serve with: crudités, chicken or fish fingers, a mixed salad, or use as a dressing for coleslaw.

852 CITRUS

Add 2 teaspoons (10 ml) grated lemon zest, and replace the white wine vinegar with 2 tablespoons (30 ml) lemon juice.
Serve with: chicken salad, crudités, or boiled new potatoes.

856 DILL PICKLE

Add 2 tablespoons (30 ml) sweet dill-pickle relish to the dressing with the herbs.
Serve with: fish, chicken or turkey burgers; chicken and fish fingers; mashed potatoes.

CHEESY

Add 2 tablespoons (30 ml) finely grated Parmesan to the dressing before adding the herbs.
Serve with: boiled, crushed new potatoes; crudités; pasta for a salad.

LEMON DILL

Make the **Citrus Ranch Dressing** and replace the parsley with 2 tablespoons (30 ml) chopped fresh dill.
Serve with: cooked fish, smoked salmon, fish cakes, or prawn or salmon salads.

APPLE CIDER WITH GHERKINS

Replace the white wine vinegar with 1 ½ tablespoons (23 ml) apple cider vinegar and add 1 tablespoon (15 ml) minced, drained and rinsed gherkins to the finished dressing.
Serve with: coleslaw, grated carrots, or a tomato salad.

BARBECUE

Reduce the sour cream to 3 tablespoons (45 ml) and add 2 tablespoons (30 ml) barbecue sauce with the mayonnaise and buttermilk.
Serve with: burgers, sandwiches, chicken salads.

861 Green Goddess Avocado Dressing

Bursting with fresh herbs and smooth, nutrient-rich avocado this refreshing and versatile dressing is delicious over lettuce, with chicken or seafood and as a dip for dunking just about anything in!

INGREDIENTS

½ medium avocado, chopped
1 clove garlic, chopped
140 g sour cream
60 ml Greek yoghurt
2 tbsp (30 ml) chopped fresh
  parsley leaves
1 tbsp (15 ml) roughly chopped
  fresh tarragon
1 tbsp (15 ml) roughly chopped
  fresh chives

2 tbsp (30 ml) roughly
  chopped fresh basil leaves
1 tsp (5 ml) anchovy paste
2 tbsp (30 ml) fresh lemon
  juice
1 tbsp (15 ml) white wine
  vinegar
½ tsp (3 ml) granulated sugar
Salt and black pepper

MAKES 370 ml

Place all the ingredients in a blender or food processor with ½ teaspoon (3 ml) salt, ¼ teaspoon (1 ml) pepper, and 3 tablespoons (45 ml) water and process until smooth. Adjust seasoning to taste. Transfer to a bowl, cover tightly with cling film and chill for 2 to 3 hours. Whisk well before serving. Store in an airtight container or jar in the fridge for up to 2 days.

Serve with: a Bibb or butter lettuce and tomato or mixed-greens salad, chicken, salmon or prawns, crudités.

HANDY TIP

For a vegetarian version replace the anchovy paste with 1 teaspoon (5 ml) soy sauce.

Variations

862 WITH LIME

Replace the lemon juice with lime juice and add the finely grated zest of 1 large lime.
Serve with: Bibb or Romaine lettuce, tacos and burritos, or chilled seafood.

863 WITH TEQUILA AND LIME

Make the **Green Goddess Avocado Lime Dressing** and add 1 tablespoon (15 ml) tequila to the blender or food processor.
Serve with: tomato or green salads, crudités, prawns, or a salmon, avocado, tomato and watercress salad.

864 WITH PISTACHIO

Add 45 g chopped pistachios to the blender with the rest of the ingredients.
Serve with: green beans, broccoli or broccoli rabe.

865 WITH GREEN OLIVE

Add 3 tablespoons (45 ml) well-chopped pitted large green olives to the finished dressing.
Serve with: crudités, a beetroot and smoked trout salad, chicken pasta salad.

Avocado makes a creamy dressing for fish and salads

SPICY CORIANDER

Add ½ to 1 jalapeño chilli, seeded and chopped, to the blender with the rest of the ingredients. (Pictured left.)
Serve with: a Cobb, tomato, or chicken, spinach and watercress salad.

WITH ROASTED PEPPERS

Add 55 g chopped, drained jarred roasted red peppers with the rest of the ingredients in the food processor. (Pictured right.)
Serve with: a rocket and watercress salad, green vegetables or mashed potatoes.

868 Carrot & Ginger Dressing

This dressing tastes like it should contain hundreds of calories, but is far healthier than you might think. The secret is in the silken tofu, which provides a creamy texture while keeping fat at bay.

INGREDIENTS

110 g chopped peeled carrot (about 2 medium carrots)

110 g silken tofu, drained

1 ½ tbsp (23 ml) chopped peeled ginger

1 large garlic clove, chopped

2 tbsp (30 ml) mirin (Japanese rice wine)

1 tbsp (15 ml) rice wine vinegar

3 tbsp (45 ml) lime juice

2 tbsp (30 ml) soy sauce, plus more as needed

55 ml rapeseed or vegetable oil

½ to 1 tsp (3 to 5 ml) wasabi paste

1 tbsp (15 ml) honey

MAKES 340 ml

Combine all the ingredients in a blender and process until smooth and thoroughly blended. Add more soy to taste, if necessary. Leftover dressing will keep in an airtight container in the fridge for up to 1 week.

Serve with: salad leaves such as rocket, watercress and mizuna; tofu, fish and chicken; chilled egg, soba or udon noodles and grated carrots.

HANDY TIP

Sharp, pungent wasabi is Japanese horseradish. You're most likely to see it as a vibrant green paste, or as a powder that is reconstituted with water before use.

Variations

869 SPICED

Replace the wasabi with ½ teaspoon (3 ml) ground cumin, ¼ teaspoon (1 ml) ground coriander and a generous pinch cayenne.
Serve with: chicken or steak salad with mixed green salad such as rocket, mizuna and watercress; shredded cabbage and carrot for an Asian-style coleslaw.

870 WITH ORANGE

Replace the lime juice with freshly squeezed orange juice and 1 teaspoon (5 ml) freshly grated orange zest.
Serve with: fish, prawns or squid, and chilled egg or soba noodles.

871 WITH MIXED HERBS

Add 1 tablespoon (15 ml) each chopped fresh chives, parsley and chervil to the blended dressing while still in the blender, and pulse until the herbs are well chopped.
Serve with: a mixed green salad with cucumber, carrots, bean sprouts and edamame, fish, steak or chicken.

WITH SPRING ONION

Add the finely sliced green and light-green parts of 3 spring onions to the finished dressing.
Serve with: chilled egg or soba noodles with toasted sesame seeds, spicy green salad leaves such as rocket, mizuna and watercress.

WITH CHILLI

Replace the wasabi with ½ to 1 seeded and chopped red chilli.
Serve with: baby spinach, romaine leaves, or mixed mesclun greens, or combine with egg or soba noodles, Napa cabbage and slivered almonds and serve chilled.

WITH MISO

Add 1 ½ tablespoons (23 ml) red miso to the blender with the rest of the ingredients.
Serve with: sushi rolls or crudités, shredded kale, cabbage and brussels sprouts, mixed salads.

WITH CARAWAY

Toast 1 teaspoon (5 ml) caraway seeds in a dry frying pan until fragrant and slightly darker. Once cool, add to the rest of the ingredients in the blender.
Serve with: a salad of Romaine leaves, cucumber, red bell pepper, bean sprouts and grated carrots, or red and Napa cabbage for an Asian-style coleslaw.

WITH APRICOT

Reduce the honey to ½ tablespoon (8 ml) and add 5 to 6 dried apricots, which have been soaked in just-boiled water for about 15 minutes until softened, then drained and chopped to the blender with the rest of the ingredients.
Serve with: vegetarian sushi rolls and summer rolls, chicken or tofu salads with a mixed green salad.

WITH SMOKY PAPRIKA

Add 1 teaspoon (5 ml) smoked paprika to the blender with the rest of the ingredients.
Serve with: green or tomato salads, or a steak salad with crunchy greens, toasted pecans, bean sprouts, carrots, red bell pepper and edamame.

DESSERT SAUCES

878 Raspberry Coulis

This is less a recipe and more a formula. Coulis sauces are supremely easy to make but they do rely on your taste buds to perfect. The key is to taste and re-taste until you're absolutely happy with the balance of sweet and tart.

INGREDIENTS

200 g fresh or defrosted
  frozen raspberries
2 ½ tbsp (38 ml) lemon juice
Icing sugar, to taste

MAKES 240 ml

Place the raspberries and lemon juice in a blender and process until completely smooth. Add 1 tablespoon (15 ml) icing sugar to the blender and pulse to combine. Taste and add more sugar as needed, ½ to 1 teaspoon (3 to 5 ml) at a time, pulsing between each addition. Pass through a fine mesh sieve. Transfer to a small jug or bowl, cover with cling film and chill for at least 45 minutes before serving.

Serve with: cheesecake, vanilla or lemon panna cotta, white and dark chocolate mousse, fruit pavlova, as a dip for fruit and marshmallows.

HANDY TIP

Make coulis in bulk in the summer when berries are at their sweetest and freeze in ice cube trays or silicon mini muffin moulds. When solid remove from the moulds, load into freezer bags, seal and keep frozen for up to 6 months. To use, transfer the frozen coulis to the fridge for about 6 hours to defrost, or defrost in the microwave on a low setting.

Variations

879 BLACKBERRY

Replace the raspberries with blackberries.
Serve with: mixed berry, vanilla, lemon and chocolate cheesecake.

882 MANGO

Replace the raspberries with chopped, peeled and seeded mango, and the lemon juice with lime juice, and start with just ½ tablespoon (8 ml) sugar.
Serve with: tropical fruit tarts; cheesecakes; mango, passion fruit or coconut panna cotta; soufflés; coconut cream pie; and ice cream and sorbet.

880 MIXED BERRY

in place of just the raspberries, use a mixture of raspberries, blackberries, strawberries and red currants.
Serve with: panna cotta, angel food cake, soufflés, fresh fruit tarts and ice cream.

883 MANGO AND MALIBU

Make the **Mango Coulis**, adding 1 to 2 tablespoons (15 to 30 ml) Malibu rum to the finished sauce.
Serve with: coconut, mango and other tropical fruit ice cream and sorbets; fresh tropical fruit; mango cheesecake; white chocolate mousse; or tropical fruit pavlova.

881 KIWI-LIME

Replace the raspberries with chopped, peeled kiwi fruit and the lemon juice with lime juice. Start with ½ tablespoon (8 ml) sugar.
Serve with: tropical fruit tarts and pavlova, tropical fruit smoothies or yoghurt parfaits, as a dip for cut fruit, and with cake or fruit sorbets.

884 PEACH

Replace the raspberries with chopped, peeled and pitted peaches and start with just ½ tablespoon (8 ml) sugar.
Serve with: pound cake, fruit tarts, poached fruit, fruit salads or ice cream.

885 PEACH AND GINGER

Make the **Peach Coulis**, adding 1 teaspoon (5 ml) grated peeled fresh ginger to the blender with the fruit.
Serve with: grilled or toasted pound cake; poached fruit; ice cream; waffles, pancakes and crêpes; soufflés and cheesecakes.

886 STRAWBERRY

Replace the raspberries with chopped, hulled strawberries.
Serve with: strawberry pavlova, panna cotta, cheesecake, fresh nectarines or peaches, ice cream.

887 MIXED BERRY AND KIRSCH

Make the **Mixed Berry Coulis**, adding 1 to 2 tablespoons (15 to 30 ml) kirsch to the finished sauce.
Serve with: mixed berry, chocolate or vanilla cheesecake; crêpes, pancakes and waffles; rich, dark chocolate mousse or tart.

888 Tangy citrus sauce

This refreshing sauce is just the thing to cut through rich, creamy desserts such as cheesecakes and flans, buttery cakes and filled crêpes.

INGREDIENTS

1 tbsp cornflour
110 g granulated sugar
2 tbsps (30 ml) unsalted
    butter, diced
85 ml lemon juice

55 ml lime juice
Grated zest of 1 lemon
Grated zest 1 lime
Salt

MAKES 340 ml

Combine the cornflour with 1 tablespoon (15 ml) cold water in a small bowl and mix until smooth. Set aside.

Place the sugar in a small saucepan with 170 to 240 ml water and set over medium-low heat, until the sugar completely dissolves. Add the butter and, once melted, increase the heat slightly and bring to the boil. Simmer briskly for 2 minutes, then add the citrus juice, zest and a generous pinch of salt. Bring back to a boil and simmer for a minute further. Pour in the cornflour slurry, stirring constantly, and cook for about 2 minutes until the sauce is thickened. Strain the sauce through a fine mesh sieve. Serve warm or chilled.

Serve with: ice cream; vanilla, lemon or orange pound cake; warm steamed puddings; cheesecakes, flans and crêpes.

HANDY TIP

This recipe makes a vibrantly flavoured, zingy sauce; however, the colour can be a little lacklustre. So, to give it more of a sunny hue, add a drop of yellow food colouring.

Variations

889 WITH RUM

Add a splash of dark rum to the saucepan with the lemon and lime juices.
Serve with: warm gingerbread pudding; steamed lemon sponge pudding; crêpes, pancakes and waffles.

890 WITH PINEAPPLE

Stir 2 tablespoons (30 ml) finely minced fresh or canned pineapple into the finished strained sauce.
Serve with: ice cream, cheesecakes, or with Greek yoghurt and pound cake.

891 MANDARIN LIME

Replace the lemon juice with fresh, sweet mandarin juice, and the lemon zest with mandarin zest.
Serve with: crêpes filled with whipped cream flavoured with Grand Marnier and sweetened with icing sugar; orange and almond pound cake; clafoutis; madeleines.

892 BLOOD ORANGE AND LEMON

Use only 55 ml lemon juice and replace the lime juice with 85 ml blood orange juice. Replace the lime zest with 1 to 2 teaspoons (5 to 10 ml) freshly grated blood orange zest.
Serve: marbled through whipped cream or Greek yoghurt; crêpes, pancakes and waffles; soufflés; cake bites.

893 LEMON LIMONCELLO

Replace the lime juice and zest with 140 ml lemon juice and add 1 tablespoon (15 ml) limoncello to the juice.
Serve with: lemon- and ricotta-stuffed crêpes, lemon and raspberry soufflés, cheesecakes, panettone bread pudding.

894 CITRUS GINGER

Add 1 teaspoon (5 ml) finely grated peeled fresh ginger with the citrus juices and zest. If desired, add 1 tablespoon (15 ml) minced crystallised ginger to the finished sauce.
Serve with: spiced steamed puddings; cheesecakes; pound cake, bundt and angel food cake; chocolate and gingerbread cake; fresh fruit tarts.

895 LEMON VERBENA

Stir 1 ½ tablespoons (15 to 23 ml) finely chopped fresh lemon verbena into the finished, strained sauce.
Serve with: lemon pound cake; panna cotta; clafoutis; ice cream; semi-freddo; lemon, orange, raspberry and peach soufflés; as a dip for doughnuts and hot fruit fritters.

896 LEMON AND ROSEMARY

Omit the lime juice and zest and use 140 ml lemon juice in total. Add 1 teaspoon (5 ml) bruised and minced fresh rosemary leaves with the lemon juice.
Serve with: ginger and apple cakes, steamed puddings, soufflés.

897 WITH LEMONGRASS

Add the chopped bruised bulb of 1 stalk lemongrass to the saucepan along with the citrus juices.
Serve with: lemon, mango and dark chocolate and chilli-spiced cheesecakes; coconut milk rice puddings; tropical fruit tarts; ice cream and tropical fruit sorbets.

898 cherries Jubilee sauce

This flambéed cherry dessert sauce was first prepared by the renowned French chef August Escoffier for the British Queen Victoria's Jubilee celebrations at the end of the 19th century.

INGREDIENTS

1 tbsp cornflour	55 g granulated sugar
30 g unsalted butter, cubed	3 tbsp (45 ml) lemon juice
400 g pitted fresh or defrosted frozen sweet cherries	1 tsp (5 ml) vanilla extract
	Salt
	60 ml kirsch or brandy

SERVES 4

Combine the cornflour and a splash of cold water in a small bowl and stir until smooth. Set aside.

Melt the butter in a large frying pan over medium heat. Add the cherries and any juices, sugar, lemon juice, vanilla extract and a pinch of salt. Cook, stirring, until the sugar is dissolved and the cherries are tender and their juices have leached into the pan.

Turn up the heat, add the kirsch, then remove the pan from the heat and carefully ignite using a long-handled match. Spoon the juices over the cherries until the flames subside. Return to the heat and whisk in half of the cornflour slurry. Simmer over medium-low heat for 1 to 2 minutes or until the sauce is thickened, adding more cornflour if you prefer a thicker sauce. Remove from the heat and leave to stand for 2 to 3 minutes before serving.

Serve with: vanilla ice cream, warm vanilla pound cake, cheesecake, rice pudding, Greek yoghurt, crêpes.

HANDY TIP

Why not serve this restaurant-style and entertain your guests by preparing the sauce table-side on a small portable gas or electric cooker?

variations

899 WITH AMARETTO AND ALMOND

Substitute the kirsch or brandy for amaretto and stir 1 to 2 tablespoons (15 to 30 ml) lightly toasted slivered almonds into the finished sauce.
Serve with: crêpes and waffles, sweet corn bread, chocolate cake, brownies, panna cotta or rice pudding.

900 WITH ORANGE

Add 2 tablespoons (30 ml) orange juice and ½ teaspoon (3 ml) finely grated orange zest to the frying pan with the cherries. Substitute Grand Marnier for the kirsch or brandy.
Serve with: pancakes, crêpes and waffles with whipped cream, cheesecake, pound or bundt cake.

901 WITH RASPBERRIES

Stir 2 tablespoons (30 ml) raspberry jam or jelly into the frying pan with the cherries, reduce the sugar to 2 tablespoons (30 g) and replace the kirsch or brandy with Chambord (a raspberry liqueur).
Serve with: Greek yoghurt, rice pudding, vanilla panna cotta, bread pudding or ice cream.

902 Butterscotch -Toffee sauce

When I think of my final meal, this sauce features prominently! What's not to love about it? The best part is that I've yet to find a dessert companion that it doesn't impeccably match.

INGREDIENTS

85 g soft light-brown sugar
85 g soft dark-brown sugar
2 ½ tbsp (38 ml) golden syrup
55 g unsalted butter, diced

Salt
170 ml double cream
½ tsp (3 ml) vanilla extract

MAKES 285 ml

Combine the sugars, corn syrup or golden syrup and butter in a heavy-based, high-sided saucepan with a scant ¼ teaspoon (1 ml) salt and set over medium heat. Stir occasionally until the butter melts and the sugars dissolve. Increase the heat slightly, bring to a boil, then simmer for about 3 minutes. Pour in the cream and vanilla extract, bring back to a boil, stirring, until the mixture is smooth. Continue to cook, bubbling briskly, for a further 5 to 6 minutes until the sauce is thickened and shiny. Remove from the heat and leave to cool for at least 5 to 10 minutes. Serve warm.

Serve with: cake bites, mini doughnuts and churros; ice cream, cream puffs, grilled bananas, pineapple and peaches; apple cake, bread pudding and sticky toffee or date pudding.

HANDY TIP

For a darker toffee and less butterscotch sauce, use all soft dark-brown sugar.

variations

903 WITH BANANA

Stir 1 peeled and diced small banana into the finished sauce.
Serve with: ice cream with warm chocolate or toffee brownies; pancakes, crêpes and waffles.

904 WITH COCONUT

Replace the double cream with coconut cream, simmering for 4 to 5 minutes until thickened.
Serve with: coconut cake, fresh coconut tart, coconut and chocolate ice cream.

905 WITH KAHLUA

Stir 1 to 1 ½ tablespoons (15 to 23 ml) Kahlua into the finished sauce.
Serve with: banana bread pudding, butterscotch pudding, chocolate pudding, apple crumble; ice cream; as a dip or drizzle for grilled or roasted pineapple and banana, fritters, cream puffs and churros.

906 White Mint Chocolate Sauce

This creamy sauce has a fresh flavour making it perfect for summer desserts.

INGREDIENTS

120 ml whole milk
240 ml double whipping cream
20 fresh mint leaves

250 g best-quality white chocolate

SERVES 6-8

Place the milk and cream in a saucepan and bring to a boil. Remove from the heat, add the mint leaves, cover, and allow to infuse for 15 minutes.

Melt the white chocolate in a bain-marie. Stir until smooth. Pour the infused milk mixture through a sieve into the melted chocolate. Stir until smooth. Return the sauce to the saucepan, bring to a boil, then remove from the heat, stirring continuously. Serve immediately.

This sauce will thicken as it cools and should be warmed in a bain-marie if necessary. Store refrigerated for up to 3 days.

Serve with: summer fruits and meringues.

HANDY TIP

To change up the minty flavour of this sauce, try using different varieties of the herb from spearmint and peppermint to fruity orange and grapefruit mint.

Variations

907 LIGHT

Replace the milk and whipping cream with skimmed milk and low-fat whipping cream.
Serve with: fresh fruit and low-fat frozen yoghurt.

908 WITH MILK CHOCOLATE

Replace the white chocolate with 250 g milk chocolate.
Serve with: warm chocolate brownies.

909 WITH VANILLA

Replace the mint leaves with 1 vanilla bean, split lengthwise.
Serve with: ice cream.

910 Hot Fudge Sauce

Remember trips to the ice cream parlour for hot fudge sundaes, where towering concoctions would emerge drenched in a thick, heavenly elixir? Well this is that taste of chocolate heaven!

INGREDIENTS

120–160 ml double cream
85 g unsalted butter, cubed
160 g soft light-brown sugar
2 tbsp (30 g) granulated sugar
Salt
45 g unsweetened cocoa powder, sifted
85 ml golden syrup

30 g extra bittersweet or unsweetened chocolate, chopped
1 tsp (5 ml) vanilla extract

MAKES 170 ml

Place the cream and butter in a small saucepan and cook over medium-low heat, stirring, until the butter is melted. Add the sugars and a pinch of salt and cook, stirring until sugar is dissolved. Simmer gently for 2 to 2 ½ minutes. Stir in the cocoa and corn syrup and cook for 2 minutes, stirring, until thoroughly blended.

Stir in the chocolate, and when melted, simmer gently for 12 to 15 minutes or until thick, glossy and smooth, stirring frequently. Remove from the heat and stir in the vanilla extract. Leave to cool for at least 10 minutes before serving. This sauce can be cooled completely then stored in an airtight container in the fridge for a week. Warm through before using.

Serve with: ice cream, chocolate cake or brownies, or use cold as a frosting to decorate cakes.

HANDY TIP

As its name suggests, unsweetened chocolate is just that – 100% processed cacao beans without added sugar. It is too bitter to be eaten but produces a rich sauce with a subtle bitter coffee edge. Bittersweet or extra bittersweet chocolate typically contains 70% to 85% cacao and will produce a slighter sweeter sauce.

Variations

911 MEXICAN CHILLI

Place the cream in a saucepan with 1 small cinnamon stick and 1 star anise and bring to a gentle simmer. Remove from the heat and leave to steep for 15 minutes. Remove the spices and continue with the recipe, adding a generous pinch to ¼ teaspoon (1 ml) of cayenne or ancho chilli powder 5 minutes before the end of the cooking time.
Serve with: vanilla, chocolate and cinnamon ice cream; crêpes and waffles; spiced chocolate brownies.

912 WITH RUM

Stir 1 to 1 ½ tablespoons (15 to 23 ml) rum into the finished sauce, once off the heat.
Serve with: ice cream, chocolate puddings and brownies.

913 SALTED

Replace the pinch of salt with ½ teaspoon (3 ml) flaky sea salt.
Serve with: brownies, chocolate cake, waffles, pancakes or fresh fruit.

914 creamy caramel sauce

This sauce is sophisticated enough to please a dinner-party crowd and tasty enough to serve at a kids party.

INGREDIENTS

140 ml double cream
200 g granulated sugar
2 tbsp (30 ml) golden syrup

55 g cold unsalted butter, cubed
¼ tsp (1 ml) flaky sea salt
½ tsp (3 ml) vanilla extract

MAKES 360 ml

Place the cream in a small saucepan and bring to a gentle simmer, remove from the heat and set aside.

Place the sugar, syrup and 2 tablespoons (30 ml) water in a heavy-based, high-sided saucepan and set it over a medium-low heat, shaking gently, until the sugar has dissolved. Don't stir the sugar, instead use a damp pastry brush to knock any sugar crystals off the sides of the pan. Bring to a boil and bubble briskly until a dark golden, amber colour, shaking the pan to ensure it colours evenly. Remove from the heat and immediately pour in the warm cream, swirling to distribute it evenly. Quickly add the butter, salt and vanilla and whisk until smooth. Serve warm or chilled.

Serve with: ice cream, chocolate cakes, baked custards, sticky toffee pudding.

HANDY TIP

To avoid burning the caramel, have a bowl of ice at the ready so you can plunge the base of the saucepan into it to stop the caramel cooking.

Variations

916 ZESTY ORANGE

Add 1 teaspoon (5 ml) finely grated orange zest to the pan with the butter, and stir 2 tablespoons (30 ml) Grand Marnier to the finished sauce.
Serve with: grilled orange slices, ice cream, roasted bananas, pumpkin bread pudding and pound cake.

917 WITH ORANGE

Whisk 1 tablespoon (15 ml) defrosted and heated orange juice concentrate and ½ teaspoon (3 ml) finely grated orange zest into the sauce with the butter.
Serve with: pumpkin, orange and almond bread pudding, vanilla, chocolate and caramel soufflés.

918 MOCHA

Dissolve 2½ teaspoons (13 ml) instant espresso powder into the hot cream.
Serve with: espresso brownies, ice cream, or blend the cold sauce into milkshakes.

915 SALTED

Increase the salt to ½ to ¾ teaspoon (3 to 4 ml).
Serve with: brownies, ice cream, sautéed or roasted bananas and poached pears.

919 VANILLA BEAN

Omit the vanilla extract and add the scraped out seeds of 1 split vanilla pod to the cream before heating it.
Serve with: warm banana cake; toasted pound cake; ice cream; crêpes, pancakes and waffles.

920 WITH BOURBON

Add 2 tablespoons (30 ml) bourbon with the butter.
Serve with: toasted vanilla pound cake; angel cake; ice cream; or blend the cold sauce into milkshakes.

921 WITH BOURBON AND PECAN

Make the **Creamy Bourbon Caramel Sauce**, stirring 25 g finely chopped toasted pecans into the finished sauce.
Serve with: warm cinnamon buns, brownies, grilled oranges and gingerbread bread pudding.

922 WITH GINGER

Add 1 ½ teaspoons (8 ml) finely grated peeled fresh ginger to the saucepan with the cream, and infuse for 15 minutes. Strain before adding to the sugar and syrup mixture.
Serve with: ice cream or as a dip for apple, pear and peach wedges.

923 SPICY APPLE

Make the **Creamy Ginger Caramel Sauce**, adding 1 small cinnamon stick, 2 cloves and 1 star anise with the ginger; ½ tablespoon (8 ml) apple cider vinegar with the sugar, and 2 tablespoons (30 ml) apple schnapps to the finished sauce.
Serve with: apple cake, apple wedges, apple filled crêpes, sponge puddings.

924 Bittersweet chocolate sauce

Chocolate sauce doesn't get much better than this.

INGREDIENTS

225 g best-quality bittersweet chocolate with 70% cocoa solids
140 ml whole milk
3 tbsp (45 ml) double whipping cream

2 tbsp (30 ml) superfine sugar
2 tbsp (30 ml) unsalted butter

SERVES 6–8

Melt the semisweet chocolate in a bain-marie or in a heatproof bowl set over a pan of simmering water, making sure the bowl does not touch the water.

Combine the milk, cream and sugar in a saucepan and bring to a boil. Remove from the heat and pour onto the melted chocolate, stirring continuously.

Return the chocolate mixture to the saucepan, quickly bring to a boil, and immediately remove from the heat. Beat or whisk in the butter a little at a time until the sauce is smooth and glossy. Serve immediately. This sauce will thicken as it cools and should be warmed in a bain-marie or in a heatproof bowl set over a pan of simmering water. Store refrigerated for up to 3 days. (Pictured opposite top.)

Serve with: ice cream and chocolate desserts.

HANDY TIP

If you can't find superfine sugar, simply use 2 rounded tablespoons (approximately 30 ml) regular granulated sugar instead.

Variations

925 ORANGE CHOCOLATE

Replace the bittersweet chocolate with 225 g orange-flavoured semisweet chocolate.
Serve with: fruit desserts.

926 MOCHA CHOCOLATE

Stir 1 teaspoon (5 ml) instant espresso granules into 1 to 2 tablespoons (15 to 30 ml) hot water and add to the saucepan with the milk.
Serve with: mocha cream puffs, apple and banana fritters and as a dip for churros.

927 MINT CHOCOLATE

Replace the bittersweet chocolate with 225 g mint-flavoured semisweet chocolate.
Serve with: vanilla cheesecake.

928 BOOZY CHOCOLATE

Stir 1 ½ tablespoons (23 ml) rum into the finished sauce.
Serve with: pound, chocolate and banana cake;
strawberries and diced pineapple chunks; pancakes, filled
crêpes and waffles; and ice cream.

929 WHITE CHOCOLATE

Replace the bittersweet chocolate with 225 g white
chocolate. (Pictured centre.)
Serve with: red fruits.

930 MILK CHOCOLATE

Replace the bittersweet chocolate with 225 g milk
chocolate. (Pictured bottom.)
Serve with: ice cream.

931 crème Anglaise

A crème anglaise is no less useful than a Swiss Army knife. Not only can you serve it with a multitude of desserts, you can also turn it into treats, such as ice cream, baked custards and even an icing for cakes.

INGREDIENTS

225 ml whole milk
285 ml double whipping cream
1 vanilla pod, split lengthwise

100 g granulated sugar
5 large egg yolks

MAKES 600 ml

Place the milk, cream and vanilla pod in a saucepan over medium heat. Bring to a gentle simmer, remove from the heat and leave for 15 to 20 minutes to infuse.

Meanwhile, place the sugar and egg yolks in a medium bowl and whisk until pale and cream-coloured. Remove the vanilla pod from the milk and set aside. Pour the warm milk into the egg mixture in a thin, steady stream, whisking constantly. Wash and dry the saucepan and pour the egg and milk mixture back into it. Scrape the vanilla seeds from the pod and stir into the pan. Return to the hob, and cook over low heat, stirring constantly, until thick enough to coat the back of the spoon. (If the heat is too high, the sauce may scramble.) Strain through a fine mesh sieve. Serve warm, or chill for at least 1 hour to serve cold. (Pictured opposite top.)

Serve with: fruit pies, tarts and crumbles; poached, baked or roasted fruit; and steamed sponge puddings.

HANDY TIP

To tell if the sauce has thickened enough, coat the back of a wooden spoon, lift it out and then run your finger down the back of the spoon. If your finger creates a clear streak without sauce running down, then the custard is ready (see page 7).

Variations

932 CARDAMOM GINGER

Infuse the milk and cream with 3 slices peeled ginger and 3 to 5 roughly crushed cardamom pods – depending on how much cardamom flavour you like. Strain the cream mixture before pouring it over the eggs.
Serve with: spiced warm puddings, tarts and fruit pies, warm chocolate pudding, Christmas pudding, steamed ginger sponge pudding and chocolate soufflés.

933 WITH LEMON

Replace the vanilla pod with the pared zest of 1 lemon, cut into strips, taking care to shave away any bitter pith. Strain the milk before pouring it over the eggs.
Serve with: baked, roasted or poached fruits; apple pie and tarte tatin; fruit tarts, cobblers and crumbles; and steamed sponge puddings.

934 LEMON THYME

Make the **Lemon Crème Anglaise**, adding 2 sprigs lemon thyme or regular thyme to the milk and cream to infuse with the lemon zest.
Serve with: warm lemon sponge pudding; treacle sponge pudding; bread pudding; fruit tarts, crumbles, cobblers and pies.

935 WITH APPLE BRANDY

Stir 2 tablespoons (30 ml) apple brandy into the finished sauce.
Serve with: apple pie and tarts, warm apple cakes and bread puddings, stuffed baked apples.

936 CINNAMON ORANGE

Omit the vanilla pod and infuse the milk and cream mixture with 1 stick cinnamon and three 2 cm by 7 cm (1-inch by 3-inch) strips of pared orange zest, taking care to shave away any bitter pith. Strain the milk before pouring it over the eggs. (Pictured centre.)
Serve with: Christmas pudding, warm apple pie, pear crumble, bread and butter pudding, sticky toffee pudding and chocolate and orange soufflés.

937 WITH LAVENDER

Infuse the milk and cream mixture with 1 tablespoon (15 ml) culinary lavender buds, then strain before pouring it over the eggs. (Pictured bottom.)
Serve with: bread and butter pudding; poached pears, peaches, and apricots; steamed sponge puddings.

938 Zabaglione sauce

In Italy they call it *zabaglione*; in France, *sabayon*. Virtually a dessert in itself, all that's needed is a handful of fresh berries or sliced, fresh fruit. Zabaglione is traditionally flavoured with aromatic, sweet wine, but if you're serving it to children, omit the alcohol and add a few drops of pure vanilla extract instead.

INGREDIENTS

3 tbsp (45 ml) double whipping cream

3 large egg yolks, at room temperature

3 tbsp (45 ml) granulated sugar

3 tbsp (45 ml) Moscato di Asti or marsala wine

MAKES 340 ml

Place the cream in a small bowl and beat using an electric whisk for about 1 minute or until softly whipped. Set aside.

Place the egg yolks, sugar and wine in a medium heatproof bowl and beat using an electric whisk for 30 seconds until the mixture starts to get foamy. Set over a saucepan of simmering water, making sure the bottom of the pan isn't touching the water. Continue to beat until the mixture is very pale, thickens considerably and at least doubles in volume. Remove from the heat, and carefully fold in the whipped cream, in two or three additions, using a metal spoon, until combined. Serve warm or cold. (Pictured opposite top.)

Serve with: fresh berries, peaches or poached fruit.

HANDY TIP

It's very important to ensure that the simmering water in the pan below isn't touching the bottom of the bowl that holds the egg yolk and sugar mixture because it will overheat and cook the egg. If you start to notice strands of cooked egg, there's little that you can do. Your best bet is to discard the mix and start again!

Variations

939 PORT BALSAMIC

Replace the marsala or Moscato di Asti with port, and whisk ½ tablespoon (8 ml) aged balsamic vinegar into the sauce mixture in the bowl just after it starts to thicken.
Serve with: mixed berries, roast plums or grilled figs.

940 WITH CHOCOLATE

Fold 55 g melted and cooled semi-sweet chocolate chips into the softly whipped cream before adding to the sauce.
Serve with: strawberries and raspberries, shortbread, ladyfinger cookies and chocolate biscotti.

941 APPLE BRANDY MINT

Replace the marsala or Moscato di Asti with apple brandy and stir 1 tablespoon (15 ml) finely shredded fresh mint leaves into the finished sauce.
Serve with: poached apples, pears and quince or vanilla shortbread cookies.

942 WITH LEMON

Beat in 1 ½ tablespoons (23 ml) lemon juice and
1 teaspoon (5 ml) finely grated lemon zest to the mixture
in the bowl or bain-marie just after it starts to thicken.
Serve with: strawberries or raspberries or toasted lemon
pound cake.

943 WITH VIN SANTO AND VANILLA

Replace the marsala or Moscato di Asti with Vin Santo,
and add the scraped out seeds of 1 small vanilla pod to the
rest of the ingredients in the bowl or bain-marie. (Pictured
centre.)
Serve with: fresh or roasted apricots with Italian cantucci
cookies, or with fruit and nut biscotti.

944 AMARETTO ORANGE

Replace the marsala or Moscato di Asti with amaretto
liqueur and add 1 teaspoon (5 ml) finely grated orange zest
to the bowl or bain-marie with the rest of the ingredients.
(Pictured bottom.)
Serve with: oranges, grapefruit, fresh or grilled pineapple.

SWEET SPREADS & DIPS

945 Lemon Curd

A delectably fresh filling for cakes, meringues and pie crusts; a luscious spread for warm toast, fresh scones and tender Muffins; and a naughty snack by the spoonful!

INGREDIENTS

2 large eggs, plus 1 large
   egg yolk
Finely grated zest 1 unwaxed
   lemon
125 ml lemon juice
110 g granulated sugar
70 g cold unsalted butter,
   cubed

MAKES 340 g

Place the whole eggs and egg yolk in a small bowl and lightly beat.

Place the lemon zest, juice, sugar and butter in a heatproof bowl. Set the bowl over a saucepan of simmering water making sure the bottom of the bowl doesn't touch the water. Stir every now and then until the butter has melted.

Slowly pour in the beaten egg, a little at a time, whisking, to incorporate into the lemon mixture. Continue to cook, now stirring (not whisking) frequently with a wooden spoon, for about 10 minutes or until the mixture is thick and very creamy and thickly coats the back of the spoon.

Remove the bowl from atop the saucepan of water and leave to cool for 5 to 10 minutes, then strain through a wire mesh sieve. Pour into a medium bowl and place a piece of cling film directly on the surface of the curd to prevent a skin from forming until completely cool and ready to use. To store, keep in the fridge in an airtight container for up to 1 week.

Serve with: scones, toast, muffins, crumpets, warm brioche and croissants; use to sandwich a Victoria sponge cake or fill cooked pastry tart cases and meringue nests.

HANDY TIP

It's important to stir and not whisk the curd once the egg has been incorporated into the lemon mixture because whisking will make it foamy rather than smooth and creamy.

Variations

946   MEYER LEMON

Replace the regular lemons with Meyer lemons and reduce the sugar to 85 g.
Serve with: scones and croissants; use to fill pastry tart cases and top with meringue for lemon meringue tart.

949   WITH LIMONCELLO

Stir 2 tablespoons (30 ml) limoncello into the finished curd.
Serve with: toasted panettone; combine with ricotta cheese and use as a filling for crêpes; layer with whipped cream for a trifle or combine with mascarpone for a lemon tiramisu.

947   WITH MINT

Bruise 6 to 8 large mint leaves to release the oils then roughly chop and add to the bowl with the lemon zest, juice and other ingredients.
Serve with: Muffins and brioche; Greek yoghurt and softly whipped double cream for parfaits; or layer between sponge cake and berries for trifle.

950   LIME CARDAMOM

Make the **Lime Curd**, adding 3 roughly crushed cardamom pods with the lime zest, juice and other ingredients.
Serve with: yoghurt and mango, kiwi or other tropical fruit; with cream puffs, eclairs and crêpes; vanilla or lime-flavoured cakes.

948   WITH LAVENDER

Add 1 tablespoon (15 ml) culinary lavender buds to the bowl with the lemon zest, juice and other ingredients.
Serve with: crumpets and croissant; with whipped cream as a filling for Swiss rolls, and use as a filling for pavlovas topped with berries.

951   WITH BLOOD ORANGE

Replace half the lemon juice with fresh blood orange juice, and reduce the sugar to 85 g, or 70 g for a more tart curd.
Serve with: scones, toast, muffins, crumpets, brioche, croissants and other breads; meringues; Victoria sponge cakes flavoured with orange; pastry cases made with orange zest; shortbread, cake and brownie bites.

952   LIME

Replace the lemon juice with 110 ml lime juice and the lemon zest with 2 teaspoons (10 ml) lime zest, and increase the sugar to 140 g.
Serve with: Greek yoghurt; with whipped cream, tropical fruit and sponge cake for a trifle; use to fill pastry tartlet cases or mini pavlovas and top with mango or kiwi fruit.

953   ORANGE

Replace the lemon juice with orange or tangerine juice, and the lemon zest with 2 teaspoons (10 ml) orange or tangerine zest, and reduce the sugar to 85 g, or 70 g for a more tart curd.
Serve with: scones, toast, muffins, croissants and other breads; use with whipped cream to fill crêpes or tart cases.

954   LIME CHILLI

Add ½ to 1 teaspoon (3 to 5 ml) chopped jalapeño chilli with the lime zest, juice and other ingredients when making the **Lime Curd**.
Serve with: scones, toast, muffins, crumpets, brioche, croissant and other breads; shortbread fingers and cake bites; dark chocolate sponge cakes; lime-flavoured angel food cake; or to fill pavlovas with tropical fruits.

955 Quick Strawberry Jam

Enjoying homemade preserves doesn't necessarily require hours of hard work, or mountains of equipment. With this recipe you can slather made-from-scratch jam on your toast in less than an hour.

INGREDIENTS

450 g ripe strawberries, hulled and quartered
100 g granulated sugar
2 ½ tbsp (38 ml) lemon juice

Salt
½ tbsp (8 ml) cold, unsalted butter

MAKES 300 g

Place the strawberries in a food processor and pulse until chopped, but not puréed. Transfer to a heavy-based medium saucepan, stir in the sugar, lemon juice and a pinch of salt and set over medium-low heat. Cover and cook, stirring every now and then until the sugar is dissolved and the fruit is tender and releasing its juices, about 5 minutes.

Remove the lid, increase the heat to medium and continue to cook for a further 15 minutes, stirring every now and then, until the strawberries have collapsed and the mixture is thick and jammy. Remove from the heat and stir in the butter. Skim off any remaining foam or scum on the surface of the jam.

Let stand for 5 minutes, then ladle or funnel into a jar or bowl and leave to cool to warm or room temperature before serving. Store for up to 2 weeks in the fridge. (Pictured opposite top.)

Serve with: toast, brioche, croissant, scones, crumpets, Muffins, and your choice of fresh sliced bread.

HANDY TIP

Adding butter is a trick veteran jam-makers use; the fat dissolves most of the foam that settles on the top of the jam during cooking.

Variations

956 WITH GINGER

Add 1 ½ tablespoons (23 ml) minced peeled ginger to the saucepan with the strawberries.
Serve with: toast, brioche, croissant, scones, crumpets, muffins and bread.

957 WITH ROSEWATER

Stir 1 tablespoon (15 ml) rosewater into the finished jam.
Serve with: toast, brioche, croissant, scones, crumpets, muffins and bread.

958 WITH ROSEMARY

Add 1 to 2 sprigs of rosemary with the strawberries. Remove before serving or storing the jam.
Serve with: toast, brioche, croissant, scones, crumpets, muffins and bread.

959 WITH APPLE

Add 1 large grated peeled and cored Granny Smith or Braeburn apple with the strawberries.
Serve with: toast, brioche, croissant, scones, crumpets, muffins and bread.

960 WITH VANILLA

Add the scraped out seeds of 1 split vanilla pod and the pod itself with the strawberries. Remove the pod before serving or storing the jam. (Pictured centre.)
Serve with: toast, brioche, croissant, scones, crumpets, muffins and bread.

961 WITH BLUEBERRIES

Replace 140 g strawberries with blueberries. (Pictured bottom.)
Serve with: toast, brioche, croissant, scones, crumpets, muffins and bread.

962 Skinny Banana, Honey & Yoghurt Dip

This dip steps in when you're craving something sweet but want to keep the calories in check.

INGREDIENTS

2 medium bananas, peeled and chopped
140 ml low-fat Greek yoghurt
3 tbsp (45 ml) honey, plus more to garnish
1 ½ tbsp (23 ml) lime juice

Generous pinch ground cinnamon, plus more to garnish

MAKES 340 ml

Place all the ingredients in a blender and process until smooth. Use immediately or chill in the fridge in a covered container for up to 2 days. To serve, transfer to a small bowl and garnish with a drizzle of honey and a dusting of ground cinnamon.

Serve with: fruit salad, fruit kebabs, shortbread, strawberries, sponge cake and brownies.

HANDY TIP

If you want to go all out, opt for luscious full-fat Greek yoghurt that will give you a creamier texture. For a dairy-free option, replace the Greek yoghurt with Greek-style cultured coconut milk or almond milk.

variations

963 WITH MAPLE

Replace the honey with maple syrup and the cinnamon with ½ teaspoon (3 ml) vanilla extract. Garnish with a drizzle of maple syrup.
Serve with: pineapple, kiwi, mango, apples, peaches and pears for dipping.

964 HONEY VANILLA

Replace the cinnamon with the scraped out seeds of 1 vanilla pod.
Serve with: fruit kebabs, frozen grapes, fruit and cookies for dipping.

965 WITH CHOCOLATE CHIPS

Use half the quantity of honey, replace the cinnamon with 55 to 85 g dark chocolate chips (60% cacao). Process until the chocolate chips are broken down into fine flakes. Add more honey, if necessary. Garnish with a few whole chocolate chips.
Serve with: fruit kebabs, strawberries, chocolate shortbread, biscotti, chocolate sponge cake or brownies.

966 PISTACHIO AND MINT

Add 2 tablespoons (30 ml) roughly chopped fresh mint leaves with the rest of the ingredients. Stir 60 g finely chopped, shelled, roasted pistachio nuts into the finished dip. Garnish with extra chopped pistachios and a sprig of mint.

Serve with: fruit salad, fruit kebabs, strawberries, nut shortbread fingers, fruit and nut biscotti.

967 WITH MAPLE AND WALNUT

Make the **Skinny Banana, Maple and Yoghurt Dip**, adding 60 g finely chopped, toasted and cooled walnuts to the finished dip. Garnish with extra chopped walnuts and a drizzle of maple syrup. (Pictured top.)

Serve with: vanilla, chocolate or nut shortbread, fruit salad, strawberries, brownies and cinnamon sugar nachos.

968 NOT-SO-SKINNY BANANA, HONEYCOMB AND YOGHURT DIP

Stir 3 to 4 tablespoons (45 to 60 ml) crushed plain or chocolate-covered honeycomb candy into the finished dip. Garnish with extra crushed candy. Serve immediately. (Pictured bottom.)

Serve with: cinnamon nachos, chocolate covered pretzel, fruit salad, strawberries, cakes and brownies.

969 Apple Pie Dip

This warm dip is the perfect antidote to brisk days, and rainy evenings as the weather turns colder. Settle into a comfy sofa and get dipping.

INGREDIENTS

1 ½ tsp (8 ml) cornflour
2 medium Granny Smith apples, peeled, cored and finely diced
1 tbsp (15 ml) lemon juice
3 ½ to 4 tbsp (53 to 60 ml) soft light-brown sugar
1 ½ tbsp (23 ml) unsalted butter

¼ tsp (1 ml) ground cinnamon
Pinch ground cloves
Pinch ground nutmeg
¼ tsp (1 ml) vanilla extract
Salt

MAKES 340 ml

Combine the cornflour in a small bowl with 1 tablespoon (15 ml) cold water and stir until smooth. Set aside.

Combine the remaining ingredients with a pinch of salt and 2 tablespoons (30 ml) water in a medium saucepan. Set over medium heat and cook, stirring, until the butter and sugar melt, apples release their juices and the liquid comes to a boil. Simmer gently, covered, stirring occasionally, until the apples are tender but not collapsed. Stir in the cornflour slurry and simmer for another minute until the liquid is thickened. Remove from the heat and cool for a couple of minutes. Serve warm or at room temperature.

Serve with: crackers, wafers, rice cakes and cinnamon nachos, ice cream, or to fill crêpes.

HANDY TIP

Use this dip to make delicious mini pies. Line muffin tins with discs of rolled-out shortcrust pastry dough, fill the cases with the dip, then top with cut-out pastry lids making sure to pinch and seal the edges to stop the filling from leaking out. Make little slits in the middle of the lids, brush the top of each pie with cream and sprinkle with sugar. Bake in a preheated oven at 190°C (375° F) for 20 minutes until golden brown.

Variations

970 WITH APPLE BRANDY

Stir in 1 ½ tablespoons (23 ml) apple brandy just before adding the cornflour slurry.
Serve with: crackers, wafers, rice cakes and cinnamon nachos, ice cream, or to fill crêpes.

971 WITH CRUMBLE

Rub 45 g unsalted butter into 2 tablespoons (30 ml) plain flour. Stir in 2 ½ tablespoons (38 ml) soft light-brown sugar, a pinch of salt, a pinch of cinnamon and 3 tablespoons (45 ml) oats. Crumble the dough into small pieces. Transfer to a baking sheet and cook in an oven at 190°C (375°F) for 20 to 25 minutes until golden brown. Leave to cool. Sprinkle over dip before serving.
Serve with: crackers, wafers, pretzels or rice cakes.

972 TWO-LAYER APPLE MERINGUE PIE DIP

Beat 110 g cream cheese until soft and light, add 55 g jarred marshmallow cream, 2 tablespoons (30 ml) icing sugar and a drop of vanilla extract and beat until thoroughly combined. Spread evenly over the top of the dip.
Serve with: crackers, wafers and cinnamon nachos and shortbread biscuits.

973 Peach, White chocolate 'n' cream Dip

Whip up this dessert dip for any celebration. If fresh peaches aren't available, substitute with jarred poached peaches.

INGREDIENTS

200 ml double whipping cream
140 g white chocolate, chopped
170 g mascarpone cheese

1 tbsp (15 ml) icing sugar
2 medium ripe peaches, finely diced

MAKES 750 g

Combine half the cream with the white chocolate in a small heatproof bowl and set over a pan of simmering water, making sure the bottom of the bowl isn't touching the water. Stir occasionally, until the chocolate has melted, remove from the heat and stir to combine the chocolate and cream. Set aside to cool completely.

Meanwhile place the mascarpone, remaining cream and sugar in a medium bowl and beat using a handheld electric mixer until combined, thickened to the soft peak stage, and light. Stir in the cooled chocolate and beat for 10 seconds. Gently fold in the chopped peach by hand using a metal spoon. Serve immediately or chill until ready to use. Serve at room temperature.

Serve with: cinnamon nachos; spiced and sugared crackers; shortbread cookies; crêpes or sponge cakes.

HANDY TIP

There are few things more indulgent than mascarpone, a cream-enriched, soft cow's milk cheese with a high butterfat content and delicate tangy flavour. For a substitute, use cream cheese and increase the sugar in the recipe to 1 ½ tablespoons (23 ml).

Variations

974 WITH STRAWBERRIES

Replace the peaches with 110 g chopped hulled strawberries.
Serve with: vanilla, almond and chocolate cookies and biscotti, scones, muffins and croissants.

975 MANGO AND LIME

Replace the peach with 110 g chopped peeled and pitted mango, and the lemon juice with lime juice, and stir ½ teaspoon (3 ml) finely grated lime zest into the mascarpone with the first addition of whipped cream.
Serve with: crackers, cookies, biscotti and plain pretzels; use as a filling for crêpes, sponge cakes and Swiss rolls; waffles, sweet breads, buns, brioche and scones.

976 WITH MINT AND HAZELNUT

Fold 1 ½ tablespoons (23 ml) chopped fresh mint leaves and 2 tablespoons (30 ml) finely chopped hazelnuts to the mixture with the chopped peaches.
Serve with: crackers, cookies, wafers, biscotti, and pretzels; pear and apple wedges; or use as a filling for crêpes, sponge cakes and Swiss rolls.

977 Classic Chocolate Fondue

No buffet table, kid's party or romantic dinner is complete without a pot of molten chocolate. Don't skimp on the main ingredient; no amount of cream can bury the taste of cheap chocolate.

INGREDIENTS

300 ml double whipping cream
2 tbsp (30 ml) unsalted butter
1 tsp (5 ml) vanilla extract
170 g 70% cacao best-quality bittersweet chocolate, well-chopped
170 g best-quality milk chocolate, well-chopped
Salt

MAKES 720 ml

Place the cream, butter, and vanilla extract in a saucepan over medium heat. Bring to a boil, stirring occasionally, and remove from the heat. Add the chocolates with a pinch of salt and stir until smooth and glossy. Serve warm, in a pre-warmed ceramic bowl or a fondue pot over a flame or heat source to keep it warm, but not hot.

Serve with: sponge cake bites, brownie bites, marshmallows, fruit, shortbread biscuits or biscotti.

HANDY TIP

For your own chocolate Nirvana, try different varieties of chocolate with varying cacao content to find just the right combination that'll make you go weak at the knees!

Variations

978 WITH ORANGE

Replace vanilla with 2 teaspoons (10 ml) grated orange zest, stir 2 tablespoons (30 ml) Grand Marnier into finished dip.
Serve with: cakes, brownies, marshmallows or fruit kebabs.

979 BOOZY RUM COCONUT

Replace the vanilla extract with ½ to 1 teaspoon (3 to 5 ml) coconut extract and add 1 to 2 tablespoons (15 to 30 ml) dark rum to the saucepan with the chocolate.
Serve with: vanilla and chocolate sponge cake bites, brownie bites, marshmallows, fruit kebabs, strawberries, shortbread, pretzels and biscotti.

980 WITH HAZELNUT

Roast 110 g whole, skinned hazelnuts in an oven at 180°C (350°F) until deeply browned, about 15 minutes. Cool completely, then grind in a food processor with 1 ½ tablespoons (23 ml) granulated sugar until a smooth paste forms. Add the paste to the hot cream with the chocolate.
Serve with: sponge cake or brownie bites, fruit, marshmallows, chocolate chip and walnut biscotti.

981 Maple Butter

A fluffy, buttery topping enriched with maple syrup and aromatic vanilla for the perfect final touch to homemade pancakes and waffles. Be sure to use the best maple syrup you can find.

INGREDIENTS

120 g unsalted butter, softened
Salt
60 ml pure maple syrup

1 tbsp (15 ml) icing sugar, sifted
½ tsp (3 ml) vanilla extract

MAKES 150 g

Place the butter with a pinch of salt in a medium bowl and beat with a handheld electric mixer until fluffy and creamy. Add the maple syrup, icing sugar and vanilla extract and beat for 20 to 25 seconds until thoroughly blended. Use immediately, or transfer to a covered container and keep in the fridge for up to 1 week. Bring up to room temperature before serving, and whip again, if desired.

Serve with: pancakes, waffles and crêpes; muffins, scones, toast, brioche, baguette and bread.

HANDY TIP

Make a log of maple butter to slice into discs to serve atop pancakes, waffles and warm muffins etc. Transfer the finished mixture to a piece of cling film or greaseproof paper and shape into a log, roll up the cling film or paper into a long sausage and twist the ends like sweet wrappers. Chill in the fridge for at least an hour, or freeze. When ready to serve, open up the paper or cling film, leave the butter to soften for a few minutes then slice.

Variations

982 WITH PECAN

Add 2 ½ tablespoons (38 g) finely chopped pecans to the bowl with the maple syrup.
Serve with: pancakes, waffles and crêpes; muffins, scones, toast, brioche, baguette and bread.

983 WITH ORANGE

Add 1 teaspoon (5 ml) finely grated orange zest and 2 tablespoons (30 ml) Grand Marnier to the bowl with the maple syrup.
Serve with: pancakes, waffles and crêpes; muffins, scones, toast, brioche, baguette and bread.

984 CINNAMON NUT CRUNCH

Omit the maple syrup and add 2 ½ tablespoons (38 ml) soft brown sugar, 2 teaspoons (10 ml) ground cinnamon and 38 g crushed candied or glazed pecans to the bowl with the whipped butter.
Serve with: whole-grain pancakes, buckwheat waffles and crêpes; muffins, scones, wholewheat toast, brioche, baguette and whole-grain bread.

985 WITH DRIED CHERRIES

Add 2 ½ tablespoons (38 g) chopped dried cherries to the bowl with the maple syrup.
Serve with: pancakes, waffles and crêpes; muffins, scones, toast, brioche, baguette and bread.

986 MILK CHOCOLATE HAZELNUT

Omit the maple syrup and add 110 g finely grated milk chocolate, 1 tablespoon (15 ml) icing sugar and 30 g finely chopped hazelnuts to the bowl with the whipped butter.
Serve with: pancakes, waffles and crêpes; muffins, scones, toast, brioche, baguette and bread.

987 STRAWBERRY MINT

Finely mince 85 g hulled ripe strawberries and add to the bowl with the maple syrup and 1 to 1 ½ tablespoons (15 to 23 ml) finely shredded fresh mint leaves.
Serve with: pancakes, waffles and crêpes; muffins, scones, toast, brioche, baguette and bread.

988 HONEY 'N' SPICE

Replace the maple syrup with 3 tablespoons (45 ml) strongly flavoured honey, and add ½ teaspoon (3 ml) ground cinnamon, a pinch cayenne and ¼ teaspoon (1 ml) ground cloves to the bowl with the honey.
Serve with: pancakes, waffles and crêpes; muffins, scones, toast, brioche, baguette and bread.

989 WITH LAVENDER

Add ½ teaspoon (3 ml) culinary lavender buds to the whipped butter with the maple syrup.
Serve with: pancakes, waffles and crêpes; muffins, scones, toast, brioche, baguette and bread.

990 RUM RAISIN

Add 2 tablespoons (30 ml) raisins that have been soaked in 60 ml rum for 20 minutes until softened to the whipped butter with the maple syrup.
Serve with: pancakes, waffles and crêpes; muffins, scones, toast, brioche, baguette and bread.

991 Peanut Butter Swirl Cheesecake Dip

When you don't have the time to bake an actual cheesecake, whip this up instead! Use digestive biscuits as dippers and you'll have a deconstructed version of the real deal.

INGREDIENTS

60 ml smooth peanut butter
110 g cream cheese, softened and at room temperature
3 tbsp (45 ml) icing sugar
85 ml sour cream, at room temperature
¼ tsp (1 ml) vanilla extract

MAKES 285 g

Place peanut butter in a heatproof bowl and warm in the microwave for 30 seconds on high until runny, stirring once after 15 seconds. Cool to room temperature.

Meanwhile, in a medium bowl combine the cream cheese and sugar, stir to combine then beat with an electric mixer until light and creamy Add the sour cream and vanilla extract and beat again to incorporate into the cream-cheese mixture, about 20 seconds. Using a metal spoon, fold the peanut butter into the cream-cheese mixture. Swirl gently to create a marble effect, being careful not to over mix. Serve immediately.

Serve with: plain or chocolate-covered pretzels, cinnamon sugar nachos and crackers, strawberries, apple and pear wedges and shortbread biscuits.

HANDY TIP

To melt the peanut butter on the hob, use a bain-marie or place in a heatproof bowl and set atop a pan of simmering water and heat, stirring occasionally, for a few minutes, or until shiny and runny.

Variations

992 CRUNCHY

Replace the smooth peanut butter with crunchy.
Serve with: sugared and spiced crackers, shortbread cookies, pretzels and chocolate-covered pretzels.

993 WITH CRYSTALLISED GINGER

Add 2 tablespoons (30 ml) finely chopped crystallised ginger to the cream-cheese mixture with the sour cream.
Serve with: fruit kebabs, frozen grapes, bananas and nut biscotti.

994 WITH CHOCOLATE CHIP

Add 55 g finely chopped bittersweet chocolate to the bowl with the sour cream.
Serve with: marshmallows, shortbread, chocolate chip shortbread, strawberries, brownie and cake bites.

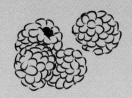

995 WITH HAZELNUT

Replace the peanut butter with chocolate hazelnut spread.
Serve with: fruit salad; brownie bites; pretzels; and vanilla and chocolate sponge bites.

996 DULCE DE LECHE

Replace the peanut butter with supermarket-bought dulce de leche caramel sauce. If the sauce is quite runny, there's no need to heat it up first.
Serve with: semi-frozen banana chunks, toffee and vanilla shortbread, nut biscotti and plain pretzels.

997 RASPBERRY MINT

Add 1 ½ tablespoons (23 ml) finely shredded fresh mint leaves to the cream cheese mixture with the sour cream, and use 4 to 5 tablespoons (60 to 75 ml) supermarket-bought or homemade **Raspberry Coulis** (see page 248) in place of the peanut butter – there's no need to heat it first.
Serve with: fruit salad; strawberries; shortbread; cinnamon nachos; vanilla wafers and lemon cake bites.

998 LEMON CURD AND BASIL

Add 1 ½ tablespoons (23 ml) finely shredded basil leaves to the cream-cheese mixture with the sour cream, and use 60 ml **Lemon Curd** (page 266) in place of the peanut butter – there's no need to heat it first.
Serve with: lemon and vanilla cake bites, gingerbread squares, vanilla wafers, lemon biscotti, strawberries and fruit kebabs.

999 ALMOND BUTTER AND COCONUT

Add 2 tablespoons (30 ml) toasted and cooled unsweetened flaked coconut or supermarket-bought dried and shredded coconut to the cream-cheese mixture with the sour cream, and replace the vanilla extract with a drop of coconut extract, and the peanut butter with almond butter.
Serve with: coconut biscuits, plain pretzels, tropical fruit, marshmallows, semi-frozen bananas and nut brownies.

1000 PUMPKIN

Beat 60 ml canned pumpkin with 2 tablespoons (30 ml) softened cream cheese until smooth. Sweeten to taste with maple syrup and season with a pinch of allspice and ground cinnamon. Use in place of the peanut butter in the main recipe – don't heat the pumpkin mixture first.
Serve with: gingerbread, lemon and coffee cake bites; shortbread; chocolate-covered pretzels; strawberries; and pear and apple wedges.

SAUCES, DIPS & DRESSINGS SELECTOR

	Asian-style snacks	Breads and sandwiches	Potato crisps and snacks	Crackers	Salads and crudités	Vegetables	Rice	Pasta and polenta	Couscous	Pizza	Pancakes and crêpes	Egg dishes	Cheese	Vegetarian dishes	Chicken and poultry	Duck and game	Beef and veal	Lamb	Pork and Ham	Meats	Offal	Seafood	Fish
EMULSIFIED SAUCES																							
Hollandaise, page 20		●				●					●	●	●		●		●					●	●
Beurre Blanc, page 24					●	●						●			●		●					●	●
Béarnaise, page 26						●									●		●	●		●		●	●
Beurre Noisette, page 27					●		●	●						●			●					●	●
Romesco Sauce, page 28	●				●										●		●	●				●	●
Tapenade, page 30	●		●	●	●								●									●	●
Mayonnaise, page 31	●				●										●		●					●	●
Aioli, page 34	●				●										●		●					●	●
Tahini Sauce, page 36	●					●									●							●	●
Garlic butter, page 38	●					●	●	●							●							●	●
CREAMY AND CHEESY SAUCES																							
Classic Béchamel, page 40						●		●				●			●		●					●	●
Four-Cheese Sauce, page 44			●			●	●	●		●			●		●		●					●	●
Saffron Cream Sauce, page 46						●									●							●	●
Cheese and Buttermilk Sauce, page 48			●		●	●	●	●		●		●	●	●	●							●	●
Roast Garlic Asiago Cream Sauce, page 50						●	●	●						●	●		●		●				
Mushroom and Onion Sauce, page 52						●	●	●							●		●					●	●
Mustard and Cider Sauce, page 54						●									●				●			●	●
Leek and Parmesan Sauce, page 56						●	●	●							●							●	●
Butternut Squash and Mascarpone Sauce, page 58						●		●						●	●			●	●				
PESTOS AND HERB SAUCES																							
Pesto, page 60	●				●	●		●		●					●							●	●
Sun-dried Tomato Pesto, page 64	●		●	●	●	●		●	●						●		●					●	●
Sweet Pea Pesto, page 66	●			●	●	●									●			●				●	●
Cashew Nut and Coriander Pesto, page 68	●			●	●	●									●	●	●	●				●	●
Mint Sauce, page 69	●			●	●	●							●	●	●			●		●			
Gremolata, page 70				●	●									●	●					●		●	●
Classic Chimichurri, page 71					●	●	●								●		●	●				●	●
English Parsley Sauce, page 73						●					●				●							●	●
Coriander and Coconut Chutney, page 74	●			●											●							●	●
STOCK-BASED SAUCES																							
Bacon and Mushroom Sauce, page 76		●				●	●	●			●				●		●						
Chicken Velouté, page 80						●	●	●							●		●						
Beef Jus, page 82							●	●							●		●						
Marsala Sauce, page 84						●	●	●							●		●						
Chocolate and Chilli Mole, page 85						●	●								●		●						
Green Peppercorn Sauce, page 86							●	●							●		●						
Rich Vegetable Gravy, page 88						●		●	●					●	●		●						
Yellow Pepper Sauce, page 90							●	●						●								●	●
Prawn Bisque Sauce, page 92							●	●														●	●
Bouillabaisse Sauce, page 93							●															●	●
Fish Velouté, page 94													●										●
Pea and Mint Sauce, page 95						●	●								●								
CHILLI AND BARBECUE SAUCES																							
Lemongrass, Ginger and Chilli Dipping Sauce, page 96	●	●			●	●									●		●	●				●	●
Pineapple-Chilli Sauce, page 99															●	●	●	●				●	●
Harissa, page 100		●			●	●				●				●	●	●		●				●	●
Southwestern Roasted Green Chilli Sauce, page 102					●	●	●				●	●			●		●					●	●
Honey-Mustard Barbecue Sauce, page 103				●	●										●		●						
Spicy Tomato Barbecue Sauce, page 104						●									●	●	●	●	●				
Hoisin Barbecue Sauce, page 106																●	●						
Old-fashioned Barbecue Sauce, page 108												●			●		●	●	●				
Piri Piri Sauce, page 109												●			●		●	●					●

	Asian-style snacks	Breads and sandwiches	Potato crisps and snacks	Crackers	Salads and crudités	Vegetables	Rice	Pasta and polenta	Couscous	Pizza	Pancakes and crêpes	Egg dishes	Cheese	Vegetarian dishes	Chicken and poultry	Duck and game	Beef and veal	Lamb	Pork and Ham	Meats	Offal	Seafood	Fish	Fruit desserts
KETCHUPS AND TOMATO SAUCES																								
Classic Tomato Sauce, page 110					●			●		●				●								●	●	
Tomato and Fish Sauce, page 113								●																
Roast Tomato and Ricotta Sauce, page 114								●							●		●							
'No Cook' Sugo Vacanza, page 116								●																
Classic Bolognese Sauce, page 118					●			●						●			●							
Tomato Ketchup, page 120	●	●										●			●		●	●				●	●	
Tunisian-style Tomato Sauce, page 124		●			●	●	●	●				●			●		●	●					●	
Curry Ketchup, page 126		●				●									●		●		●				●	
Banana Ketchup, page 127															●		●	●	●				●	
SAVOURY FRUIT SAUCES																								
Cranberry and Orange Sauce, page 128											●		●	●	●	●	●	●						
Apple and Sage Sauce, page 132															●	●		●	●	●	●			
Classic Orange Sauce, page 134					●										●	●	●	●			●	●	●	
Peach Chutney, page 136		●											●		●	●			●					
Grilled Lemon Parsley Sauce, page 137															●		●	●				●	●	
Dark Cherry and Port Sauce, page 138															●	●	●	●						
Plum and Star Anise Sauce, page 140															●	●	●		●			●	●	
Pear and Raisin Relish, page 142	●	●											●		●	●			●					
Mango Cream Sauce, page 143		●												●	●							●	●	●
ASIAN SAUCES																								
Teriyaki Sauce, page 144						●									●		●						●	
Chinese Black Bean Sauce, page 147						●	●								●		●		●			●	●	
Red Thai Aubergine Curry, page 148						●																		
Spicy Kung Pao Sauce, page 150						●									●		●		●					
Tomato, Onion and Prawn Sambal, page 151		●				●																		
Spicy Peanut Satay Sauce, page 152					●										●		●	●				●	●	
Nuoc Cham Dipping Sauce, page 154	●														●		●					●	●	
Madras Curry Sauce, page 156		●			●	●								●	●		●							
Creamy Tikka Masala Sauce, page 157		●			●	●								●	●									
Filipino Adobo Sauce, page 158						●	●								●	●		●						
Tamarind Sauce, page 159	●			●										●	●							●	●	
SALSAS AND VEGETABLE DIPS																								
Tzatziki, page 160		●		●	●										●		●						●	
Wild Mushroom 'Caviar' Dip, page 163		●	●	●	●			●							●	●								
Beetroot and Ginger Dip, page 165	●	●			●										●									
Luscious Artichoke Dip, page 166		●	●	●	●										●							●	●	
Courgette, Chilli and Caper Dip, page 168		●	●	●	●										●		●					●	●	
Aubergine Dip with Walnuts, page 170	●	●	●										●	●	●									
Classic Guacamole, page 172		●	●		●										●			●						
Charred Sweetcorn Salsa, page 174		●	●	●											●		●	●				●	●	
Pineapple Salsa, page 176	●	●													●		●	●				●	●	
Pepita Salsa, page 177		●													●		●	●						
Salsa Cruda, page 178		●	●												●	●		●				●	●	
MEAT AND SEAFOOD DIPS																								
Creamy Salmon Rillettes, page 180		●	●	●	●	●	●	●														●		
Prawn and Almond Dip, page 184		●		●	●	●							●								●			
Hot Crab Dip, page 186		●	●	●	●																			
Smoked Mackerel Pâté, page 187		●																						
Bagna Cauda, page 188					●	●																		
Beef Rendang Dip, page 189		●		●	●	●	●																	
Chilli Con Carne Dip, page 190		●	●		●												●		●					
Spinach and Sausage Dip, page 192		●	●	●	●																			
Chicken Liver Pâté, page 194		●		●	●																			
Buffalo Chicken Dip, page 196		●	●		●	●								●										

	Asian-style snacks	Breads and sandwiches	Potato crisps and snacks	Crackers	Salads and crudités	Vegetables	Rice	Pasta and polenta	Couscous	Pizza	Pancakes and crêpes	Egg dishes	Cheese	Vegetarian dishes	Chicken and poultry	Duck and game	Beef and veal	Lamb	Pork and Ham	Meats	Offal	Seafood	Fish	Cakes and biscuits	Cheesecakes	Ice cream and sorbets	Soufflés	Chocolate desserts	Fruit desserts
CREAMY CHEESE, BEAN AND LENTIL DIPS																													
Hummus, page 198		●	●	●	●	●	●								●				●			●							
Edamame and Tofu 'Hummus' Dip, page 202		●	●	●	●	●				●					●				●		●								
Cannellini and Pesto Dip, page 203		●	●	●																									
Mexican Three-Layer Dip, page 204		●	●		●	●																							
French Green Lentil Dip, page 205		●	●	●	●																								
Indian Lentil Dip, page 206		●	●	●										●											●				
Tomato, Black Pepper and Feta Dip, page 208		●	●	●	●	●		●	●										●										
Queso al Horno, page 209		●	●			●																							
Baked Cheesy Artichoke and Spinach Dip, page 210	●	●	●	●																									
Roasted Fennel and Mascarpone Dip, page 211		●		●	●								●	●					●		●								
Caramelised Onion and Goat's Cheese Dip, page 212		●	●	●										●															
Olive Dip, page 213		●		●										●									●						
OIL AND VINEGAR DRESSINGS																													
Classic Vinaigrette, page 214					●	●	●	●							●			●				●	●						
Red Onion, Mint and Cucumber Vinaigrette, page 217														●				●				●	●						
Raspberry Vinaigrette, page 218					●	●							●		●	●						●	●						
Warm Bacon Vinaigrette, page 220				●	●										●		●												
Champagne, Walnut and Grape Vinaigrette, page 222					●	●							●			●													
Classic Italian Dressing, page 223					●	●	●	●					●		●		●	●											
Tomato and Herb Vinaigrette, page 225															●		●		●			●	●						
Miso-Ginger Dressing, page 226				●	●	●									●		●					●							
Rice Vinegar and Sesame Oil Dressing, page 228	●			●	●										●			●				●							
CREAMY DRESSINGS																													
Classic Caesar Dressing, page 230		●			●	●							●	●	●							●	●						
Tarragon Buttermilk Dressing, page 234					●	●									●														
Creamy Maple-Mustard Dressing, page 236					●	●									●	●	●												
Russian Salad Dressing, page 237		●			●	●									●														
Red Pepper and Basil Dressing, page 238						●									●							●							
Peanut and Sesame Dressing, page 239					●	●	●	●							●							●	●						
Blue Cheese Dressing, page 240		●			●	●	●	●							●		●	●											
Best-ever Ranch Dressing, page 242		●		●	●	●	●	●			●				●				●	●	●	●	●						
Green Goddess Avocado Dressing, page 244		●			●	●	●	●							●		●					●	●						
Carrot and Ginger Dressing, page 246					●	●	●	●							●	●	●					●	●						
DESSERT SAUCES																													
Raspberry Coulis, page 248											●													●	●	●	●	●	●
Tangy Citrus Sauce, page 252											●													●	●	●	●	●	●
Cherries Jubilee Sauce, page 254	●										●													●	●	●			
Butterscotch-Toffee Sauce, page 255											●													●		●		●	●
White Mint Chocolate Sauce, page 256																									●			●	●
Hot Fudge Sauce, page 257											●													●		●		●	●
Creamy Caramel Sauce, page 258											●													●		●		●	●
Bittersweet Chocolate Sauce, page 260											●													●	●	●		●	●
Crème Anglaise, page 262																												●	●
Zabaglione Sauce, page 264																								●					●
SWEET SPREADS AND DIPS																													
Lemon Curd, page 266		●									●													●					●
Quick Strawberry Jam, page 270		●																						●					
Skinny Banana, Honey and Yoghurt Dip, page 272			●																					●					●
Apple Pie Dip, page 274		●	●			●	●				●													●		●			
Peach, White Chocolate 'n' Cream Dip, page 275		●	●								●													●					●
Classic Chocolate Fondue, page 276			●																					●					●
Maple Butter, page 277		●									●													●					
Peanut Butter Swirl Cheesecake Dip, page 280			●																					●					●

INDEX

ACKNOWLEDGEMENTS

Many thanks to Julie Brooke, Jacqui Caulton, Val McArthur
and the team at Quintet.

Peter, *First Assistant to the Chef, Chief Taster and Director
of Dishwashing*, I applaud with loving gratitude your
unwavering devotion to the cause and boundless
enthusiasm for saucing!

PICTURE CREDITS